THE SIXTIES

Second Edition

Terry H. Anderson
Texas A & M University

PEARSON
Longman

New York • San Francisco • Boston
London • Toronto • Sydney • Tokyo • Singapore • Madrid
Mexico City • Munich • Paris • Cape Town • Hong Kong • Montreal

Vice President and Publisher: Priscilla McGeehon
Acquisitions Editor: Ashley Dodge
Executive Marketing Manager: Sue Westmoreland
Supplements Editor: Kristi Olson
Media Editor: Patrick McCarthy
Production Manager: Joseph Vella
Project Coordination, Text Design, and Electronic Page Makeup: Thompson Steele, Inc.
Cover Designer/Manager: Wendy Ann Fredericks
Cover Photos: *Clockwise from top:* Washington, D.C., Dr. Martin Luther King, Jr., during
    massive civil rights demonstration, August 28, 1963, © Topham/The Image Works; Civil
    Rights Marchers, Forsyth County, Georgia, USA, © Superstock; Student Mary Ann Vecchio
    screams as she kneels over the body of fellow student Jeffery Miller during an anti-war
    demonstration at Kent State University, Ohio, © Hulton/Archive by Getty Images; and
    Children frolic around a colorful psychedelic bus with hippies on the roof at Golden Gate
    Park in San Francisco in 1967, © Gene Anthony/Black Star Publishing/PictureQuest.
    Background image: © PhotoDisc
Photo Research: Photosearch, Inc.
Manufacturing Buyer: Lucy Hebard
Cover Printer: Phoenix Color Corp.

For permission to use copyrighted material, grateful acknowledgment is made to the copyright
holders on p. 230, which is hereby made part of this copyright page.

Library of Congress Cataloging-in-Publication Data

Anderson, Terry H.
   The sixties / Terry H. Anderson.--2nd ed.
      p. cm.
   Includes index.
   Filmography: p.
   ISBN 0-321-15637-4
      1. United States--Politics and government--1961–1963. 2. United States--Politics and
   government--1963–1969. 3. United States--Social conditions--1960–1980. I. Title.

E841.A54 2003
973.923--dc21

                                                                              2003045816

Copyright © 2004 by Terry H. Anderson

Please visit our Website at http://www.ablongman.com

ISBN 0-321-15637-4

4 5 6 7 8 9 10   06 05

Contents

Additional Reading • 223

Filmography • 228

Photo Credits • 230

Index • 231

Preface

In their December 1969 issue, the editors of *Life* magazine published a special issue on the sixties, labeling it "The Decade of Tumult and Change." They noted that the era came in two stages: the "brisk feeling of hope, a generally optimistic and energetic shift from the calm of the late '50s," followed by "a growing swell of demands for extreme and immediate change" when the decade "exploded—over race, youth, violence, lifestyles, and, above all, over the Vietnam War." The editors declared that these issues would "carry over into the '70s, and it is impossible to predict when they will end."

Indeed, the sixties had not ended a generation later. In 1999 conservative Pat Buchanan declared, "Woodstock values have triumphed. Divorce, dirty language, adultery, blasphemy, euthanasia, abortion, pornography, homosexuality, co-habitation . . . permeate our lives." Former activist John Judis responded that it was not the counterculture but "consumer capitalism" who "razed redwoods . . . flooded cyberspace with spam, used sex to sell detergents, and helped to transform many American teenagers into television zombies." *Time* magazine simply asked, "Most decades have the good grace to go away. Why won't the '60s?"

This book is about the sixties era, 1960 to the early 1970s. It is an attempt to take the reader beyond the rhetoric of pundits and politicians and to explore *why* many citizens at that time felt change was not only necessary, but mandatory. This is an attempt to provoke readers, and to make sense of the sixties.

Historians have written surveys of the era. Some have ended the liberal decade with the election of conservative Richard Nixon in 1968, assuming that politics defined the sixties. In fact, liberal politics and programs did not end with Nixon's inauguration, and as we shall see, the Democratic Congress passed and the Republican president signed many liberal ideas into law during his first term. Other historians have used an organizational or ideological approach, tracing the rise of groups such as the Student Nonviolent Coordinating Committee (SNCC) or the Students for a Democratic Society (SDS) that espoused a New Left ideology; these authors have ended their books in the late sixties with the demise of SNCC or SDS. In fact, neither ideology nor any organization defined the era, and social activism and cultural change blossomed for years after the collapse of those groups. Finally, some historians have adopted a thematic approach, tracing one social movement such as the civil rights struggle from beginning to end, then writing about another movement such as the demand for student rights or women's liberation. That method, however, is out of context and results in a skewed account. Unlike the relatively stable fifties, the sixties changed almost daily. One event, one movement, affected the next; all were related, not independent.

The Sixties is different; it does not end the era after Nixon's election, focus on organizations or ideology, or employ a thematic approach. After a brief introduction on the postwar years, this book explores the significant political, foreign policy, social, and cultural events from the 1960 Greensboro sit-ins and presidential campaign to the high tide of women's liberation and American withdrawal from Vietnam in 1973. Along the way I demonstrate that what really made the era unique were the various "movements" that merged together during and after 1968 to form a "sixties culture" that advocated liberation and empowerment. *The Sixties* also is different because it examines the dramatic era as it unfolded, both chronologically and thematically. Here, one event builds on another until the decade "exploded" and reached its climax in the early seventies.

I am indebted to the readers who wrote or e-mailed with comments and suggestions for improving the first edition of *The Sixties*, many of which I have incorporated into this second edition. One female student at Bard College, for example, asked why I used the word *coed* when discussing college women in the 1950s and 1960s. In this edition, I have cut its usage, but during that era *coed* was the term that meant the institution was co-educational, accepting both male and female students. The word was discarded later in the sixties with the rise of women's liberation.

Terminology used in this book reflects the fact that our American language is fluid. Until his assassination in 1968, the Reverend Martin Luther King Jr. called himself a *Negro*, a label generally abandoned later when the preferred terms became *black* and *African American*. Terms used also respect geographical differences. *Hispanic* is the word usually used in Texas, while it might be *Latino* in California. I have employed these terms carefully and hope readers will understand that sensitivity about labels for our citizens is one of the legacies of the sixties.

In response to other suggestions from readers of the first edition, I have added more material on women's history and integrated it throughout the text. I also have placed more emphasis on gays and lesbians and on environmental issues, topics added to the Suggested Readings section. Finally, I have added a Filmography of noteworthy movies dealing with the sixties with annotations on each film. In making these changes, however, I have been especially careful to retain the book's essential identity and characteristics—a balanced and objective discussion and a lucid and stimulating read.

Naturally, a book of this size cannot be definitive, nor can it cover every important event and topic, but it can attempt to explain *why* America experienced a "Decade of Tumult and Change."

T. A.
College Station, Texas
March 2003

Acknowledgments
for the Second Edition

M any historians read this book in draft, and their comments have helped shape the style and substance of this work. For their comments, I am grateful to Barbara Klemm, Broward Community College; Mark Dalhouse, Truman State College; Thomas Greene, Villanova University; George Lubrick, Northern Arizona University; David Culbert, Louisiana State University; David Bernstein, California State University, Long Beach; Michael Kurtz, Southeastern Louisiana University; Allan Winkler, Miami University; Brian Gordon, St. Louis Community College; James Lorence, University of Wisconsin Marathon Center; Steven Lawson, University of North Carolina at Greensboro; and Robert Divine, University of Texas. Reviewers of the first edition whose comments and criticisms have been especially useful in making revisions for this second edition include Saul Lerner, Purdue University Calumet; Alexandra Mina Stern, University of California at Santa Cruz; Eric Newhall, Occidental College; and Ernesto Chavez, University of Texas at El Paso. I thank as well readers of the first edition—professors and students alike—who took the time to write or e-mail me with their questions, critiques, and recommendations for changes and improvements. The team at Longman—Ashley Dodge, Jacob Drill, and Sue Westmoreland—were helpful and supportive throughout the publication process.

At Texas A&M University, many colleagues and friends shared information, gave advice, or simply made the working environment pleasant: Sara Alpern, Daniel Bornstein, Jim Bradford, Al Broussard, Chuck Brooks, Walter Buenger, Jonathan Coopersmith, Chip Dawson, Chester Dunning, David Hudson, Mary Johnson, Andy Kirkendall, Robyn Konrad, Arnold Krammer, John Lenihan, Brian Linn, Di Wang, and Jude Swank. Shane Bernard, my former graduate student, served as my research assistant for a year, and so did two outstanding undergraduates, Amy Todd and Steve Smith. Shane, Amy, and Steve tracked down quotes and citations and surprised me with their resourcefulness. A faculty development leave again was generously funded by the Texas A&M Association of Former Students.

My brothers, Steve and Jeff, shared their good humor and camaraderie, and so did my parents, Howard and Emily. Sadly, my mother passed away before this second edition appeared. Our spirited conversations and her sense of humor always will be missed.

Many others contributed in their own way. Dion Ross Kasakoff opened my eyes to Brazil, sent me fishing in the Pantanal, and bluffed my nonexistent visa all the way through Paraguay. Joe Golsan kept me apprised of numerous college scandals while he sliced his way to victory on the tennis court. David Ogden suffered 29 straight set defeats, probably more, yet afterwards still had the energy to drink brews and tell jokes and lies as big as the state of Texas. Rose Eder was my hiking, fishing, skiing, and scuba buddy, as usual, and still had time to travel with me to another dozen countries, from riding the Marrakech Express to hiking Sri Lanka's Sigiriya fortress to diving with Manta Rays off Komodo Island; at other times we resolved all domestic and international problems while walking our Labs—Singha, Kona, and Bear.

Finally, I would like to thank those fine people who have influenced and helped my career: historians H. W. Brands, Robert Divine, George Herring, Betty Miller Unterberger, and the late Merle Curti and Charles DeBenedetti, and editors Sheldon Meyer, Bruce Borland, Noel Parsons, Peter Ginna, Ashley Dodge, and Jacob Drill.

At Indiana University, three professors took an alienated Vietnam veteran and changed him into a professional historian. For that considerable feat, this book is dedicated to Robert H. Ferrell, Richard S. Kirkendall, and David M. Pletcher.

For

Robert H. Ferrell

Richard S. Kirkendall

David M. Pletcher

About the Author

Terry H. Anderson is professor of history at Texas A&M University. A Vietnam veteran who has traveled to over 50 countries, he has taught in Malaysia and Japan and was a Fulbright professor in China and the Mary Ball Washington Professor of American History at University College Dublin, 2001–2002. He has written many articles on the sixties and the Vietnam War, is a coauthor of *A Flying Tiger's Diary* (with fighter pilot Charles Bond Jr.), and is the author of *The United States, Great Britain, and the Cold War, 1944–1947*, *The Movement and The Sixties*, and the forthcoming book, *The Pursuit of Fairness: A History of Affirmative Action*.

Cold War America: Seedbed of the 1960s

old war America, the era after World War II and until 1960, has been described by numerous writers. At the end of the fifties liberals lambasted those years for conformity, among the "dullest and dreariest in all our history," and they complained about the emphasis on money and consumerism—the "age of the slob." Conservatives disagreed. Praising the robust economy, status quo politics, and traditional families, one proclaimed that the era was the "happiest, most stable, most rational period the western world has ever known since 1914."

Whatever one thinks of the years following World War II, one thing is certain: some events then not only created cold war America, but planted the seeds that germinated later, creating the sixties. What were the political, diplomatic, social, and cultural themes of cold war America, and how did they sprout into the "Decade of Tumult and Change"?

Won the War, Lost the Peace

As U.S. troops came home from World War II, most agreed with an idea proposed by Henry Luce in *Life*—the next era of history would be the "American Century." Egypt, Greece, Rome, France, and Britain all had experienced their eras of greatness, and now America must "assume the leadership of the world." America's overwhelming victory boosted beliefs that most citizens held before the war, and for the future. As Luce said, the United States was "the most powerful and vital nation in the world." If Americans had the will, then they could beat any adversary. Moreover, most Americans agreed that in a world of good and evil, they represented the beacon of hope, the defender of freedom. In this sense, then, the war became known as the "good war," for it not only ended the Great Depression at home, but it extended U.S. power abroad and boosted national pride.

Armed with these ideas, the proud veterans came home to a grateful nation. Americans anticipated a future that would be, as entitled in a popular 1946 movie, *The Best Years of Our Lives*. Some veterans rejoined their families and returned to their civilian jobs; others, aided by the GI Bill, attended college in record numbers. African American vets hoped for what they called during the war the "Double V," victory over U.S. enemies abroad and over racism and segregation at home, and young females who had worked in defense plants, "Rosie the Riveters," eagerly awaited the return of their special heroes. Many fell in love. The census bureau reported issuing more marriage licenses in 1946 than in any other year, an increase of 40 percent over 1945. There were so many weddings, in fact, that the U.S. Department of Agriculture pleaded with the public during the postwar food shortage: "Don't throw rice. Try confetti."

Shortly thereafter, doctors reported a stunning increase in the number of pregnant wives. The birthrate had been rather low during the depression and war, but returning veterans and their new brides quickly reversed that trend—the first years of the baby boom. By 1950 there were 8 million more children than demographers had predicted.

Naturally, these new families searched for apartments and homes, but due to depression and war, residential construction had lagged since 1929: the nation faced a housing shortage. Some veterans slept in automobiles, and as many as 2 million young couples shared residences with relatives. "Needed," declared the *New York Times Magazine*, "Five Million Homes." The federal government helped, establishing guaranteed housing loans for veterans, and construction companies addressed the crisis by doubling housing starts between 1946 and 1950. On the East Coast, William Levitt bought 1,200 acres on Long Island, and soon his army of workers was finishing a house every 15 minutes. The "General Motors of the housing industry," he called his firm, and *Time* magazine put him on its cover. In 1947 construction firms in Los Angeles built 60,000 homes and apartments. America was becoming suburbanized, and during the fifties construction teams bulldozed a million acres a year, larger than Rhode Island, to build tract housing; by 1960 as many lived in the suburbs as in cities.

Couples moved into new homes and started families, but soon it was a troubled peace. In 1946 the economy sputtered, inflation soared, and strikes became so common that President Harry Truman lamented, "Peace is hell." Overseas, the wartime alliance of Britain, the United States, and the Soviet Union was crumbling over postwar issues. Russian leader Joseph Stalin broke agreements and refused to allow democratic elections in areas his army had liberated from Nazi Germany, resulting in communist governments throughout Eastern Europe. In response, former Prime Minister Winston Churchill declared that the Soviets were establishing an "iron curtain" across the Continent, and Truman refused to grant a postwar reconstruction loan to the Russians. In just two years the hot war against the Nazis had become the cold war against the communists. By 1947 the president announced he would "contain" communist expansion into Greece and Turkey and declared his Truman Doctrine. The next year the Soviets seized the government of Czechoslovakia and closed access into the German capital. The United States responded by initiating the Berlin Airlift, beginning to rebuild Western Europe with the Marshall Plan, and laying the groundwork for a defense pact that eventually became the North Atlantic Treaty Organization (NATO). An article in *Life* summarized the popular mood: "How We Won the War and Lost the Peace."

In Asia, Mao Zedong's army was victorious in the Chinese civil war, establishing communism in the nation with the largest population on earth, and in 1950 the communist government of North Korea attacked South Korea. Truman viewed Korea as the "Greece of the Far East," and in an attempt to contain communist expansion in Asia, he sent the U.S. military. In less than five years of peace, Americans again were marching off to war.

The Korean War confirmed many Americans' suspicions: most citizens agreed with pundits who declared that all communist nations were Russian "puppets," or as *Newsweek* magazine proclaimed, "All Roads Lead to Moscow." Consequently, the United States began abandoning a traditional policy: once a colony themselves, Americans always had supported nationalists fighting for self-determination against their colonial masters. By 1950, however, the administration came to believe "all Stalinists masquerade as nationalists," and Truman backed a colonial power, France, in its war against the people fighting for independence in Indochina, which included Vietnam. Korea also confirmed a lesson of World War II. War was caused by evil forces—Nazis or "commies," Hitler or Stalin—and Americans could not "appease" them as the British had done with Germany in 1938 at the Munich Conference. The United States had to stand up and declare that "aggression does not pay," for if it did not, one nation after another would "fall like dominoes" until the enemy was at America's gate. Most agreed with President Truman when he told the nation, "We are fighting in Korea so we won't have to fight in Wichita, or in Chicago, or in New Orleans, or on San Francisco Bay."

The Korean War had menacing implications. At home, many American men were called back into the military, disrupting families. Abroad, both the United States and the Soviet Union possessed the atomic bomb. Soon, both nations were accumulating large stockpiles of nuclear weapons, including the more powerful H-bomb. In an age of long-distance bombers and rockets, the United States was no longer sequestered from its enemies by the Atlantic and the Pacific—for the first time in history, Americans felt vulnerable to annihilation. This being the case, most social scientists felt that the atomic future would be stressful, and journalists Joseph and Steward Alsop predicted "constant, aching, mounting fear," the conditions for a "world-wide nervous breakdown."

Searching for Subversives

The breakdown already had begun inside America—the anticommunist crusade. In March 1947 Truman announced his strategy to combat domestic communism: the loyalty program. By executive order the president established procedures to investigate federal employees and dismiss them if the government believed there were "reasonable grounds for belief in disloyalty." Those reasons naturally included treason and espionage, but also affiliation with any so-called subversive organization. By 1951 the administration expanded the program, so one could be fired if there was "reasonable doubt" of loyalty, and later employees could be dismissed if their behavior was not "reliable or trustworthy," which led to attacks against anything unusual for the time. "One homosexual can pollute a Government office," a congressional committee declared as officials labeled gays a "security risk."

"Those who do not believe in the ideology of the United States," declared Truman's attorney general, "shall not be allowed to stay in the United States." By 1948 Congress and the administration were setting up committees, increasing the powers of the FBI, and beginning countless investigations. The administration invoked the Smith Act, stating it was a crime to teach or advocate overthrow of the government. Congress passed the McCarran Act, demanding that subversives register with federal authorities, and by 1952 the government established 33 provisions that would exclude immigrants and even tourists from the Land of the Free if they were communists or "sexual deviants."

The search for subversives, then, was already under way when its greatest advocate joined the crusade, the Republican senator from Wisconsin, Joseph McCarthy. In February 1950 he announced, "I have here in my hand a list of 205 that were known to the secretary of state as being members of the Communist Party, and who, nevertheless, are still working and shaping policy in the State Department." Reporters rushed to the scene, demanding the list, and during the next few weeks the senator played the numbers game: there were 83, and later 57, "card-carrying members of the Communist Party."

Alarmed, Congress formed a committee to investigate the charges, and after months concluded that McCarthy's statements were "a hoax and a fraud."

In saner times the Senate committee's report would have ended McCarthy's career, but 1950 was not a sane time. The previous August the Russians had detonated their first atomic bomb; because U.S. experts had predicted the Soviets would not have such a device for years, many Americans began to wonder about spies: who gave them the secret? Then a few months after McCarthy's speech, in June, communist North Korea attacked South Korea, and with U.S. troops engaged there, no American politician wanted to be known as "soft on communism." That gave McCarthy a free hand to continue his reckless charges and to slander anyone in his way. The senator attacked the Truman administration by denouncing the secretary of state, Dean Acheson, as the "Great Red Dean." McCarthy charged that the "hard fact is that those who wear the label Democrat wear it with the stain of an historic betrayal." He mesmerized his audiences as he spoke of red spies involved in "a conspiracy on a scale so immense as to dwarf any previous such venture in the history of man."

Not to be outdone, the Democrats no longer questioned McCarthy's wild charges but joined the frenzy. Truman's attorney general claimed, "There are today many Communists in America. They are everywhere—in factories, offices, butcher shops, on street corners, in private businesses—and each carries in himself the germs of death for society. These Communists are busy at work—undermining your Government, plotting to destroy the liberties of every citizen, and feverishly trying, in whatever way they can, to aid the Soviet Union."

The nation was riddled with commies, supposedly, and the only thing missing from a legion of charges was proof: the Republic sank into rule by innuendo that became known as McCarthyism.

State and local governments eagerly joined the anticommunist crusade. Almost all states introduced loyalty pledges for state employees, especially for teachers. Most states also passed antisubversive or sedition laws, excluded the Communist Party from the ballot, and passed laws making it a criminal offense to advocate overthrowing the government or to join such a group. Residents of Connecticut broke the law if they used "abusive words" about the U.S. government, and the penalty for speaking or writing subversive words in Michigan could be life in prison; in Tennessee it could be death. Penalties for being a Communist Party member varied from absurd to draconic: in New York a member could not buy a fishing license; in Ohio one was ineligible for unemployment benefits; and in Texas the member could be sentenced to 20 years in prison. In Indiana the official aim of the state was to "exterminate communists." A popular saying was "Better Dead than Red."

How would the government find the "subversive" lurking in the American society? The government began an inquisition; critics labeled it a witch-hunt. During the Truman administration the FBI conducted 25,000 full-scale investigations, but that was a fraction when compared to the number conducted by all state and federal agencies during those years: 6.5 million citizens were checked for loyalty. Officials accused, and suspects benefited from neither judge nor jury—they were without legal recourse. Apparently, Americans were no longer innocent until proven guilty.

The crusade included academia and Hollywood. Colleges, even distinguished liberal universities such as Michigan and Minnesota, banned "radical" speakers from talking on their campuses. As public concern grew, administrators initiated searches for so-called subversive professors. In 1948 the University of Washington terminated three faculty members, and the next year the University of California dismissed 26 for refusing to sign a loyalty pledge. During the next few years faculty members who were called to testify in front of congressional committees, and who refused, were fired at most schools, including Ohio State, Columbia, MIT, and Harvard. Hollywood also was suspect. In 1947 the House Committee on Un-American Activities (HUAC) began investigations by calling "friendly" witnesses, those who would "name names" of actors they felt might be communists, and "unfriendly" witnesses, those who refused to cooperate with the committee. During the next years conservative actors and producers introduced loyalty pledges and the blacklist. Although president of the Screen Actors Guild, Ronald Reagan, proclaimed, "We will not be a party to a blacklist," his union adopted a "clearance system" and banned suspected communists and unfriendly witnesses from membership.

It was a purge. During the late forties and early fifties schools and colleges fired more than 600 teachers and professors, and TV and radio producers discharged 1,500 employees. The blacklist made 350 actors and writers unemployable, while the federal government fired about 2,700 workers for questionable loyalty, and another 12,000 resigned.

Ike Takes Charge

The anticommunist crusade and cold war dominated national events as a new president took office in 1953. Candidate Eisenhower had pledged to end the war in Korea, and after his election his administration did that by signing a truce. But the truce did not relieve the fear of communism. The president signed an act that ended "all rights and privileges" for the Communist Party, and his new secretary of state, John Foster Dulles, advocated a more aggressive foreign policy. Containment, he charged, was a treadmill that would "keep us in the same place until we drop exhausted." Instead, the United States should "roll back" the communists, should "liberate" Eastern Europe from Moscow. Dulles spoke in tough terms about getting the American way in world affairs, even if this meant confronting Russia and going "to the brink" of war. In his "brinkmanship" Dulles advocated the idea that conventional forces were too expensive. The United States needed to take a "new look" at its policy, and that meant the nation should rely on nuclear weapons, on "massive retaliation." These weapons were cheaper, "more bang for the buck," and during the administration the U.S. stockpile of nuclear weapons grew from about 1,200 to over 22,000.

Throughout the Eisenhower years his administration talked tough. The president declared his domino theory: "You have a row of dominoes set up," he said, "you knock over the first one" and all the rest will follow. One nation falls to communism, and the entire world would be in peril. To keep the world "free," the United States and Britain joined security pacts, so many that journalists dubbed the policy "pactomania." NATO would keep Europe secure; CENTO would do that for the Middle East; and SEATO would stop the "Red Chinese" from rolling into Southeast Asia. The Eisenhower administration gave massive amounts of arms and funds to nations on "our side," and to keep wayward governments in line, the CIA intervened into the affairs of many nations; it helped overthrow the rulers in Iran and Guatemala. The United States signed numerous unilateral military agreements, and so by the sixties the country had military commitments to 47 nations and hundreds of bases overseas. No one seemed to mention that there never had been more than a handful of democracies in world history, and that most of the new allies were dictatorships, albeit anticommunist ones.

A case in point was South Vietnam. As mentioned, after World War II the French colony of Indochina erupted into a war for independence. The leader of the revolt was Ho Chi Minh, a man who was not only a nationalist but also a communist. The conflict lasted from 1946 to 1954, and to resolve it the major nations held the Geneva Conference. They decided that Vietnam would be divided temporarily into two nations: North Vietnam ruled by Ho Chi Minh and South Vietnam eventually led by Ngo Dinh Diem. Elections were to be held in two years, reuniting the nation. Dulles was outraged at Geneva, walked out of the meeting and called it appeasing the communists, an "Asian Munich," another falling domino. Eisenhower realized that if a referendum was held then Ho would have won 80 percent of the vote, and so he supported Diem's refusal to hold the 1956 elections. During cold war America, democracy was important only if the U.S. side won.

Creeping Conformity

The cold war abroad, and McCarthyism at home, had a significant social impact. Generally speaking, Americans are individualistic and independent. But the continual threats from beyond, and supposedly within, created a society in the early fifties unusually concerned about security, a people bent on conformity and consensus.

Conformity was important. Americans moved into suburbs filled with similar homes, similar people, who held similar ideas. Musician Bruce Springsteen recalled that in the town where he grew up, parents and officials were "very intent on maintaining the status quo. Everything was looked at as a threat." Individualism seemed in demise, William H. Whyte Jr. wrote in *The Organization Man*, and he lamented that traditional American values such as independence and competition were being replaced by group activities and bureaucracies. The "junior executive" was more important than the independent thinker, and *The Man in the Grey Flannel Suit* was not only a popular book and movie, but a symbolic image of the fifties: clean cut, suit and tie.

High schools across the nation enforced dress codes, as the fifties became the decade of rules and regulations: no jeans for boys; skirts for girls. In San Antonio, officials banned tight blue jeans or ducktail haircuts on the grounds that "there is a connection between undisciplined dress and undisciplined behavior." Thus teens looked remarkably like their parents. Girls wore hair that resembled Mom's perma-press head, and dear ol' Dad cropped his son's hair in World War II style, the crew cut.

Conformity also appeared on college campuses. Many professors and students had been intimidated by McCarthyism and so the tendency was to fit in, be on the team, and avoid controversy. At the University of Michigan nine out of ten students were afraid to sign a document—it was the Declaration of Independence without the first sentence. When a professor confronted his students, complaining they were conformists, one responded, "Why should we go out on a limb about anything? We know what happened to those who did." A social scientist reported in 1957 that "students today tend to think alike, feel alike, and believe alike," and commencement orators that spring lamented "a whole nation of yesmen," "prefabricated organization men," new graduates "more concerned with security than integrity, with conforming than performing, with imitating than creating."

Professors labeled their students the "silent generation," and silence was particularly expected from female students, then called "coeds." As an increasing number of women flocked to college, advisers guided them toward traditional female disciplines: education, nursing, or home economics. The professions were for men, and many universities had higher admission standards for women, and even *quotas* at graduate and professional schools—to reserve space for the men. Faced with limited opportunities, coeds realized that it was in their interest to embrace the traditional role, to find Mr. Right, the lifetime husband and provider. "I remember the deans telling us an educated person made the best mother," a Radcliffe graduate recalled. "She could sing French songs to her children." College was the "world's best marriage mart," an educator declared, and in fact half of the coeds in the mid-fifties dropped out to marry. When asked about her future ambitions, a Smith senior got right to the point: "I would like to be married to a Princeton graduate." Not being engaged by their last year on campus meant "senior panic," and one female admitted, "On every blind date we all hoped to meet the handsome, smart, witty young man—with shining prospects and a beautiful soul—we would marry." According to one observer, a "legion of coeds" were "far more intent on getting their man than the FBI."

Marriage equaled security, which was coveted during cold war America. Teens were "going steady" at record rates during the fifties, women married younger than at any time in the century, and the divorce rate plummeted. Marriage also equaled success. *Ladies' Home Journal, McCall's, Redbook,* and other women's magazines pumped out articles: "Marriage Is Here to Stay," "Making Marriage Work," "Can This Marriage Be Saved?" Divorce equaled failure. Opinion polls demonstrated in 1957 that only 9 percent of the public believed that an unmarried person could be happy: no female wanted to remain single and become an "old maid."

Most women conformed to the conventional role—wife and mother. According to the accepted message of the decade, a woman could feel fulfilled only if she had children. *Life* declared in a special issue on women in 1956, "Of all accomplishments of the American woman, the one she brings off with the most spectacular success is having babies."

And they did. The number of births soared from 2.8 million in 1945 to over 4 million in 1954, where it remained for the next ten years—the baby boom. The number of families with three kids doubled, with four kids tripled, and by 1960 there were 56 million kids age 15 or under. On TV, one sitcom advocated that children were *Cheaper by the Dozen,* and most students agreed. As one Harvard business major said, "I'd like to have six kids. I don't know why I say that—it just sounds like a minimum production goal."

America embraced tradition: husband in the lead and wife with kids at home. A survey found that concerning the repetitive but essential chores around the house of cleaning and washing, only 10 percent of husbands helped their happy homemakers. She embellished the home and then created another recipe for dinner. In 1955 the two nonfiction best-sellers were *Better Homes & Gardens' Decorating Book* and *Betty Crocker's Cookbook*. Six years later when Jacqueline Kennedy was asked what was the role of the first lady, she stated the endorsed answer: "to take care of my husband." As for the men, they too had responsibilities. As one recalled, "Those of us who came of age in the fifties had no choice. You had to be a husband, a provider, and a success."

In other words, one was supposed to be "normal," for being "different" in the fifties usually was avoided: fit in, play the game, don't rock the boat.

Happy Days

Years later, many Americans referred to the fifties as "happy days." From the perspective of the older generation, the decade was an immense improvement over the previous era of depression and war. In 1957 a poll asked, "Taking all things together, how would you say things are these days—would you say you're very happy, pretty happy, or not too happy?" A resounding 89 percent were either very or pretty happy.

Why? During the Eisenhower years the Korean conflict was history and politics were returning to normalcy. Stalin had died and the new Soviet leaders seemed more moderate. The cold war thawed, and McCarthyism was on the wane; the senator was discredited by 1954 and later died an alcoholic. At the White House, General Ike was in charge: "I Like Ike" was his slogan for these simple times. Whether he was in the White House or on the golf course, his popular approval ratings remained high, averaging 64 percent. In fact he was so popular, journalist Walter Lippmann quipped, "Ike could be elected even if dead." All the while, his administration practiced the politics of moderation. He balanced the budget three times in eight years, signed the Democratic bill that funded the first interstate freeways, and tried to avoid contentious social issues. Peace seized the nation.

So did prosperity. Americans were busy buying a record number of homes in the suburbs, and most of these buyers were first-time home owners—they were obtaining the American Dream. Meanwhile, the economy boomed. *Time* declared "1955 showed the flowering of American capitalism," and two years later an expert proclaimed, "Never before in all the world's history has any nation known such a flood tide of prosperity." Exports soared, resulting in large profits and high wages; almost every year managers and workers looked toward a bonus or raise. The gross national product (GNP) nearly doubled during the decade, inflation remained low, and the invention of credit cards contributed to massive consumption. The purchasing power of citizens increased 50 percent during the decade. The average home contained seven times more equipment than one in the twenties, and for the first time that included a television; Americans bought 50 million TVs by 1960. Detroit revved into high gear, manufacturing almost 60 million automobiles, meaning that for the first time almost every American family could own at least one car. The era was symbolized by the drive-in—either for fast food or for movies. Parents smiled as they drove to new shopping malls, and kids smiled as they received an endless supply of fads—saddle shoes, Barbie dolls, stacks of 45 rpm records. Parents bought $100 million worth of Davy Crockett coonskin hats, while in just a few months of 1958 kids bought 20 million hula hoops. More high school guys had cars, and their girls dressed better and could afford more cosmetics, than at any previous time in history. As one youth declared, "We are the luckiest teenagers in the history of the world."

Furthermore, the fifties were happy days because of kids and family. After Dad returned from coaching his son in Little League, after Mom picked up her daughter at the Girl Scout meeting, families sat in their living rooms and watched TV shows that emphasized traditional values and wholesome life: *Leave It to Beaver, Ozzie and Harriet, The Donna Reed Show, Father Knows Best*. There were only three national TV networks then, and unlike later times when numerous channels emphasized sensationalism and negativism, the message in the fifties was patriotic, positive, and homogenized. The fifties were the Wonder Bread decade: Campbell's soup, Jell-O, Velveeta. Everyone seemed the same—and that happy message was broadcast prime time.

Peace, prosperity, and family provided a well-fed picnic for the depression generation and their numerous children. For most Americans, the fifties were nifty, an "American High," gushed one historian, "a time of hope, a time of growth . . . even a time of glory."

Indeed, these were happy days for many white Americans, especially men, at a time when a common saying was "It's a Man's World." Yet for others the fifties were not so nifty, and during the last years of the decade some citizens were becoming concerned because there were national problems not being addressed—problems that would plant the seeds for the Decade of Tumult and Change.

Seeds of Discontent

In 1957 the Soviets shocked the world by becoming the first nation to launch a satellite, *Sputnik*, into space. "The Russian success in launching the satellite has been something equivalent to Pearl Harbor," wrote a British observer, and an American professor added, "It's our worst humiliation since Custer's last stand." In response the Eisenhower administration began a massive effort to build more powerful rockets and compete with the Soviets in space, while Congress provided some student loans for studying the sciences and established the National Aeronautics and Space Administration (NASA).

The space race had begun, and it renewed atomic fear as both the United States and the USSR continued atmospheric bomb testing. A *McCall's* article in 1957 asked a haunting question, "Will Tomorrow Come?" The next year radioactive strontium 90 began to show up in the milk supply, and two-thirds of Americans listed nuclear war as the nation's most urgent problem. Norman Cousins and others formed the National Committee for a Sane Nuclear Policy (SANE), and the organization grew rapidly and pressured the administration. In 1958 President Eisenhower signed a moratorium on testing with the Russians, but atomic fear continued to be a popular concern, one described in successful books such as Walter Miller's *A Canticle for Leibowitz* and later in popular movies like *On the Beach, Fail-Safe,* and *Dr. Strangelove.* The last scene from *On the Beach* was an empty city with a banner waving in the radioactive breeze: "There is still time, Brother."

Another problem that began to disturb some citizens by the end of the fifties was the role of women. During the decade a record number had earned college educations, and the number of females in the work force also soared, usually part-time sales jobs at the new malls. With husband, kids, spare change, and a home in the suburbs, supposedly, women should have felt fulfilled. Yet some were not. "The problem lay buried, unspoken, for many years in the minds of American women," wrote Betty Friedan. "As she made the beds, shopped for groceries, matched slip-cover material, ate peanut butter sandwiches with her children, chauffeured Cub Scouts and Brownies, lay beside her husband at night—she was afraid to ask even of herself the silent question—'Is this all?'" Friedan called it "the problem that has no name," and it was confirmed by a survey by *Redbook* and published as "Why Young Mothers Feel Trapped." The editors found that many young wives were "desperately anxious and dissatisfied," mostly because of "the crushing commitment to home and community." When *Redbook* asked readers to respond, they were swamped with an astonishing 24,000 letters, demonstrating a discrepancy between reality and image.

That discrepancy appeared on the job, where discrimination was rampant. The workplace was segregated by sex and employment ads listed "Help Wanted Male" and "Help Wanted Female," meaning that managerial and executive positions were for men and lower paying jobs were for women. Most companies would not allow a female employee to apply for management, and many firms required women to quit when they married, particularly airline stewardesses. Except for nursing and teaching, men dominated the professions, and at those schools, deans had quotas that usually admitted only about 5 percent female. As a result white men were about 95 percent of the attorneys, physicians, and professors.

The discrepancy also appeared in sexuality. During the late forties Alfred C. Kinsey conducted his famous research demonstrating that private sexual practices were more permissive than public morality. Community fathers rejected such ideas and passed numerous rules, regulations, and laws to uphold American virtue. Cohabitation among unmarried couples was unlawful in cities, and some states had laws similar to Alabama's, where it was criminal to participate in extramarital sexual intercourse. In Florida, nursing a baby in public was obscene, "indecent exposure, lewd and lascivious behavior." Some local governments passed ordinances prohibiting the sale of bikinis as a way to "control promiscuity," and New York City had an ordinance allowing police to remove people from a public place if they were sexually provocative—or gay. In many states, using birth control, even by married couples, was banned, and in Massachusetts the penalty for dispensing a can of contraceptive foam could be five years in jail. If a woman did get pregnant, there was no recourse to birth; abortion was illegal. The federal government censored racy books such as *Fanny Hill, Tropic of Cancer,* and *Lady Chatterley's Lover,* and television networks did the same with their media. In 1956, when Elvis Presley appeared on *The Ed Sullivan Show,* the performer with the gyrating pelvis was broadcast as a half man—only from the waist up.

The moral code also included something perplexing to some—the "double standard," the idea that men and women had different sexual urges and responsibilities. Hannah Lees wrote in her 1957 *Reader's Digest* article that "women are not supposed to want or need as much love-making as men," and if they did, then the wife would "make him feel inadequate, and then hostile." Supposedly, a young man had a large sexual appetite, and so on a date he would try to "get as much" as he could. The young maiden would fight him off, for if she gave in she was "easy," a "slut," which soon became campus news. In cold war America there were good and bad nations and good and bad girls—and the good girls carried the heavy responsibility of upholding the moral fiber of the boys, and of the nation. Good girls said "no, not 'til we're married," and opinion polls demonstrated that 80 percent supported female virginity until matrimony. After the ring was on her finger, she became his property. The term *spousal abuse* did not exist in the fifties, and the thought that a husband could rape his wife was inconceivable.

To maintain fifties morality, authorities levied heavy fines for unsanctioned behavior. High schools expelled pregnant girls, who were not allowed to graduate, and universities monitored coed behavior in dorms and off campus. After a Michigan State student was raped in 1960, she did something quite unusual—she publicly pressed charges. At that time, most Americans believed that females who endured such tragedy really had "asked for it," and she was expelled.

Sexual standards, of course, only demonstrated hypocrisy in cold war America. Actually, half the marriages in the fifties were between teenagers, and half of those brides were pregnant—they "had to get married." Obviously, teens were doing something else at the drive-in theater besides watching the movie in the '57 Chevy. Yet most citizens refused to face such facts. During the cold war, it was almost unpatriotic to see things unpleasant in America.

Some things were best left unsaid, and that included discussions about sexual orientation. Girls who didn't play with dolls were "tomboys," boys who didn't play sports were suspect, and in any college locker room one could get a laugh by calling someone a "faggot" or "homo." In 1949 *Newsweek* printed an article, "Queer People," which labeled "homosexuals" as "sex murderers," and as late as 1963 an article in the *New York Times* referred to them as "deviants" and "degenerates." In the years between, the psychological and medical community debated how to "treat" them—that is, make them "normal" heterosexuals. Abstinence with psychoanalysis, of course, yet for females the so-called cures also included hormone injections and hysterectomy and for men electroshock—even castration or lobotomy. With such views widespread, local police departments routinely entrapped, harassed, and arrested gays and lesbians. A New Orleans bar raid netted over 60 lesbians, and after a teenage male in Boise admitted to gay sex with local men, 9 males were sentenced to 5 to 15 years for the crime of homosexuality. The repression led gays to organize, and during the decade men formed the Mattachine Society in Los Angeles and women the Daughters of Bilitis in San Francisco.

While sexual orientation was usually kept in the closet during the fifties, race was a problem that was being discussed openly. For those African Americans who lived in the South, usually in small towns or rural areas, the status quo was just a step away from slavery; it was a system of segregation called Jim Crow. Based on the 1896 Supreme Court ruling of *Plessy v. Ferguson* allowing "separate but equal" public facilities for the two races, 17 southern and border states had passed laws that established Jim Crow segregation. State laws established segregated hospitals, jails, and homes for the indigent, deaf, dumb—even for the blind. White businesses, such as motels or restaurants, did not serve blacks, and public facilities like swimming pools did not admit them; in bus and railway stations, signs hung over toilets and water fountains that declared, "Whites Only" or "Colored." Throughout the South whites sat in the front of public buses, blacks in back. When the Reverend Jesse Jackson's father, a proud black veteran of the U.S. Army, returned home to South Carolina after victory over the Nazis, he had to sit behind defeated German prisoners of war.

As for education, Southerners saved money at the black schools, which often were shacks where teachers made only about a third the salary of white counterparts. In Clarendon County, South Carolina, officials spent $179 on every white student in 1950 and $43 on each black one; in Mississippi, those figures were over $123 for a white and $33 for a black: that year less than 3 percent of African Americans in Mississippi had completed high school! The few blacks who remained in school and graduated faced the same situation in higher education. In Texas, approximately three-fourths of federal land-grant funds were spent at white Texas A & M while the remainder went to black Prairie View A & M. This was the South's interpretation of "separate but equal."

Southern states also restricted black voting rights by legal gimmicks, such as white primaries, literacy tests, poll taxes, and even good-character tests. White registrars simply would ask potential black voters an unanswerable question. "How many bubbles are in a four-ounce bar of Ivory soap?" an official asked Carey Cauley in Alabama. When Cauley could not answer, he was deemed illiterate, unable to vote. In 1958 the Civil Rights Commission found that in Alabama only 9 percent of blacks in the state were registered to vote, and that figure was only 4 percent for Mississippi. The commission also found 16 counties across the South that had a majority of black residents but not one black voter.

To be sure, blacks had made some progress during and after World War II and their lives were better in the North. With white males heading off to war first, African Americans residing in the South began the "Great Migration" to northern and western industrial cities where they often worked in integrated factories, made decent salaries, and faced less overt racism. After the war, President Truman ordered the integration of the armed forces, which was implemented slowly, and the Supreme Court ruled that blacks could not be kept out of public graduate schools because of their race. In professional sports, Jackie Robinson broke the color line by taking the field for the Brooklyn Dodgers. Northern universities, public facilities, and many businesses were integrated, yet de facto segregation existed, especially for residential areas and public schools. In 1957 some 60,000 people lived in the suburb of Levittown, Pennsylvania, and not one was black. Schools usually were segregated because district lines followed discriminatory housing practices: suburbs had white schools, and ghettos had black schools. Northern blacks did have voting rights, but white politicians rarely addressed their issues so few African Americans turned out on Election Day.

In both the North and South, most white Americans were racists. Popular opinion polls revealed that 97 percent of southern and 90 percent of northern whites opposed interracial dating; three-fourths of southern and half of northern whites opposed having a black neighbor. Racial slurs and "nigger jokes" were common throughout the nation, for before the civil rights era white society was intolerant and insensitive toward minorities: Mexicans = greasers or wetbacks; Puerto Ricans = spicks; Asians = chinks; and Jews = kikes, yids, or jewboys. Anyone who gave something and then wanted it back was an "indian giver." Racism infected even the wealthy and educated. Ivy League colleges often limited the number of Jewish students, and consequently that community established Brandeis University. Public universities allowed discriminatory practices; almost all sororities or fraternities were segregated. The fifties was for White Anglo-Saxon Protestants, the WASP Decade.

Laws and slurs were minor compared to the problem of making a living, for being a minority was being poor. The fifties economic boom benefited whites, for they held the good jobs, either by law or custom. Most black men were laborers, and a third of black working women in New York City were domestic servants. In 1960 the Department of Labor reported that the average black worker made less than 60 percent of white counterparts. Because many Mexican Americans worked as migrant labor, over half lived in poverty, usually working for a dollar a day. As musician Bo Diddley recalled, "Some of us didn't have the down payment on a Popsicle."

Racism was a national problem, but it was more brutal in the South. Black musician Gabriel King kissed a white teen behind a swamp pop club in Louisiana; he was arrested for "indecent behavior," and although the girl confessed her love for King, the judge sentenced him to one year in prison. A more flagrant miscarriage of justice occurred when a 14-year-old black from Chicago, Emmett Till, visited Mississippi. Unaware of "southern customs," he supposedly whistled at a white woman. Shortly thereafter, the woman's husband and another man captured him, cut off his testicles, shot him in the head, and dumped his mangled body in a local river. Although the killers later confessed, the white jury acquitted them. This murder was not atypical—between the 1880s and the 1950s Southerners lynched over 3,800 blacks.

The Eisenhower administration avoided the plight of African Americans, but not the Supreme Court. The president had appointed the Republican governor of California, Earl Warren, as chief justice, and in 1954 the Court made a landmark decision—*Brown v. Board of Education.* The National Association for the Advancement of Colored People (NAACP) filed on behalf of a young black student, Linda Brown, who, instead of attending a white school in her neighborhood only three blocks away, was bused a mile to attend a black school in Topeka, Kansas. Chief Justice Warren read the opinion: "Does segregation of children in public schools solely on the basis of race, even though the physical facilities and other tangible factors may be equal, deprive the children of the minority group of equal educational opportunities? We unanimously believe that it does." The Court ruled that separate educational facilities were "inherently unequal," and in 1955 the chief justice ordered states to begin a "prompt and reasonable start" to desegregate their public schools.

The southern response was immediate—massive resistance. Southern politicians proclaimed that their racial traditions were not a federal issue but a state's right. Thus they would not abide by *Brown,* and they reaffirmed states' rights by passing more than 450 laws and resolutions to prevent or limit integration. The attorney generals of Louisiana, Alabama, and Texas issued injunctions to prohibit the NAACP from operating in their states, while Louisiana conducted hearings on racial unrest and published their conclusions: the "Communist conspiracy originating with Joseph Stalin . . . is now widely acknowledged as the origin and guiding influence behind the move to integrate the public schools of the South." Opinion polls demonstrated that over 80 percent of white Southerners opposed school desegregation, and a quarter felt that using violence was justified to maintain white supremacy.

Law versus Tradition: The *Brown* case challenged the accepted custom in the South. President Eisenhower had the constitutional duty to uphold the Court's ruling, to begin desegregating schools, but he was not interested in changing the racial status quo. He did not endorse the *Brown* ruling and privately declared that his appointment of Warren was the "biggest damn fool mistake I ever made."

Rosa Parks also challenged law and tradition. On December 1, 1955, a white bus driver in Montgomery, Alabama, demanded that African American Parks give up her seat to a white passenger. She refused, violating the local segregated seating law, and was arrested. In response, local black leaders formed the Montgomery Improvement Association (MIA), and named as its president 26-year-old Martin Luther King Jr., who promoted his idea of nonviolent direct action. The MIA started a bus boycott that lasted over a year. The organization forged a local coalition between black groups and churches that previously had been in competition, it received financial aid from northern blacks and liberal whites, and it eventually led to the formation of a larger organization, which by 1957 became the Southern Christian Leadership Conference (SCLC). Most importantly, the boycott was victorious: it demonstrated that average people could organize nonviolent direct action. While the bus company lost revenue, a federal court ruled against the Montgomery segregation ordinance and in favor of black demands for integrated seating. The buses desegregated, bruising Jim Crow in Montgomery.

For the most part, Montgomery was a local affair, but that was not the case at Central High School in Little Rock, Arkansas. By 1957 the city had worked out a plan to comply with the *Brown* case. Nine black students who lived in the district would desegregate the high school. But public pressure mounted, and to prevent integration the governor surrounded the school with the Arkansas National Guard. When one black girl appeared at the school she was met by an angry white mob screaming, "Lynch her! Lynch her!" The governor's action challenged the federal government. Reluctantly, President Eisenhower federalized the state National Guard and ordered a thousand U.S. Army troops into Little Rock.

The president integrated one segregated high school, and that provoked a strident southern response: "Thus Spake King Ike," declared one Louisiana newspaper. Another proclaimed that Eisenhower had ended democracy and established a "frightening monster—A MILITARY DICTATORSHIP." The Little Rock affair demonstrated that federal attempts to integrate southern schools would be met with massive resistance, perhaps even violence.

By the late fifties, then, a careful observer would have noticed that behind the smiles of happy days were seeds of discontent in America—social discrimination at home and intense anticommunism abroad—which would germinate for the next few years and sprout as protest in the next decade. But it is easy to look back and discover the antecedents of change. In the baby boom era, most families focused their attention on their jobs and kids.

Rebels Without a Cause

Teens seemed to dominate the media, especially as a new problem—"juvenile delinquents." The young were growing restless, especially in the suburbs, and Hollywood explored the topic in many perceptive movies such as *The Wild One, East of Eden, Splendor in the Grass, Blackboard Jungle,* and *Rebel Without a Cause.* In these movies the usual cause of youthful rebellion was that father had been fighting the war when the kids were young, and the message was clear: Dad was the authority, the leader, and delinquency was a threat to the family and therefore to the nation. Juvenile delinquency, of course, had little to do with nationalism and instead reflected a rising population of teens by the late fifties. Many of them sitting in theaters could relate to the characters portrayed by Montgomery Clift, Marlon Brando, and James Dean. When Judy (Natalie Wood) asked her new neighbor Jim Stark (James Dean) in *Rebel*, "Do you live around here?" Stark's response became a classic statement of teenage alienation for the decade: "Who lives?" "Whatever it was," said a youth, "after you saw something like *Rebel Without a Cause*, you felt like going out and breaking a few windshields. And once in a while, you did, or at least you chucked a couple of water balloons at passing cars. That was you, man, a brooding nobody with something silent inside just seething to get out."

Other teenagers turned to an increasing number of new rebels without a cause. Jules Feiffer's cartoons and the comedy of Lenny Bruce or Mort Sahl satirized society. *Mad* magazine brutalized traditional values and mocked national leaders with its grinning moron in the nuclear age, Alfred E. Neuman, always asking, "What, me worry?"

The beatniks didn't worry, especially about mainstream society. In 1957 Jack Kerouac's unusual novel *On the Road* became a best-seller, and suddenly the nation was introduced to the beats. These young writers and poets included Kerouac, Allen Ginsberg, William Burroughs, Gregory Corso, Lawrence Ferlinghetti, Gary Snyder, and others who mingled in the Greenwich Village area of New York City or North Beach in San Francisco. America disturbed the beatniks. They were appalled by the cold war, McCarthyism, the FBI, the CIA, and the Organization Man. The average American, according to Ginsberg, accepted the "dogmatic slumber" in the suburbs and worshiped the "square God of the Garden of Eden." Life to the beats was not conformity or complacency; they wore black, grew beards, talked hip lingo, and frantically hitchhiked around the nation, smoking marijuana, reading poetry, having orgies. "He could hardly get a word out," Kerouac wrote about one beat, "he was so excited with life." As they opted out of contemporary society they viciously attacked cold war America. Ginsberg wrote the poem *Howl* and declared that America was "Moloch! Solitude! Filth! Ugliness! Ashcans and unobtainable dollars! Children screaming under stairways! Boys sobbing in armies! Old men weeping in the parks!" Appropriately for the decade, federal officials declared it obscene and seized the volume.

Beats ridiculed society, which attracted some intellectuals and students, but many times more teens were tuning in their radios, for during the last years of the fifties the younger generation began to shake, rattle, and roll. Rock demonstrated a type of rebellion, the first sign there would be a generational revolt in the sixties. It was vibrant, exciting, and drums and electric guitars moved a younger generation to watch *American Bandstand* and dance, dance, dance—everything from the stroll, to the twist, to the jitterbug. Rock was for the kids, or as a baby boomer noted, it "held us together like some kind of mystic glue." The music also introduced many white youth to black musicians; both races could twist to Chubby Checker or sing along with Diana Ross and The Supremes, and that eventually promoted integration. The message, however, was not rebellious, simply romance and dance; in fact, until the next decade rock lyrics reflected the status quo: Girls were looking for security in Mr. Right (Shelley Fabares's "Johnny Angel"); the double standard ruled (Big Bopper's "Chantilly Lace"); and it was a man's world (Beach Boys' "I Get Around"). Elvis might wiggle his hips in a provocative way, but he sang the oldest theme in music, "Love Me Tender," while Martha and The Vandellas were "Dancing in the Street." Rock demonstrated that Johnny and Sue were restless, not rebelling, for in the fifties the only discord most teens had with society was the jitterbug.

Great Expectations

Eventually, most parents realized that the music was not a threat, and in the long run rock helped ease the fears of cold war America. By the end of the fifties, high school dances, "sock hops," were common—and they were fun—which contributed to fond memories of happy days. "Around my high school," Tom Mathews recalled, "guys were . . . padding the halls in saddle shoes and humming 'Sh–Boom.' A Nice girl was a virgin who didn't smoke cigarettes. Ideology? No one had even heard of it. There were no issues." And as a record number of students packed off for college, they intended to obey the rules, study, cheer their team, and, they hoped, participate in panty raids. "The employers will love this generation" of students, wrote Clark Kerr, the president of the University of California. "They aren't going to press many grievances. They are going to be easy to handle. There aren't going to be any riots."

After all, most Americans were satisfied. The end of the fifties marked social calm and economic prosperity. Of course, there was communism, atomic fear, double standards, and especially the "southern problem"—all of which planted the seeds of the sixties. But at the end of the decade most citizens felt America would prevail over the commies, were comforted by the bomb moratorium, agreed with the sexual status quo, and thought that, somehow, segregation would be resolved. Besides, suburban parents were busy at the shopping malls or laughing along with Jackie Gleason, Jack Parr, or *I Love Lucy.* Their children, meanwhile, were watching the adventures of Spin, Marty, and Annette on *The Mickey Mouse Club* while remembering that *Superman* was saving us with his "never-ending battle for Truth, Justice, and the American Way." For most, life was good, and it was simple, during happy days.

National expectations were soaring at the beginning of 1960. A survey found that nearly 80 percent of adults felt "children born today can look forward to a wonderful future," and in January *Look* magazine published a poll that revealed citizens were happy with their home life, work, community, and expected to "go on enjoying their peaceable, plentiful existence—right through the sixties and maybe forever."

Then, the next month, four young black college students in the South ended what *Life* labeled "the calm of the late '50s." They sat down at a lunch counter—and began the sixties, the Decade of Tumult and Change.

Chapter 1

The Years of Hope and Idealism, 1960–1963

O n the afternoon of February 1, 1960, four African American students at North Carolina A & T College walked into the local Woolworth's in Greensboro, North Carolina. Two of them bought toiletries, and then they all walked over and sat down at the lunch counter. A sign on the counter declared the Jim Crow tradition throughout the South: "Whites Only."

A waitress approached, and Ezell Blair Jr. ordered. "I'd like a cup of coffee, please." The waitress answered, "I'm sorry. We don't serve Negroes here," but Blair responded, "I beg to disagree with you. You just finished serving me at a counter only two feet away from here. . . . This is a public place, isn't it? If it isn't, then why don't you sell membership cards? If you do that, then I'll understand that this is a private concern." "Well," the waitress responded heatedly, "you won't get any service here!" She refused to serve the black students for the remainder of the afternoon. When the store closed at 5:30 P.M., the students left, and one of them said to the waitress, "I'll be back tomorrow with A & T College."

They became known as the Greensboro 4, and that evening on their campus they spread the word of the sit-in. The next morning about 30 male and female black students walked into Woolworth's and sat at the lunch counter. Occasionally a student would try to order but was not served. After two hours they ended the sit-in with a prayer. Next day about 50 sat at the counter. This time they were joined by three white students, and by the end of the week hundreds of black students from a half dozen nearby campuses appeared.

The second day of the Greensboro sit-in; from left, Joseph McNeil, Franklin McCain, Billy Smith, and Clarence Henderson.

The sit-in movement spread rapidly across the South. Always dressed nicely, acting politely, some students read Henry David Thoreau's classic essay *Civil Disobedience* while others read the Bible. In the weeks after Greensboro, black students started sit-ins at lunch counters in Winston-Salem, Durham, Raleigh, and other cities across North Carolina, and during the spring activists were using the tactic in most southern states, from Nashville to Miami, from Baltimore to San Antonio. Blacks also began read-ins at libraries, paint-ins at art galleries, wade-ins at beaches, and kneel-ins at white churches. In Philadelphia, 400 ministers asked their congregations not to shop at businesses that did not hire blacks. Throughout 1960 and the next year about 70,000 participated in various protests in 13 states, and a newspaper in Raleigh noted that the "picket line now extends from the dime store to the United States Supreme Court and beyond that to national and world opinion."

The sit-ins were the first phase of the national civil rights movement, and the reasons for that activism had been clear for some years. In the land of the free, some citizens were more free than others, although all were guaranteed the same liberties by the U.S. Constitution. Although blacks made some progress boycotting buses in Montgomery and a few other cities, victories were only local triumphs. Much more typical was that southern states and cities simply *ignored* federal court rulings, and to appease conservative voters, presidents enforced those decisions only when confronted—such·as at Little Rock. Although the U.S. Constitution guaranteed the right to vote for all citizens, the vast majority of southern blacks could not vote in 1960 because local white officials would not allow them to register. Although the Court mandated integration at public parks, beaches, golf courses, and in interstate travel, those facilities and transportation remained segregated. And although the Court ordered integration in the *Brown* case in 1954, not even 1 percent of southern schools integrated per year, meaning that all black children would be attending integrated schools in the year 2054.

Law versus Tradition: The sixties became the era when those two clashed, a main reason why the decade became one of "Tumult and Change." In 1960 law was the underdog, so if blacks wanted civil rights they would have to use other tactics to change the segregated South. Martin Luther King Jr. called for nonviolent direct action, or as activist James Lawson said, he and his companions were going "to love segregation to death." Sit-ins were the first example of that tactic in the sixties, and they not only integrated lunch counters, but also stimulated many more students to become activists. They formed an organization, the Student Nonviolent Coordinating Committee (SNCC), and they began calling their activism a new name: "the movement."

Yet being part of the movement could be dangerous. In Greensboro, white youths appeared at Woolworth's, threatened blacks, and eventually someone telephoned that if the sit-in did not stop a bomb would be detonated. The manager closed the store, and the mayor called for talks. That was a typical white response: officials formed committees to "study" proposals to end segregated seating while at the same time they applied pressure on older black leaders to control their youth and demanded that black college presidents expel activists. During the first year of the sit-ins, black college administrators expelled over 140 students and fired almost 60 faculty members. Nevertheless, the sit-ins spread, and so local police arrested peaceful activists for "inciting a riot," jailing about 3,600 in the year after Greensboro. Short jail time did not stop the sit-ins, and so some white Southerners began the unofficial response—violence. In Atlanta, a white threw acid into a demonstrator's face, and during sit-ins in Houston, a white teenager slashed a black with a knife. Three others captured a protester, flogged him, carved "KKK" in his chest, and hung him by his knees from a tree. When blacks tried to integrate public beaches in Biloxi, Mississippi, white men chased them with clubs and guns, eventually shooting eight; local police arrested blacks for "disturbing the peace."

Repression in the past usually had worked, but not in 1960. Just the opposite; it created a common bond for black students, gave them a new sense of pride, and encouraged many of them to try harder to beat segregation. These were "ordinary" folks, often local people, doing the extraordinary—putting their lives on the line— and this time there was no turning back.

Why? Why would a student or a sharecropper get involved and become an activist? Some had been inspired by parents, older civil rights workers, teachers, or by Martin Luther King Jr. Ezell Blair had heard King preach two years before he joined the Greensboro sit-in, and recalled the sermon being "so strong that I could feel my heart palpitating. It brought tears to my eyes." Others were inspired by decolonization in Africa, where at that time a dozen nations were obtaining independence, and activists were wondering when they would get equality in the land of the free; the sit-ins, one wrote, were a "mass vomit against the hypocrisy of segregation." Many more were simply fed up with being humiliated. As black students in Atlanta proclaimed, "Every normal human being wants to walk the earth with dignity and abhors any and all proscriptions placed upon him because of race or color."

Significantly, these issues now were being televised at prime time. It is difficult to overestimate the importance of TV in the sixties. Numerous authors have debated the impact of the media on the Vietnam War and antiwar movement, and one wonders if bus boycotts during the fifties would have remained local incidents if more white and black homes had televisions or if network coverage had been more extensive.

By 1960, however, Americans had purchased 50 million TVs, and during the next years the network evening news expanded from 15 minutes to a half hour, provoking interest in national issues. The sixties became the first televised decade, and the first show was civil rights. At predominantly black Howard University, Cleveland Sellers recalled students staring at the TV news, so quiet "you could hear a rat pissing on cotton. . . . My identification with the demonstrating students was so thorough that I would flinch every time one of the whites taunted them. On nights when I saw pictures of students being beaten and dragged through the streets by their hair, I would leave the lounge in a rage." With more extensive TV coverage virtually every citizen could witness—and judge—Jim Crow segregation.

Another reason for becoming an activist was that this generation of students had been raised in cold war America. The fifties were an unusually patriotic era in which teachers had baby boomers begin the school day with the Pledge of Allegiance, "with liberty and justice for all," and then students memorized the words of the Constitution, "We the People," and the Declaration of Independence, "All Men Are Created Equal." Yet when these students turned on the TV or read newspapers, they quickly realized that such words rang hollow. "The whole country was trapped in a lie," said activist Casey Hayden. "We were told about equality but we discovered it didn't exist."

The movement aroused hope and idealism during 1960, and so did the campaign of John F. Kennedy, another demonstration that the nation had entered a new era—the sixties.

Passing the Torch

Senator John Kennedy inspired many during his bid for the Democratic nomination. Previously, Kennedy had not displayed much support for civil rights, but the sit-ins forced the candidate to consider the issue. In June 1960 the senator met King, and he later told a group of African diplomats that "it is in the American tradition to stand up for one's rights—even if the new way to stand up . . . is to sit down." Just two weeks before the November election, King and 50 other activists were arrested during a sit-in at a department store in Atlanta. The others were released, but King was held in jail. The Republican candidate, Vice President Richard M. Nixon, had no comment, but JFK called Coretta Scott King, who was pregnant, and expressed his concern. Shortly thereafter, King was released and praised Kennedy; King's father, who had favored Nixon, now declared his support for JFK. Although the episode was neglected in the white press, it was publicized in African-American papers and celebrated at their churches, resulting in a large turnout of the black electorate in key northern cities.

Yet civil rights was not the central issue of the 1960 election; the main concerns were the cold war and the economy. A year earlier, guerrilla leader Fidel Castro had ousted the U.S.-supported dictator in Cuba, and then Castro alarmed his neighbor to the north by announcing he was a communist and by expropriating American businesses on the island. Communism emerged just 90 miles from Florida. In response, President Eisenhower protested throughout 1960 and eventually broke diplomatic relations. Relations with the Soviet Union were not much better. In May, the Soviet Union shot down an American U-2 spy plane above their country. Soviet Premier Nikita Khrushchev demanded an American apology for violating Russian airspace. When President Eisenhower refused, tempers flared at the Paris summit meeting and the Soviet leader marched out of the conference, denouncing "American aggression." At home during the 1960 campaign, the economy had lapsed into a short recession resulting in industrial stagnation and rising unemployment.

During the first months of the campaign, Kennedy had one "character" problem: he was a Catholic, and none ever had been elected to the presidency. He confronted the issue directly, flying to Houston to meet a convention of Protestant ministers, declaring on television, "I believe in an America where the separation of Church and State is absolute," where no church or parochial school should be granted "public funds or political preference." That seemed to dismiss the doubts of most voters.

The campaign heated up, and the vice president focused on his years of apprenticeship under Eisenhower, who remained popular. Nixon talked about experience and leadership, presented himself as the successor to Ike, and promised continuity, not change. Kennedy spoke of change: "The old era is ending. The old ways will not do." But Kennedy's idea of change was not to move away from previous policies. Indeed, he would be tougher on communism. He declared a "missile gap" supposedly in favor of the Soviets, and he claimed that he would be better for the economy, promising to "get the nation moving again," pledging a 5 percent growth rate. He asked the nation to reach out:

We stand today on the edge of a New Frontier—the frontier of the 1960s—a frontier of unknown opportunities and perils—a frontier of

unfulfilled hopes and threats. . . . The New Frontier of which I speak is
not a set of promises—it is a set of challenges.

JFK confronted the nation. "Can a nation organized and governed such as ours
endure? That is the real question. Have we the nerve and the will?" And he
declared, "If you are tired, then stay with the Republicans," but "America cannot
stand still . . . this is a time of burdens and sacrifice; we must move."

The polls showed a very close race as the candidates held the first televised
presidential debates. Interest soared, and 70 million Americans watched the first
encounter. Nixon appeared tired from the campaign, dark and haggard, struggling
to make a good impression. Kennedy was the opposite—fresh and vibrant, handsome and relaxed, eager to address the nation, optimistic about the future. The candidates differed little on the issues, but that was not the point: the message was
image, and the Kennedy image won on TV.

The election was one of the closest in history. Over 68 million votes were cast,
and Kennedy won by only 112,000 votes in the heaviest turnout since 1908. Nixon
won the West, the farm states, and some of the Midwest, but Kennedy won the
other midwestern states, New England, the Atlantic states, and most of the South.
Kennedy's vice presidential pick, Texas senator Lyndon B. Johnson, proved invalu-
able in his home state and the South, and in the North, the Catholic blue-collar and
the urban black votes were decisive. African Americans delivered Illinois and
Michigan—and the election—to Kennedy.

"Let us begin anew," the youngest president ever elected said in his inaugural
speech. "Let the word go forth from this time and place, to friend and foe alike, that
the torch has been passed to a new generation of Americans." The new chief executive quickly set the mood of the nation—hope and idealism. He confronted the
complacent fifties by challenging citizens to get involved, to make a commitment:
"And so, my fellow Americans: ask not what your country can do for you—ask what
you can do for your country." He appointed advisers from Ivy League colleges who
the press dubbed "the best and the brightest," and they talked about "new frontiers"
and a social agenda that would spread affluence and middle-class status to all. With
his flash and dash the new president ushered in an era of rising expectations—he
stirred America out of its fifties slumber.

Camelot, it was later called—the handsome 43-year-old president, his beautiful
young wife, 32, and the best and brightest advisers. They moved into Washington
in January 1961, and the media buzzed with terms such as *glamour, vision,*
progress, vigor. Times were changing. This was not Grandfather Ike on the golf
course; this was Jack and friends playing touch football on the White House lawn.
The president initiated a physical fitness program, and soon youngsters were ex-
ercising in schools and soldiers were trying to outdo each other on 50-mile hikes.
At the White House, a parade of famous actors, artists, and musicians entertained
the president and first lady. Washington seemed to glitter, or as adviser Arthur

Schlesinger Jr. observed, "to make itself brighter, gayer, more intellectual, more resolute. It was a golden interlude."

Kennedy appealed to liberals, naturally, and also to intellectuals and youth. A philosophy professor remembered that "Kennedy created a climate of high idealism—it was evangelical. It was marvelous that we would make a beautiful world, a more compassionate world." And the president also excited a large crop of teenagers as they began thinking about their future. He aroused them by asking if they would give their time and energy in a "peace corps" aimed at helping people in emerging nations. He inspired them to think about a hopeful, bright future. "The whole idea," stated a teen, "was that you can make a difference. I was sixteen years old and I believed it. I really believed that I was going to be able to change the world."

That was the Kennedy promise—you could make a difference—and such ideas stimulated optimism. He asked Congress to pass his legislative program, the New Frontier, which included a raise in the minimum wage and surplus food distribution to alleviate poverty, an education bill to reduce overcrowding in public schools, a tariff reduction to increase trade, a cut in taxes to stimulate the economy, and a health care program for the elderly.

Less than two months after his inauguration, JFK established the Alliance for Progress, an attempt to combat Castro's revolutionary appeal in Latin America and to help those nations have a future "bright with hope" by directing U.S. foreign aid not only toward economic development but also for social justice. More importantly, JFK initiated the Peace Corps, calling on young Americans to help in the "great common task of bringing to man that decent way of life which is the foundation of freedom and a condition of peace." The *Washington Post* called it an "exciting idea," the *New York Times* labeled it "a noble enterprise," and the response was immediate and overwhelming, demonstrating a new decade of idealistic students. Within an hour after the announcement of the corps, the government switchboard could not handle all the calls from potential volunteers: "some 6,000 letters of suggestion, inquiry, and open application. None mentions salary."

College students seemed to come alive that spring, partly because of JFK and also because of civil rights sit-ins and atomic fear; for the first time in years they began organizing, questioning, and debating. Many joined the most popular group then, the National Student Association, while conservative ones organized Young Americans for Freedom (YAF), and progressive activists formed Students for a Democratic Society (SDS). Collegians also began publishing dissident journals such as *New Freedom* at Cornell, *Studies on the Left* at Wisconsin, or *Alternatives* at Illinois, and such publications eventually appeared on 20 campuses. Some students also formed political parties concerned with national and local issues, from VOICE at Michigan to Political Action Club at Swarthmore to SLATE at Berkeley, and members began picketing businesses that discriminated. Many students began going to coffeehouses and listening to a new type of music—folk—that avoided the usual lyrics of romance and dance and addressed issues—first civil rights and later war.

On a few select campuses, spring semester 1960 witnessed the first pulse of student activism. At Harvard, a thousand students held a walk for nuclear disarmament, and students joined over 15,000 who attended a rally at Madison Square Garden aimed at ending the nuclear arms race and creating a test ban treaty. Yet activism troubled the older generation, who remained steeped in cold war culture. In response, HUAC held hearings in the Bay Area to investigate "communist activities." That prompted a thousand Berkeley students to protest the investigations at City Hall in San Francisco. On the second day, while students were singing "the land of the free, home of the brave," police appeared with billy clubs and fire hoses. They drenched the protesters, and as Betty Denitch remembered, students were "dragged by their hair, dragged by their arms and legs down the stairs so that their heads were bouncing off the stairs." Students labeled the affair "Black Friday," and Denitch later stated, "That was the start of the sixties for me."

Communism Abroad

Black Friday was a cold war response to what some considered communism at one university; a more significant reaction came from the Kennedy administration toward Cuba. In just the third month of the Kennedy presidency a sobering theme emerged: JFK and his advisers would not spend most of their time initiating a New Frontier. Instead, they would be responding to two issues—communism abroad and civil rights at home.

In April some 1,500 Cuban émigrés invaded Cuba at the Bay of Pigs. The invasion force had been conceived during the Eisenhower years, trained by the CIA, and aimed at ending the rule of Fidel Castro. Soon after his inauguration, Kennedy quietly sought the advice of his military and domestic advisers, and almost all urged him to proceed with the operation. JFK agreed, hoping an invasion of exiles would stimulate anti-Castro feelings and result in an anticommunist Cuba. Kennedy would get credit for "rolling back" communism from the Western Hemisphere.

The Bay of Pigs, according to historian Theodore Draper, was "one of those rare events in history—a perfect failure." The invasion force was poorly trained, did not receive the necessary air support, and Cubans saw the attack as American imperialism. Castro rushed to the scene, rifle in hand, rallied his army and people, and won credit for crushing the invasion and defending the nation. Publicly, Kennedy stated that the reason for the invasion was that Cuban refugees wanted to return their homeland to independence and liberty. Privately, he wondered to an aide, "How could I have been so stupid . . . to let them proceed?" The president accepted "full responsibility" for the disaster. The Cuban army captured over 1,200 prisoners and JFK later agreed to pay a $53 million ransom for their release. The president also ordered Operation Mongoose, a covert scheme to assassinate Castro using organized crime and the CIA; in an era of James Bond movies the agency tried everything from poisoned fountain pens to exploding cigars.

Kennedy's fiasco made him look weak and inexperienced in foreign affairs. The *New York Times* editorialized, "We looked like fools to our friends, rascals to our enemies, and incompetents to the rest."

But not to the American public: JFK's popularity ratings soared to over 80 percent. Most citizens hated Castro, who had called former president Eisenhower the "senile White House golfer." Any action against Castro was better than none. The president had restored vigorous leadership, supposedly, and that was more apparent the next month when JFK announced the nation's new challenge—space.

Since the Soviets launched *Sputnik,* America had lagged behind in space achievements. Then, in April 1961, the Russians again stunned the world by launching cosmonaut Yuri Gagarin, who completed an orbital flight around the earth. Upon his return to Moscow, throngs jammed Red Square for a massive parade, and in the first live television broadcast out of the Soviet Union, Premier Khrushchev boasted, "We are proud that the world's first cosmonaut is a Soviet man!"

That was too much for JFK and for the American people. Two weeks later, on May 6, America responded with its first space success. Navy Commander Alan Shepard Jr. made a suborbital flight of over 100 miles. A week later the president stood before Congress, pledging to land a man on the moon and return him safely to earth by the end of the decade. "In a very real sense, it will not be one man going to the moon . . . it will be an entire nation." The administration got Congress to increase the space budget 50 percent that year, and during the summer Air Force Captain Virgil "Gus" Grissom made the second suborbital flight. Only eight months after Kennedy's speech, Colonel John Glenn completed the nation's first orbital flight, which boosted American pride and morale.

Civil Rights at Home

The space race was on—while back on earth, the civil rights movement continued to gain momentum. By 1961 the first tactic of the movement, sit-ins, had achieved impressive results. Activists had integrated lunch counters and theaters in nearly 200 cities. Success was contagious: more black and white students joined the movement, and that provoked participation from parents and many prominent blacks, such as Sidney Poitier, Harry Belafonte, and Sammy Davis Jr. Comedian Dick Gregory led many sit-ins, and when whites told him, "We don't serve Negroes," he responded, "No problem, I don't eat Negroes."

Feeling hopeful, black activists in May began the second tactic of the movement—the freedom rides. Seven black and six white volunteers boarded two buses in Washington, D.C., and began their ride into the South. The Congress of Racial Equality (CORE) organized the ride to protest that southern states had ignored an earlier Supreme Court ruling that segregated buses and terminals were unconstitutional in interstate travel. CORE's national director, James Farmer, wanted to end such segregation by "putting the movement on wheels." To ensure press coverage,

Farmer invited reporters, and the two buses left Washington and traveled without serious incident through Virginia, the Carolinas, and Georgia.

Then they reached Alabama. When the first bus arrived in Anniston, whites armed with blackjacks, iron bars, clubs, and tire chains met the riders. They attacked the bus, broke windows, and slashed tires before the driver could execute an escape. Whites followed the bus, and when it was forced to stop eight miles out of town because of flat tires, the mob hurled a smoke bomb inside the vehicle. That forced the freedom riders out, into the hands of the angry crowd; as the bus burst into flames, whites beat the riders. After the melee, local hospital workers refused to treat the riders, and when the second bus appeared in Anniston, whites forced their way aboard and beat the passengers. One white rider, a 61-year-old retired professor from Michigan, was left with brain damage.

The riders on the second bus decided to continue to Birmingham, where another white crowd met them. The police had been warned to expect trouble, but although their headquarters was only two blocks from the terminal, no policemen appeared. The chief of police later explained it was Mother's Day and most of his boys were home "visiting their mothers" as the armed mob charged the bus. According to a CBS reporter who was on the scene, white toughs grabbed the pas-

Freedom rider bus burns near Anniston, Alabama.
Such violence put pressure on the Kennedy administration
to uphold federal law in the South.

sengers, dragged them into alleys, "pounding them with pipes, with key rings and with fists." When a white rider, James Peck, was pulled off the bus, he was knocked unconscious and later needed over 50 stitches to stop the bleeding. Police did not appear for ten minutes, and by that time local whites had left in waiting cars; there were no arrests. Governor John Patterson told the riders to "get out of Alabama as quickly as possible." The Justice Department arranged a flight, and the first freedom ride ended bruised—but not defeated.

Events in Anniston and Birmingham were widely reported, which forced the Kennedy administration to order the FBI to investigate, send 400 U.S. marshals, and pressure the Alabama governor to uphold the law. Also, television coverage enraged other student activists, and eight blacks and two whites quickly organized the second freedom ride.

Their bus left Nashville and headed south for Birmingham. After they arrived in that city, police commissioner Eugene "Bull" Connor took them off the bus and put them in the city jail for two days. Eventually, they left Birmingham with a police escort and traveled to Montgomery. When they arrived, activist John Lewis recalled, the police disappeared. No one was in sight until they got off the bus; then local whites charged. A Justice Department official on the scene immediately called Washington, D.C., shouting into the phone, "It's terrible. It's terrible. There's not a cop in sight. People are yelling, 'Get 'em, get 'em.' It's awful."

And they did get 'em. Armed with pipes and baseball bats, 300 whites attacked 21 freedom riders and a few newsmen. They clubbed Lewis to the ground, leaving him in a pool of blood with a brain concussion. When they spotted a white rider, several local women screamed, "Kill the nigger-loving son of a bitch!" They almost did, bashing his head, kicking in his front teeth, and injuring his spinal cord. One rider suffered a broken leg, and another had gas poured on him and his clothes set aflame. Local men slapped two white female riders, and when a federal official tried to help them into his car, the men beat him to the ground, knocking him unconscious. The crowd swelled to a thousand, and after 20 minutes of mob rule, the Montgomery police finally arrived and quelled the riot. When a newspaperman asked the police commissioner why ambulances had not been called, he responded that all were "broken down," and concerning why the police had not arrived sooner, he stated, "We have no intention of standing guard for a bunch of troublemakers coming into our city."

The activists informed the Kennedy administration that they intended to leave Montgomery in a bus the next day for Jackson, Mississippi. The president expressed concern and asked them to cease rides for a while and to participate in a cooling-off period. Black leaders said no. James Farmer replied that blacks had been "cooling off for a hundred years. . . . If we got any cooler we'd be in a deep freeze." The bus left Montgomery and this time it was protected by the National Guard, seven patrol cars, two helicopters, and three planes. There was no violence. But when the riders reached Jackson they were arrested for attempting to use the white rest room in the bus station, charged with "breach of peace," and jailed. They spent the next two months in a brutal Mississippi prison.

As in the previous year, white repression in 1961 did not stifle the movement, and in fact it inspired others to join the struggle for civil rights. The chaplain of Yale University, William Sloane Coffin Jr., remembered watching John Lewis on televised news "laying on the ground, his head split open, blood all over his face. . . . I doubt that I'd ever been angrier and certainly never more ashamed of the United States." Shortly thereafter, Coffin joined his first freedom ride. Other activists during the summer held sit-ins and demonstrations at bus, railroad, and airport terminals, creating more disruptions in interstate travel.

The activists forced President Kennedy to act—to uphold the law in the South. The administration ordered the Interstate Commerce Commission to issue rules prohibiting racial discrimination in interstate facilities, and although there was resistance, by the next year most interstate travel and facilities had integrated. JFK also sent his brother, Attorney General Robert Kennedy, to meet with the leaders of CORE, SCLC, and SNCC. The administration wanted the students to abandon direct and confrontational tactics and start voter registration drives, which officials felt would be less threatening to whites and therefore less violent. Also, the president hoped, registering black southern voters would appeal to northern liberal supporters and bring about peaceful change in the South before his reelection campaign in 1964.

A few activists began the third tactic for civil rights—voter registration—while at the same time international events again returned the administration's focus to foreign affairs.

Khrushchev

In June 1961 President Kennedy met West European leaders and Soviet Premier Khrushchev in Vienna. Relations with the Russians had soured since the Bay of Pigs. Furthermore, Khrushchev had made numerous declarations supporting "wars of liberation" in developing nations, and rebels were fighting in the Congo, Laos, and South Vietnam. Importantly, the Kremlin had threatened to close Western access routes to Berlin, routes that had been guaranteed by agreements at the end of World War II. Berlin was unique. Situated deep in the Soviet zone of Germany it was alone, exposed, or as strategists often called it, "the testicles of the West." The city was divided into two sections, and so East Germans could escape communism easily by crossing into capitalist West Berlin, and because many did every year, East Germany was being drained of its skilled workers while being an embarrassment for all communist governments.

The Vienna summit meeting resolved little. Khrushchev could not "stop change" against colonialism and capitalism, he said; the Soviets would continue supporting revolution abroad. Kennedy was just as firm on Berlin. "If we don't meet our commitments in Berlin, it will mean the destruction of NATO and a dangerous situation for the whole world. All Europe is at stake in West Berlin."

To boost his image as the leader of the West, the president addressed the nation in July. He declared that he was mobilizing 158,000 reserve and national guardsmen and was dramatically expanding the military. Shortly thereafter, JFK increased the defense budget, tripled draft calls, extended enlistments, enlarged the armed forces by 300,000, and sent 40,000 additional troops to defend Europe. The secretary of defense, Robert McNamara, discarded the previous administration's policy of "massive retaliation" for employing a "flexible response" to fight any conflict, from an atomic war to a small insurgency. The president then enlarged the Army Special Forces, or "Green Berets," who were trained in guerrilla warfare to combat wars of liberation, and he began sending them to South Vietnam. And the administration boosted the nuclear arsenal, even though they knew there was no "missile gap." In fact, American satellite reconnaissance in 1961 discovered the U.S. advantage in missiles over the Soviets was 17 to 1.

Khrushchev called Kennedy's speech belligerent, and in August he startled the world. While the Soviet army encircled Berlin, the East Germans built a wall that closed the border crossing in that city. President Kennedy protested, but eventually the wall solved the Berlin issue: the Russians were willing to allow West Berlin to exist deep in their eastern section of Germany as long as the city did not drain eastern workers. In the future, East Germans attempting to escape to the West were shot, a bloody testimony to communism. As tensions rose, Khrushchev again shocked the West. He announced he was breaking the American-Russian moratorium on nuclear testing. Kremlin leaders not only resumed testing, but they exploded an enormous weapon—3,000 times more powerful than the atomic bomb dropped on Hiroshima.

Atomic brinkmanship. President Kennedy responded by resuming underground testing. When that did not hush critics, he ordered 30 atmospheric tests, which began the next year. As Russia and America polluted the skies, their tanks faced each other in East and West Berlin.

Prodding JFK

Atomic brinkmanship, concerns about nuclear pollution, along with civil rights in the South, provoked more activism throughout 1961. Dagmar Wilson and her friends formed Women Strike for Peace, and in November some 50,000 housewives organized events in 60 cities. "This movement was inspired and motivated by mothers' love for children," one member explained. "When they were putting their breakfast on the table, they saw not only the Wheaties and milk, but they also saw strontium 90 and iodine 131." Many protested with banners: "End the Arms Race— Not the Human Race." *Newsweek* wrote the marchers were "like the women you would see . . . attending PTA meetings," yet some conservatives were alarmed,

Dagmar Wilson and Coretta Scott King
lead a Women's Strike for Peace demonstration.

charging that the "pro-Reds have moved in on our mothers and are using them for their own purposes." Shortly thereafter, Wilson and other leaders were called to testify before HUAC.

In the South, tensions also remained high, especially as African Americans attempted to register to vote. The administration's hope that the Old Confederacy would allow black citizens to register, and thus gain political power, was an illusion.

Instead, the white response was brutal. When Fannie Lou Hamer attempted to register in Mississippi, she lost her job, was jailed, and then given a $9,000 water bill—even though her house had no running water. A more vicious response came from another town in that state, McComb. When black activist Bob Moses took three locals to the courthouse to register, he was arrested and jailed. His second attempt resulted in a beating and stitches. Later, Herbert Lee, a black man who had helped Moses and had tried to register, was shot in the head by a Mississippi state representative. When the FBI investigated, a black witness was gunned down in his front yard. At the trial the white jury ruled that the politician shot and killed the unarmed Lee in "self-defense."

More publicized, however, was the voter registration drive in Albany, Georgia, for its leaders, Ralph Abernathy and Martin Luther King Jr., aimed to use the city to reveal the injustice throughout the South. Forty percent of Albany's inhabitants were black, but not one of these taxpayers ever had been elected or appointed as a city official, police officer, or jury member. Almost none had the right to vote. Strict segregation existed; black citizens were barred from all public facilities— parks, swimming pools, and the library. From the "colored waiting room" in the bus station it was eight blocks to a "colored restaurant" and six miles to a "colored motel." Throughout winter 1961 and spring 1962 activists marched, sat-in, and attempted to register voters, but after months of demonstrations only a handful had won the right to vote. White officials responded by throwing over 1,000 activists in jail, including Abernathy and King. When blacks peacefully marched on public streets out of their neighborhood toward white districts, police simply arrested them for disorderly conduct, parading without a permit, loitering, even "*tending* to create a disturbance."

This was the South's view of "states' rights," and to civil rights demonstrators it meant one thing: federal intervention was needed to overrule "states' wrongs," to uphold the U.S. Constitution. Activists demanded that the Kennedy administration protect them from racist attacks during peaceful sit-ins, voter registration drives, or any nonviolent activities. "Must we die before the federal government stops compromising with bigots?" asked activist Charles Sherrod. He confronted administration officials, "If we are murdered . . . our blood will be on your hands." Without federal intervention, activists only registered a small percentage of black voters in the Deep South.

The administration continued to act cautiously during 1962. While all citizens over 21 at that time had a constitutional right to vote, discrimination at businesses such as lunch counters or in department stores broke no federal statutes, and the Justice Department felt more comfortable upholding the traditional federal-state arrangement; that is, as officials wrote to King, "law and order in any locality is the primary responsibility of local officials." Although activists charged the federal government did have power under numerous federal codes, the Kennedy administration did not want to irritate local authorities, and lose southern white votes, by sending an occupation army into the Old Confederacy.

Yet the Old Confederacy would force the issue—and President Kennedy—at the University of Mississippi. Federal courts had ordered integration at southern universities, and some of them had begun the process. But not Ole Miss. In September, Governor Ross Barnett and the university declined admittance of black Air Force veteran James Meredith. Like Eisenhower during the Little Rock crisis, JFK felt he had to uphold the law. The president called the governor, urging him to yield, but to no avail. JFK then mobilized the state National Guard and sent 3,000 troops and U.S. marshals to Ole Miss. Meredith arrived on campus, and whites sparked a riot, besieging the university administration building and attacking troops. Tear gas and shots rang out in the night. Kennedy sent reinforcements, and eventually 5,000 troops occupied the campus. Three men were killed, 50 injured, and 6 marshals were shot, one critically wounded. The federal government integrated Ole Miss in what some locals called the "Last Battle of the Civil War."

Kennedy's policy divided the nation. Most Southerners and conservatives jeered, "an attack on our traditions and states' rights," while most liberals cheered, "upholding the U.S. Constitution for all citizens." Civil rights at home dominated the news, but only for a short time, for three weeks later, the issue again became communism abroad—missiles in Cuba.

"One Hell of a Gamble"

After the Bay of Pigs, the Soviets pledged to defend Castro from U.S. aggression. To do that, Khrushchev sent antiaircraft missiles, bombers, technicians, and even troops to Cuba, which an American U-2 spy plane observed in August 1962. Kennedy then secretly cautioned the Russians not to place offensive, or ground-to-ground, missiles on the island. Yet Khrushchev did not heed the warning and sent over 40 Intermediate Range Ballistic Missiles (IRBM) to Cuba. He felt JFK was preparing the U.S. Marines to invade his new ally, and he was irritated that a few years earlier the Americans had positioned offensive missiles in Europe and Turkey, close to Soviet borders. As Khrushchev told the Cuban ambassador, now the Americans "will know what it feels like to live in the sights of nuclear weapons."

In October U-2s took photographs over Cuba that stunned the White House. The Russians were building a launch pad that could fire IRBMs. Those weapons would have a 2,200-mile capability—placing New Mexico, Minnesota, Maine, and of course Washington, D.C., in atomic range.

Khrushchev's atomic brinkmanship placed Kennedy in a pressure cooker. Congressional elections were only three weeks away, and Republicans and the conservative press had been grumbling about integration at home while demanding a tougher policy toward the Soviet Union and Cuba. The administration had to be firm, but none of the options were appealing. An invasion of Cuba might result in a belligerent Soviet response or, more likely, a long guerrilla war on the island. That left either an air strike on the launch pads or a blockade so Soviet ships or planes could not deliver missiles to Cuba—both acts of war.

On October 22 the president addressed the nation. In a speech of profound gravity, Kennedy informed the public of the missiles in Cuba. Then he drew the line, not with Cuba, but with the Soviet Union. The president charged that, contrary to promises, the Kremlin was building "offensive missile and bomber bases in Cuba." Although there was not yet evidence of atomic weapons on the island, he said, he was putting the armed forces on alert and ordering a "quarantine" of the island. The U.S. military would stop all ships and aircraft suspected of carrying weapons to Cuba; if they refused to stop, they would be attacked. After years of attempting to avoid a Soviet-American showdown, Kennedy bluntly confronted the Kremlin with the possibility of war. The president declared that if any missile was launched from Cuba on nations of the Western Hemisphere, he would regard it "as an attack by the Soviet Union on the United States, requiring a full retaliatory response upon the Soviet Union."

Atomic high noon. During the next week American B-52s flew bombing patterns, U.S. Marines assembled in Florida for a possible invasion, and citizens rushed to grocery stores in a frenzy of panic buying. Meanwhile, the president met with congressional leaders. Some hawks urged an immediate invasion, to which Kennedy responded, "If we go into Cuba, we have to all realize that we have taken the chance that these missiles, which are ready to fire, won't be fired." That, JFK continued, would be "one hell of a gamble."

On October 23 Khrushchev sent a message to Kennedy, complaining bitterly that American actions were illegal, "outright banditry . . . the folly of degenerate imperialism." He accused the president of pushing mankind to the "abyss of a . . . nuclear war" and privately told his colleagues, "This may end in a big war." Soviet ships continued steaming toward Cuba.

Kennedy remained tough, and three days later the Soviet premier again wrote, this time making a proposal: Russia would send no more weapons to Cuba and would withdraw or destroy antiaircraft missiles already there if Kennedy would end the quarantine and promise not to invade Cuba. Kennedy assembled his advisers, but then a third Khrushchev message arrived, demanding that JFK withdraw U.S. missiles from Turkey. A missile for missile deal, but that was no deal to Kennedy. Secretly, he had ordered the removal of the missiles in Turkey months earlier; they were obsolete, but now he did not want to appear as if he was compromising. The president sent his brother to talk with the Soviet ambassador. Robert Kennedy informed the ambassador that the administration would remove the missiles in Turkey eventually—but there would be no announced deal or compromise. The USSR must first extract all missiles from Cuba. That satisfied Khrushchev, and he ordered Soviet ships to return home. The missiles of October did not bring about atomic Armageddon.

During the missile crisis most Americans rallied to the colors and supported the president. Again, JFK's popular approval ratings soared, this time to 74 percent. He had forced Khrushchev to back down; Americans stood tall, and when they went to the polls the next month they returned the Democratic majority to Congress. The early sixties were dominated by Kennedy, Khrushchev, and King—and that again was revealed during spring 1963 when King decided to march on Birmingham.

King

Birmingham was an appropriate choice. Public facilities, businesses, and virtually everything were completely segregated, so much that officials had removed a book from the library that featured white and black rabbits. Blacks had no votes, nor could they get jobs in the public sector. The city was so violent that local blacks called it "Bombingham" and their neighborhood "Dynamite Hill." Police commissioner Bull Connor predicted that "blood would run in the streets of Birmingham before it would be integrated."

King realized the danger, but felt the campaign would reveal southern "brutality openly—in the light of day—with the rest of the world looking on." That would force Kennedy to act. "The key to everything," King said, was "federal commitment, full, unequivocal, and unremitting."

On April 3 black activists peacefully began sitting-in and picketing restaurants and businesses. The police arrested and jailed them. Next day, about 50 activists marched on city hall, and they too were arrested, and the same fate awaited King's brother, the Reverend A. D. King, when he led a march on Palm Sunday. Each day more black citizens joined in, and the stream of marchers became a river, which prompted officials to secure an injunction barring demonstrations.

That raised an issue: should the activists follow local law and end their demonstrations? King said no, proclaimed the injunction immoral and that it was his duty to violate unethical orders and laws: he and his supporters would march to city hall on April 12, Good Friday. He promised to lead demonstrations until "Pharaoh lets God's people go," and accompanied by volunteers, King and Ralph Abernathy marched and chanted, "Freedom has come to Birmingham!" But it had not. Police this time were assisted with growling, snapping dogs, and they again arrested and jailed the marchers.

King used his time to compose his eloquent "Letter from the Birmingham Jail." The essay detailed the humiliation of discrimination and segregation, and explained *Why We Can't Wait*, which became a best-selling book in the decade. Eight days later he was released and began planning the next confrontation—the "children's crusade."

On May 2 black children, most of them teenagers, met at the Sixteenth Street Baptist Church and then began marching toward city hall singing freedom songs. When Bull Connor's forces corralled them for arrest, they prayed and then skipped to the paddy wagons. The demonstration the next day, however, was different. As a thousand teens left the church, Connor finally snapped—with television cameras rolling, he ordered his men to charge the peaceful demonstrators. They did, with nightsticks swinging, dogs snarling. Blacks responded by hurling stones, and the police turned on the high-pressure fire hoses, ripping into the crowd, blasting citizens off their feet.

Hundreds were arrested, but police brutality did not stifle the movement. The next day several thousand blacks took to the streets and the savage scenes again appeared on front pages of newspapers and on national television. *Time* reported,

> There was the Negro youth, sprawled on his back and spinning across the pavement, while firemen battered him with streams of water so powerful that they could strip bark off trees. There was the Negro woman, pinned to the ground by cops, one of them with his knee dug into her

throat. . . . The blaze of bombs, the flash of blades, the eerie glow of fire,
the keening cries of hatred, the wild dance of terror in the night—all this
was Birmingham, Ala.

Birmingham prompted sit-ins and demonstrations in nearly 200 cities across the South, boosted King's reputation as the greatest black leader, and proved to be a turning point in the movement. King's strategy worked: again, black activists revealed their plight to the nation and forced federal action. Like most Americans, President Kennedy and his brother watched the riots on television and were "sickened" by the police brutality. When King was jailed, the Kennedy brothers called Birmingham officials, and Bobby dispatched assistant attorney general Burke Marshall to negoti-ate a settlement. With more and more blacks marching in the streets, with jails over-flowing, and as the city faced social disintegration and economic collapse, officials and businessmen agreed to talk.

For three days Marshall helped both sides work out a compromise agreement that eventually integrated public facilities and provided jobs for blacks. In response, vengeful whites bombed King's motel headquarters and his brother's home. Riots ensued, 50 people were injured, and Kennedy announced his administration would not permit the agreement "to be sabotaged by a few extremists on either side." JFK ordered 3,000 federal troops into position near Birmingham.

Kennedy's action was too much for Alabama governor George Wallace. He had been opposed to federal orders aimed at integrating the University of Alabama, and in May when federal officials insisted, the governor declared, "Segregation today, segregation tomorrow, segregation forever." Yet forever was rather short in Alabama. Two weeks later, Kennedy federalized the state National Guard, and the governor stood aside and allowed the admission of two black students.

The events in Alabama inspired JFK to address the nation. On June 11 the president delivered a landmark speech. He reminded citizens that America was founded "on the principle that all men are created equal, and that the rights of every man are diminished when the rights of one man are threatened." He contin-ued that the nation was confronted with a moral issue. "The heart of the question is whether all Americans are to be accorded equal rights and equal opportunities." He looked into the camera and declared,

We preach freedom around the world, and we mean it, and we cherish it
here at home, but are we to say to the world, and much more importantly,
to each other that this is the land of the free except for the Negroes; that
we have no second-class citizens except Negroes, that we have no class or
caste system, no ghettoes, no master race except with respect to Negroes?

Kennedy then asked Congress to pass a comprehensive civil rights act—a fed-eral law granting the right of all citizens to be served in facilities open to the public.

The president also put his administration behind the movement's aims to end school segregation and provide voting rights. The president concluded by asking white citizens a question pertinent ever since: "Who among us would be content to have the color of his skin changed?"

A few hours after the address, JFK's appeal took on special meaning. A white man shot and killed NAACP field secretary Medgar Evers in his front yard in Jackson, Mississippi. Later that summer, a white supremacist dynamited Birmingham's Sixteenth Street Baptist Church, killing four girls. It was the twenty-first bombing attack against blacks in that city in eight years. Not one case had been solved.

Kennedy's dramatic speech split the nation. King wrote the president that the address constituted "one of the most eloquent, profound, and unequivocal pleas for justice and the freedom of all men ever made by any president." Southern politicians and many conservatives condemned it. Mississippi Senator James Eastland called the proposal a "complete blueprint for a totalitarian state." Northern legislators and liberals praised the act, and so did most college students, for now the president had again rekindled idealism. JFK had spoken out for equality and for the American Dream.

Two weeks later the president also sparked idealism when he arrived in Berlin. Over a million West Berliners welcomed him as their defender, and as JFK's motorcade passed, citizens cheered, waved flags, and threw flowers. Standing at city hall in front of 150,000 people, he delivered a rousing speech, saluting Berlin as the front line of humanity's struggle for freedom, and proclaiming, "Today, in the world of freedom, the proudest boast is 'Ich bin ein Berliner.'"

After the cheering stopped, diplomats from Washington, Moscow, and London began serious negotiations to improve East–West relations. The primary issue was atomic bomb testing, specifically tests in the atmosphere and potential ones underwater and in outer space. By early August, officials reached such an accord, and that reduced tensions. "Yesterday a shaft of light cut into the darkness," proclaimed President Kennedy. The accord "offers to all the world a welcome sign of hope. . . . It is not a victory for one side—it is a victory for mankind."

During the summer of 1963 it appeared that President Kennedy finally was delivering the hope and idealism he had promised in 1960. College students were picketing for racial justice or joining the Peace Corps, American astronauts were orbiting the earth, the economy was booming, Congress was debating his Civil Rights Act, and the Senate was discussing ratification of the Test Ban Treaty.

Yet it was not Kennedy who brought the years of idealism to their evangelical zenith—it was King.

To urge Congress to pass the Civil Rights Act, black leaders called for a March on Washington. On August 28 some 200,000 blacks and whites arrived. Many held hands and sang as they walked past the Capitol. They continued on to the Lincoln Memorial, and on the steps folksinger Joan Baez greeted them with "We Shall Overcome." She then joined Peter, Paul, and Mary and sang "Blowin' in the Wind." Bob Dylan sang about the recent murder of Medgar Evers, and Mahalia Jackson led the massive crowd with spirituals. Then came the speeches. All the major black organizations were represented—NAACP, CORE, SCLC, the Urban League, and SNCC—and their leaders gave short addresses. SNCC's new chairman, John Lewis, told of Mississippi sharecroppers who worked 12 hours for starvation wages and of students in jail on trumped-up charges. He warned those who advocated patience that blacks "do not want to be free gradually. We want our freedom and we want it now." And he urged blacks to "stay in the streets of every city, every village and every hamlet of this nation . . . until the unfinished revolution of 1776 is complete."

Lewis's speech demonstrated a growing militancy of some young activists, but it was overshadowed by the more hopeful and idealistic words of Martin Luther King Jr. He began by recalling the "sacred obligation" promised by the Emancipation Proclamation and Declaration of Independence, and he stated that "*Now* is the time to make real the promises of Democracy. . . . *Now* is the time to open the doors of opportunity to all of God's children." He reminded Americans that blacks could not be satisfied as long as they "cannot gain lodging in the motels of the highways and the hotels of the cities. . . . We can never be satisfied as long as our children are stripped of their selfhood and robbed of their dignity by signs stating: 'For Whites Only.'" Instead, King had a dream,

Martin Luther King Jr.: "I have a dream."

I have a dream that one day on the red hills of Georgia the sons of former slaves and the sons of former slaveowners will be able to sit down together at the table of brotherhood. . . . I have a dream that my four little children will one day live in a nation where they will not be judged by the color of their skin but by the content of their character. I have a dream today. . . .

"I have never been so proud to be a Negro," declared participant and baseball legend Jackie Robinson. "I have never been so proud to be an American." King's speech marked the pinnacle of hope—for the civil rights struggle, and for the sixties.

After listeners roared their approval, opinion polls indicated that for the first time a majority of citizens considered civil rights a pressing national issue. Finally, America seemed to be moving forward, moving toward equality for all. After the speeches, President Kennedy invited civil rights leaders to the White House. He was glowing, and in his private quarters he complimented the activists on their march. John Lewis admitted, "It seemed like the beginning of a new era for America."

Diem

Yet in the summer and fall of 1963 the issue of communism again confronted the Kennedy administration, this time in South Vietnam. The president there, Ngo Dinh Diem, had been installed with American help, but it was becoming very apparent that he was not popular. A Catholic in a Buddhist nation, he was repressive and corrupt, and most Vietnamese considered him an American puppet. After he refused to hold the 1956 elections guaranteed by the Geneva Conference, many South Vietnamese formed a rebel government, the National Liberation Front (NLF), an army labeled the Vietcong (VC)—and the VC began attacking the South Vietnamese Army (ARVN). Aided by the North Vietnamese, the VC won many battles, and it became obvious to the Kennedy administration that the only way to keep Diem in power, and prevent the unification of the nation under Ho Chi Minh, was to expand the number of U.S. military advisers in South Vietnam. Furthermore, Kennedy knew that opinion polls demonstrated that over 60 percent of Americans supported sending U.S. troops overseas to stop communist expansion. Thus JFK quietly increased U.S. advisers in South Vietnam from 1,600 in 1960 to 16,000 by 1963.

JFK's policy did not work, and Vietnam became news during the summer when Buddhist monks and students held protests in Saigon. Diem responded by ordering his police to fire into peaceful demonstrators, killing many, and by jailing hundreds of monks. Buddhist leaders replied in shocking fashion: a senior monk sat down in a busy Saigon intersection, and before a crowd and television cameras, he poured gasoline over his body—and lit a match.

During the summer six monks performed immolations, and by August many Americans were wondering what type of regime the United States was supporting in South Vietnam. From Saigon, the CIA secretly reported that Diem's "harsh and thoughtless rule" had alienated most South Vietnamese. What to do with Diem? To answer that question the president and his advisers conducted ten meetings during the autumn, and declassified documents reveal that JFK was frustrated and wanted a Saigon government that could prosecute the war more effectively. Thus Kennedy secretly approved a plot to overthrow the ruler, and on November 1 ARVN generals conducted the coup: Diem and his brother were captured and assassinated.

Eight years later, Americans discovered Kennedy's role in the Diem murder, but in 1963 no one would have believed that a president would have supported a coup against another head of state, especially not the charming, sincere JFK. Americans trusted their leaders then, a conviction that would be questioned later during the Vietnam War and be extinguished by Nixon and his Watergate scandal in 1974. Yet in 1963, the Kennedy administration simply granted diplomatic recognition to the new military government in Saigon, and the *Washington Post* optimistically noted that, compared to the repressive Diem, the United States now "can hope for working out mutual problems with a sovereign government more representative of its people."

Kennedy

Administration officials stayed above the fray in Vietnam during 1963 and instead concentrated on pushing and passing Kennedy's programs, thereby promoting him for the 1964 election. Prompted by women's organizations, he signed the Equal Pay Act. Business groups opposed the bill, citing additional "costs of hiring women"; labor unions supported it because it would reduce the probability of employers hiring females at lower wages than union men. Most congressmen, and the public, favored the bill, and it passed easily, prohibiting discrimination in the payment of wages for "equal work on jobs" requiring "equal skill, effort and responsibility."

The Equal Pay Act had too many loopholes, so it would not have much impact until the rise of women's liberation, but of more immediate importance was the deteriorating environment. By the early sixties suburban sprawl, industrial pollution, urban smog, atomic fallout, and the heavy use of pesticides all were attracting attention. "For the first time in the history of the world," Rachel Carson declared in her 1962 best-seller *Silent Spring*, "every human being is now subjected to contact with dangerous chemicals." Pesticides, she claimed, "have been found in fish in remote mountain lakes, in earthworms burrowing in soil, in the eggs of birds—and in man himself." Moreover, she declared, "We tolerate cancer-causing agents in our environment at our peril." This, she wrote prophetically, as she lay dying from a cancerous lump in her breast.

Silent Spring was an alarm clock, or as one historian called it, "The *Uncle Tom's Cabin* of modern environmentalism." President Kennedy read the book, and so did his interior secretary, Stewart Udall, and while they considered action, Udall began expanding the meaning of *conservation*. Historically, the word had meant preservation of America's natural treasures in national parks and forests, but with the baby boom and a growing middle class of automobile owners there was pressure to increase the number of outdoor recreational facilities. Thus Kennedy signed a bill that made national seashores of Cape Cod, Padre Island in Texas, and Point Reyes in California.

To promote these and his other policies, JFK began a series of speeches and political trips that autumn. In October, after the Senate ratified the Test Ban Treaty, he signed it, declaring a "message of hope . . . a clear and honorable national commitment to the cause of man's survival." In Philadelphia, he urged the passage of his Civil Rights Act so all citizens "can regard one another with the quality for which this city is noted—brotherly love." To the western states, Montana, Washington, and conservative Utah where he declared that "history has begun to flow in the direction of freedom." Back to cheering crowds in New York City, and on to Florida where he inspected the flourishing space program and received a rousing welcome. Then to Texas—San Antonio, Houston, and Dallas.

On November 22 Lee Harvey Oswald fired a rifle from a sixth-floor window and shot and killed John Kennedy. The president's assassination shocked the nation. "It was too big, too sudden, too overwhelming, and it meant too much," reporter David Brinkley told a grieving television audience who watched three days and nights of images: a smiling president in a black limousine waving to crowds . . . the slow-motion scene, JFK in the backseat, his head jerking forward and back to his wife's shoulder . . . secret service agents climbing on the car's trunk as it rushed off to the hospital . . . a distraught Vice President Johnson taking the oath of office on *Air Force One* . . . a crowded hallway in the Dallas jail as Jack Ruby suddenly stepped out, pointed a pistol, and shot suspect Lee Harvey Oswald . . . the riderless horses pulling the slain president's casket, a family in black, and the farewell salute from his son, John Jr.

To the nation, the assassination was a crucial event. In the first month after his death more than 700,000 mourners paid their respects at his grave in Arlington National Cemetery. Like Pearl Harbor and September 11, the assassination was one of those rare events that stirred Americans to remember where they were, what they were doing on that fateful day. "I'll never forget that cold drizzly day" in 1963, one baby boomer recalled. "I was in high school study hall with two hundred other restless teenagers when we got the news. First there was shock, then disbelief, and in a few minutes the girl in front of me put her head down on her desk and started gently weeping. Within minutes, most of us joined her."

After the assassination, rumors swept Dallas and then the nation. Who killed Kennedy? To answer the question the government established a commission of two Democrats and five Republicans (including Representative Gerald Ford), led by Supreme Court Chief Justice Earl Warren. After lengthy deliberations, the Warren Commission answered: Lee Harvey Oswald. Yet the answer did not satisfy the curiosity of most citizens. Like the aftermath of Lincoln's assassination a century before, scores of writers saw a conspiracy and had a theory; during the next three decades authors pumped out over 400 books on the topic. Yet none were able to prove there was more than one gunman, that there was some shadowy conspiracy or cover-up. It seemed too painful to grasp, author Gerald Posner noted, that Oswald, a "misguided loser with a $12 rifle could end Camelot."

More importantly, the assassination provoked Americans to evaluate the charismatic chief executive. In death John Kennedy's stature grew to almost epic proportions, and by the eighties citizens ranked him their favorite president. Yet most historians judge he has been overrated and they do not rank him in the top dozen. Scholars usually give JFK high marks for the space program and Peace Corps, but they also note that during his first two years his other foreign policies were unsuccessful, especially the Alliance for Progress and the Bay of Pigs. Kennedy's initial approach toward the Soviet Union only intensified the cold war, and for no other reason than pride he brought the world to the brink of atomic holocaust during the Cuban missile crisis. After all, what would have happened if Khrushchev had not backed down? As for Vietnam, Kennedy became the great question mark: if he had lived, would he have gotten us involved in a massive war? JFK remembered that conservatives had charged Truman with "losing China," and the young president feared "losing Vietnam." Aware that stopping communist expansion was popular at home, he greatly increased U.S. advisers in South Vietnam. Documents released since demonstrate that JFK was confused and frustrated with Vietnam, but theories that he would have gotten America out of that country after his reelection in 1964 remain without solid evidence.

Perhaps the most balanced assessment of Kennedy was that he promised so much, and while he did that with grace and vigor, he did not actually produce much during his short presidency. At home, his administration could not get Congress to pass his New Frontier programs, and for over two years he irritated activists because he did not take the lead on the nation's most pressing problem—civil rights. Indeed, Kennedy's visions often were interrupted by Khrushchev and King—by responding to communism abroad and civil rights at home.

Yet it was Kennedy's eventual response in the summer of 1963 that helped rekindle what *Life* called the "brisk feeling of hope" of the early sixties. In June, JFK proclaimed it was time to "reexamine our own attitudes" in foreign affairs, that his administration would seek "not merely peace in our time but peace for all time." Then he acted, reducing world tensions by signing the Test Ban Treaty. That same month, after watching the brutal scenes from Birmingham, he finally seized the high road and addressed the nation, calling for an end to segregation, advocating the American Dream for all citizens. In a struggle filled with bigotry and reaction, Kennedy became the martyr for equality and progress.

Throughout the remainder of the decade, the slain president and the early sixties represented hope and idealism, and that was described a few years later when

Kennedy idealism in the summer of 1963: Almost 17, Bill Clinton
meets President Kennedy in Washington, D.C.

Samuel Eliot Morison published his massive history of the American people. He
concluded his book,

> *With the death of John Fitzgerald Kennedy something seemed to die in
> each one of us. Yet the memory of that bright, vivid personality, that
> great gentleman whose every act and appearance appealed to our pride
> and gave us fresh confidence in ourselves and our country, will live in us
> for a long, long time. . . .*

And then Morison cited lyrics from a popular Broadway musical that seemed to
summarize popular feelings toward the Kennedy years:

> *Don't let it be for-got*
> *That once there was a spot*
> *For one brief shining moment that was known*
> *As Cam-e-lot.*

Chapter 2

The Pinnacle
of Liberalism,
1964–1965

A few days after the assassination of John Kennedy, President Lyndon Johnson gave his first speech to the nation. He reminded his fellow citizens that JFK had said, "Let us begin," and then he simply added, "Let us continue." The meaning was clear. Kennedy had proposed legislation, but passed little. LBJ would succeed, and the mid-sixties would become a great American reform era—the pinnacle of liberalism.

At that time, liberalism had less to do with foreign policy than domestic affairs. Both political parties opposed communist expansion and supported containment, although staunch conservatives advocated a more aggressive policy toward the Soviet Union and its allies. Liberalism was more important in domestic policy and had been since Franklin Roosevelt's New Deal enacted legislation that increased federal power, extended regulation of the economy, and changed the traditional relationship between government and citizens by establishing policies such as unemployment compensation and social security. Such policies disturbed conservatives, who advocated more local control and state power, limited federal programs, balancing the budget, and maintaining the status quo. After Eisenhower, most liberals during the Kennedy years thought the government should become more activist, promoting economic growth and increasing federal programs and funding to the states. And after McCarthyism, many liberals felt that federal agencies should advance personal liberties, especially civil rights.

Warren Court and the Rights Revolution

Liberalism, of course, had been emerging since the Supreme Court of Chief Justice Earl Warren declared the landmark *Brown* case that ordered the integration of public schools. The Court usually follows national norms, but during the conservative fifties the Warren Court made decisions that led America toward liberalism by ripping apart the legal remnants of McCarthyism and by increasing individual liberty and equality.

Generally speaking, there were three major themes of the Warren Court. The first was civil rights, demonstrated by *Brown* and many other cases that mandated integration of public facilities and interstate travel. The Court continued this theme in the early sixties with *Garner v. Louisiana* and *Edwards v. South Carolina,* which declared that black demonstrators had the right to peaceful protest, from sit-ins to marches, and that southern states could not "make criminal the peaceful expression of unpopular views." Later in the decade, as we shall see, the Court ruled that all of the federal civil rights acts were constitutional, and it continued to order desegregation of school districts.

A second and related theme was libertarianism, or increasing a citizen's political and personal liberty. States and the federal government had curtailed those liberties throughout history, and especially during the anticommunist crusade. For example, the Smith Act outlawed "advocating" the overthrow of the government; the McCarran Act demanded that members of the Communist Party register with the government, and executive orders, states, and local agencies had mandated loyalty pledges.

These were popular acts during McCarthyism, but later in the fifties the Warren Court made rulings that surprised the nation. In *Pennsylvania v. Nelson, Yates v. United States, Scales v. United States,* and *Albertson v. Subversive Activities Control Board,* the Court attacked the Smith, McCarran, and Communist Control acts. By overturning convictions of several communists for conspiring to advocate the overthrow of the government, or for being a party member, the Court upheld the First and Fourteenth Amendments, which included freedom of speech and association. Loyalty was resolved in *Peters v. Hobby* and *Greene v. McElroy,* which essentially found loyalty pledges unconstitutional: in America, advocating something still was freedom of speech, and unlike other nations, a citizen still was innocent until proven guilty.

By the early sixties, then, the Court was questioning federal and state restrictions on political freedom, and the justices did the same concerning personal liberty. A contentious issue was school prayer. Some states then had mandatory Bible readings, and it was common in public schools to begin the day with a Christian prayer, even in districts where some students were not religious or not Christians. In *Engel v. Vitale* and other cases, the Court found these laws unconstitutional, in violation of the First Amendment, and ordered separation of church and state.

The Court also ruled against other state laws that restricted individual behavior and instead favored "privacy rights." Obscenity had been an issue for years. State censors banned what they considered obscene magazines and books. The Court struck down these restrictions, thus allowing individuals to decide for themselves what was obscene. Many state laws also prohibited birth control, although contraception devices were common and "the pill" won government approval in 1961. Connecticut had an 1879 law that outlawed these devices even for married couples, and Planned Parenthood director Estelle Griswold sued the state. The Warren Court ruled in her favor, and women were free to decide about contraception. Other states had laws prohibiting black and white adults from cohabiting, but in *McLaughlin v. Florida* the Court ruled those laws unconstitutional; citizens could live with whomever they desired. Fifteen states had laws banning interracial marriages. "The Constitution cannot control such prejudices," declared the Court, "but neither can it tolerate them." The Court found those restrictions unconstitutional in a case concerning a white man and his black wife, *Loving v. Virginia.*

A final theme of the Warren Court was egalitarianism. Engraved on the Supreme Court Building are the words EQUAL JUSTICE UNDER LAW. Yet all citizens were not equal at the ballot box or in court. Rural areas had controlled many state governments for decades, although citizens had migrated from farms to cities. For the 140,000 people living in Burlington, Vermont, there was one legislator, the same representation for 1,400 rural dwellers in the state. Tennessee had not reapportioned its voting districts in 60 years, and in *Baker v. Carr* the Court struck down malapportionment and declared the doctrine of "one man, one vote." Since then, states reapportion after each census.

Another issue concerned police behavior and the rights of suspects. Surveys demonstrated that the wealthy received better police treatment or more lenient sentences than the poor, and the Court attempted to correct that in *Gideon v. Wainwright, Mapp v. Ohio, Escobedo v. Illinois,* and *Miranda v. Arizona.* Clarence Gideon was charged with theft; too poor to hire an attorney, he was found guilty and incarcerated. In *Gideon* the Court ruled that all citizens have the right to legal defense; if they cannot afford an attorney, then the state must provide one, resulting in an expansion of public defenders. In *Mapp,* the Court ruled that police must obtain evidence legally, upholding Fourth Amendment rights of "unreasonable searches and seizures." And in *Escobedo* and *Miranda* the Court stunned the nation; it declared that suspects in custody had the right to an attorney during interrogation and police must inform them of their constitutional rights because "the real trial often takes place in the police station." These cases changed traditional police behavior, and by the mid-sixties cops on the beat were discussing "probable cause" and issuing the Miranda warning to suspects.

Conservatives were appalled. In the Bible Belt billboards declared, IMPEACH EARL WARREN. "They put the Negroes in the schools," declared an Alabama congressman. "Now they have driven God out." Police chiefs complained that the Court seemed more concerned with criminals than with victims, and one said, "I guess now we'll have to supply all squad cars with attorneys." But liberals cheered, declaring that the Court finally had curtailed state restrictions and dubious police practices and in the process had given individuals more liberties and privacy rights.

Whatever the case then, most scholars since agree that the Warren Court brought about a "rights revolution," and that its place in American history was surpassed only by the Court of Chief Justice John Marshall, 1801–1835, which laid the foundations of American constitutional law. The Warren Court made decisions that changed the judicial status quo. It ruled to bring about the legal equality of races, of rural and urban citizens, of the wealthy and poor, of prosecutors and defendants, and the result, wrote Justice Abe Fortas, was "the most profound and pervasive revolution ever achieved by substantially peaceful means."

Johnson Liberalism

By the mid-sixties, then, the Court was actively promoting liberalism while at the same time the Johnson administration was doing that politically. During the president's first speech to the nation, he urged the passage of a civil rights act to "eliminate from this nation every trace of discrimination and oppression that is based upon race or color." And in January 1964 LBJ declared his "unconditional War on Poverty."

During the booming economy of the fifties there was little interest in poverty, but that changed in the Kennedy years. In 1960 CBS correspondent Edward R. Murrow aired "Harvest of Shame," and during the next years television began to expose pockets of poverty as cameramen followed civil rights activists into the Deep South and social workers into Appalachia. Scholars wrote books such as Harry M. Caudill's *Night Comes to the Cumberlands,* Leon Keyserling's *Poverty and Deprivation in the U.S.,* and most importantly, Michael Harrington's *The Other America.* Television exposure, books, and numerous articles jolted citizens, and provoked the Kennedy administration to begin studies that revealed that about 35 million citizens, or 20 percent of the nation, languished in poverty. Over 70 percent were white, although half of black citizens and single women with children were poor, as were a third of the elderly. Most distressing, one scholar noted, was that "poverty breeds poverty."

Since the Great Depression, most citizens felt that government should try to help Americans break the cycle of poverty. Kennedy put his economic adviser Walter Heller in charge of formulating a program, but the task was daunting. Not only would poverty programs be expensive, but there were the questions of which agency had the mandate to address the issue. Was it a federal or state responsibility, and what determines "poverty"? For example, is a farmer poor if he earns a small annual income but grows abundant food for his family? Are college students poor if they support themselves and make a part-time income below some poverty line? And what amount of annual income determined poverty? The government set the poverty line at $3,100 for a family of four and $1,500 for an individual living alone.

When Johnson became president he was aware of the issues, and he told Heller to give the poverty program the "highest priority. Push ahead full tilt." The president appointed R. Sargent Shriver to direct the poverty task force, a group of 137 scholars and experts who examined and then devised a program that became law when Congress passed the Economic Opportunity Act of 1964.

"The war on poverty is not a struggle to support people," declared Johnson. "It is a struggle to give people a chance." To "open the door of opportunity," Shriver's new Office of Economic Opportunity coordinated the $15 billion that the federal government *already* spent on social welfare programs, along with the additional funds Congress approved to fight the poverty war—less than $1 billion annually. The total went to a host of new programs, many aimed at inner cities in what became know as Community Action Programs.

The war battled poverty by attempting to help those below the poverty line. In 1964 the nation witnessed rising youth unemployment, over 20 percent, and that year the first baby boomers were beginning to graduate from high school. Thus the administration established the Job Corps to train males for skilled employment, and the Neighborhood Youth Corps, which put the semiskilled to work in their cities. For those low-income families who wanted to send their children to college, the administration established Upward Bound to help gifted students, and work-study, in which the government and colleges shared the cost of hiring student workers. To mobilize youthful idealism, LBJ began his domestic peace corps, Volunteers in Service to America (VISTA). The volunteers (paid small wages) worked with the physically and mentally impaired and helped alleviate the chronic poverty of migratory workers and Native Americans.

Other issues were population and hunger. In 1964 the world's population surpassed 3 billion, provoking scores of conferences and articles about the "explosion of the population bomb." No president had addressed the issue, but LBJ told the United Nations that "five dollars spent on population control was worth one hundred spent on economic aid." His administration began giving foreign aid to help developing nations establish family planning and at home began funding birth control clinics, both of which resulted in lowering the birthrate. Concerning hunger, American farmers produced food surpluses, yet some citizens starved. To remedy this, the Truman administration had begun subsidized school lunches, and later the government occasionally gave away food. By 1959 farmers produced over $9 billion worth of surplus, and the government gave most of it away to over 5 million poor citizens. Senator Hubert Humphrey advocated a more systematic federal "food stamp" program, and the Kennedy administration began a pilot program in eight areas, giving out stamps to the poor who could redeem them at grocery stores. The program received little press, either from farmers or conservatives, and in 1964 LBJ proposed the Food Stamp Act "to help achieve a fuller and more effective use of food abundances" and "provide improved levels of nutrition among low-income households." The federal and state governments shared the cost, and the food stamp program began nationally the next year without fanfare.

Americans were more interested in a tax cut. During the early sixties taxes remained high, a legacy of the Korean War. Kennedy had proposed the cut that he felt would stimulate the economy, but conservatives called it fiscally irresponsible and blocked the measure. In 1964 LBJ tried again, and the result was an act that lowered rates for individuals and for corporations and contributed to a booming economy for the decade with high growth and very low unemployment; by 1968 the average family income was $8,000, double what it had been a decade earlier.

National attention also was focused on the Civil Rights Act. The heart of the bill concerned the issues of job discrimination and public facilities. Can employers discriminate, especially if they are contractors that have received funds paid by all taxpayers to build public works such as a post office or an interstate freeway? Should all citizens have equal access to public facilities, from libraries to parks to sports arenas? And should private businesses such as motels, restaurants, or theaters that cater to the public be allowed to discriminate by only serving whites? (The bill did not address membership clubs such as private golf courses.) Opinion polls demonstrated that about two-thirds supported integrating these facilities, even though over 70 percent of Southerners opposed. LBJ pushed for passage during spring 1964, and conservatives put up a massive attempt to block the act, claiming it was federal interference in states' rights. In Congress, a Virginia senator punctuated his speech by waving a small Confederate flag, and a Georgia senator introduced a plan for the federal government to spend $1.5 billion—to distribute blacks equally among the 50 states. Republican Senator Barry Goldwater declared the act would create a "federal police force of mammoth proportions" and lead to the "destruction of a free society." Conservative senators began what became the longest filibuster in history.

Job discrimination was addressed in Title VII of the act. As was traditional, employers hired white male workers first and jobs were segregated by gender. When the House debated the act, an 80-year-old conservative, Democratic Representative Howard K. Smith of Virginia, moved to add the word sex to the list of those protected by Title VII. "This bill is so imperfect," he said, "what harm will this little amendment do?" He then ridiculed the idea of "rights," contending that as females outnumber males in the nation, women were being deprived of their "right to a husband," which Congress should resolve "particularly in an election year." Amid laughs, another congressman rose and felt compelled to reveal the secret for his marital harmony: "I usually have the last two words, and those words are 'Yes, dear.'" Although liberals were not prepared for the levity, they were for Congressman Smith's ploy, because conservatives had tried to add sex discrimination bans to all the titles of the act, which was aimed to divide supporters and defeat the bill. Then Michigan's Democrat Martha Griffiths surprised most liberals by declaring her staunch support for the amendment, stating that the bill protects job discrimination based on race, but without adding sex, white female job applicants would have "no

The "Johnson treatment" on Abe Fortas.

rights at all." Griffiths's argument carried the day. The House passed the amendment in two hours, an incredibly short time for an addition that eventually would have a profound impact on the American workplace.

Meanwhile, LBJ gathered support for the act by calling senators into the Oval Office for the "Johnson treatment." Powerful and overbearing, the *New York Times* declared that "Lyndon Johnson seems 20 feet tall—when he really measures no more than 10." The president bore down on senators, coaxing, flattering, sometimes threatening, and always reminding them of promises due. As one politician described it, "Lyndon got me by the lapels and put his face on top of mine and he talked and talked. I figured it was either getting drowned or joining."

Johnson prevailed, and moderates and liberals broke the filibuster and passed the 1964 Civil Rights Act. After blacks had resided in America for three centuries, the United States recognized that in all states they were citizens protected by the U.S. Constitution. The act provided aid to school districts that integrated, prohibited discrimination in national elections, and importantly, desegregated all public facilities. Southern motels and restaurants quickly sued the federal government, and the Warren Court ruled the act constitutional. Finally, Title VII stated that a private business with more than 25 employees could not discriminate in hiring because of an individual's race, color, religion, sex, or national origin, and to begin the long process of enforcing equal opportunity the government established the Equal Employment Opportunity Commission (EEOC).

Yet the Civil Rights Act failed to address another important issue for African Americans—the right to vote in state and local elections—and so again activists launched the movement, this time in Mississippi.

Freedom Summer

Mississippi was over 40 percent African American, a third of its counties had black majorities, but in three years SNCC activists had registered only about 5 percent of those eligible voters. Thus a coalition of civil rights organizations decided to change tactics and invite about 1,000 white northern students to invade Mississippi for "Freedom Summer" 1964 to help register black citizens. They assumed northern public opinion and federal officials would not tolerate Southerners assaulting white college students from prominent families.

In June, students from over 200 universities and colleges met with representatives of the Council of Federated Organizations (COFO) in Oxford, Ohio. Earlier, COFO flyers had been distributed on some northern campuses: "A Domestic Freedom Corps will be working in Mississippi this summer. Its only weapons will be youth and courage. We need your help now." Because the volunteers were not paid for the summer and had to provide their own transportation and bond in case they were jailed, most of them came from affluent families and they attended the finest universities; almost 60 percent came from Harvard, Yale, Stanford, Princeton, Berkeley, Michigan, or Wisconsin. They all came for different reasons, but most of them held common views that segregation was morally wrong and America was not living up to its own creed: All Men Are Created Equal. Most also shared hope and idealism. "There is a moral wave building among today's youth," one declared, "and I intend to catch it!"

As the volunteers arrived in Ohio, the COFO staff greeted them. Bob Moses stated, "Mississippi has been called 'The Closed Society.' It is closed, locked. We think the key is in the vote." The older activists then trained the students to register voters and to protect themselves in case of attack. In mid-June they moved into Mississippi.

On June 21, three volunteers disappeared—Michael Schwerner, Andrew Goodman, and James Chaney. Schwerner and Goodman were whites from New York, the former a graduate of Cornell and the latter a student at Queens College. Chaney was a black Mississippian. Because there had been four "mystery killings" of blacks in the state during the first half of 1964, activists feared for their coworkers' lives and immediately called for a search. Governor Paul Johnson scoffed, calling them communists and declaring, "They could be in Cuba."

Two days later authorities found the volunteers' burned-out car. President Johnson ordered sailors from a nearby navy base to conduct a massive search with the help of the FBI. Federal agents searched for six weeks before they discovered the bodies buried in an earthen dam. Goodman and Schwerner had been shot in the heart, and a physician stated that Chaney "had been beaten to a pulp. . . . In my twenty-five years as a pathologist and medical examiner, I have never seen bones so severely shattered, except in tremendously high-speed accidents or airplane crashes."

Schwerner's widow told the nation, "We all know that this search with hundreds of sailors is because Andrew Goodman and my husband are white. If only Chaney was involved, nothing would've been done."

Rita Schwerner was right, unfortunately, and her husband's death was just the beginning of violence. Throughout the summer racists beat 80 civil rights workers and shot at 30 volunteers, killing 4. Southern policemen arrested over 1,000 activists on trumped-up charges. Terrorists bombed or burned 30 black homes and businesses. In McComb there were 17 bombings in three months, and racists burned 37 black churches. Mississippi was burning.

Freedom Summer schoolteacher and her students, 1964.

"It was the longest nightmare of my life," wrote activist Cleveland Sellers. Nevertheless, volunteers continued working throughout the long, hot Mississippi Freedom Summer. They traveled throughout the state, talking to black croppers. They built "freedom schools" so illiterate, poor blacks could learn to articulate their desires and demands, and community centers to "strengthen a homegrown freedom movement," which would survive when the volunteers returned to college campuses for fall semester. Activists also attempted to register blacks in the state's Democratic Party and soon realized that white Democrats would not budge. In fact, after 1,000 volunteers worked an entire summer, they had registered fewer than 1,600 black voters with the Mississippi Democratic Party. That had been expected, so activists established an alternate party, the Mississippi Freedom Democratic Party (MFDP). The volunteers enrolled nearly 60,000 disenfranchised blacks into the MFDP, and those newly franchised voters elected 44 "freedom delegates" to attend the 1964 Democratic Convention.

In August the Democratic Party held its convention in Atlantic City. The "Freedom Democrats" stated that they would support the party's nomination and platform, whatever the outcome. White Mississippi delegates reminded others of the 1948 convention; when Harry Truman proposed civil rights then, white Southerners walked out and formed the Dixiecrats. Black delegates testified in front of the party's credentials committee, stating that because they were not allowed to participate in state elections, the MFDP represented the only freely elected party in Mississippi. They demanded to be seated as the true delegates for the state. On national television, many described violence and intimidation in Mississippi. Fannie Lou Hamer, the granddaughter of slaves, revealed her efforts to register voters—being fired, shot at, beaten until she could no longer walk: "I question America, is this America, the land of the free and the home of the brave?" Martin Luther King Jr. pleaded with the Democrats: "If you value your party, if you value your nation, if you value the democratic process, you must recognize the Freedom Party delegation."

The credentials committee refused to seat the Freedom Delegation. Southern white delegations had told LBJ they would walk out of the convention if the party supported the MFDP, and that might bring about a Republican south and perhaps even throw the election to the GOP. The president would not take that chance. Furthermore, Johnson had signed the Civil Rights Act and begun his War on Poverty, which helped minorities, and he would need some southern support next year to pass his Great Society. To buy off the liberals, Johnson offered the vice presidency to their candidate, Senator Hubert Humphrey, and a compromise: the white Mississippi delegation would be seated at the convention—but for the last time. In the future only state delegations that enfranchised all citizens would be allowed at the convention of the Democratic Party.

The compromise meant that the 1968 Democratic Convention would be a raucous affair—for many unforeseen reasons—and that the 1964 convention was a watershed in the civil rights crusade. It highlighted a growing division within the movement. At Atlantic City some older activists saw progress in the compromise and continued to participate in coalition politics in an attempt to liberalize the Democratic Party. King and most mainstream blacks agreed with Bayard Rustin that the compromise was "not what any of us wanted, but it's the best we could get." Change was possible; after four years of the movement the status of black citizens had jumped a light-year when compared to their first three centuries in America. Most blacks shared the optimism of white liberals, and they overwhelmingly supported the Democratic Party; in the 1964 election over 90 percent of black voters cast their ballots for Johnson. Other younger activists were discouraged by the convention. Some had been in the movement since the Greensboro sit-ins in 1960, and now after four years of violence, they had achieved only an agreement that in another four years, in 1968, southern blacks would be allowed to participate in the democracy. Freedom Now! had been their demand, and as they left the convention they grew disillusioned with liberals—and with King. Some young activists began questioning King's leadership, his nonviolent activism, and they started discussing a more militant movement.

Sixties Generation

By 1964, then, youthful activism was becoming a mainstay of the sixties, and that certainly was true as the first baby boomers arrived on college campuses for the fall semester. Because of the low birthrate during the depression and war, the nation had grown old. In 1960 the average age was 34, and the number of youth (18 to 24) was only 16 million. But then the baby boom; it began in 1946 and lasted for 18 years, until 1964, resulting in an enormous crop of youngsters. The nation turned young, and by the mid-sixties the average age plummeted to 17 and by the end of the decade the number of youth soared to about 25 million. The result was the "sixties generation," those who turned 18 between 1960 to 1972, which comprised over 45 million.

The enormous size of the sixties generation would have an impact on America— even if they had never demonstrated. The numbers meant the sixties would witness more juvenile problems (delinquency, crime, violence, unwed mothers) than the small fifties generation. The sixties also would have more disruptions on campus, some of it due to overcrowding. When the population surge hit California, for example, the state had to build 49 new campuses. Moreover, the size of the generation meant that explaining, exploiting, or catering to youth became a national obsession. Ford Motor Company developed a car for kids, the Mustang, and a soft drink company proclaimed the "Pepsi Generation." The Associated Press declared, "1964 would have to go down as the Year of the Kids." The next year *Newsweek* claimed that "never before have the young staked out so large a claim to the present," and *Time* named their 1966 "Man of the Year" the "man—and woman—of 25 and under."

The sixties generation began to express their own values, which often shocked their parents. Spring break 1964 found Fort Lauderdale deluged with students looking for "sex, sand, suds, and sun." On Easter weekend some 75,000 collegians held a huge bash at Daytona Beach, which ended in a riot when a girl "lost" her bikini;

police arrested 2,000 for public promiscuity and drinking. The summer was filled with "hootenannies" with folksingers, surfing with the Beach Boys, and the "British invasion" of the Beatles, and by autumn crew cuts and culottes suddenly were being replaced by bangs and miniskirts: America was becoming sexy. By Labor Day weekend the party had moved to Hampton Beach, New Hampshire, where 10,000 kids practiced the new fad, "bundling," sleeping together on the beach. A "boy used to date two girls simultaneously, a nice girl and a not-so-nice girl," explained a Michigan female student. "Now he wants two girls in one." A Vassar female added, "It's a load off my mind, losing my virginity."

The older generation was shocked, but the sixties generation didn't seem to mind, for compared with their parents they were more idealistic and tolerant and less concerned with money, security, and communism. A third of high school graduates headed off for college, three times more than their parents' generation, and when they got on campus they were angered to find the hidden hand of their parents present in the form of *in loco parentis.*

The term meant "in the place of parents" and translated to volumes of campus rules and regulations. Like most universities, at Texas females had to live on campus until they were 21 before they could "apply" to the dean of women to live on their own. On most campuses, dorms were segregated by sex and visitation restricted, often only to Sunday. Then the question was how wide the room doors had to be opened. Officials demanded the "width of a book," which students often interpreted as a "book of matches." At Barnard College, a man could visit a woman in her dorm room if the "three-foot rule" was enforced—three of their four feet had to be on the floor at all times. Students had strict curfews. The University of Massachusetts, for example, listed penalties for females arriving late at dorms: five "minutes means loss of the next Friday night," 10 eliminated Saturday night, and 15 sent the wayward gal to women's judiciary. At Illinois, female dorms were shut and locked on weekends at 1 A.M., and girls were prohibited from kissing their dates goodnight while leaning up against the building—no bumping and grinding. A journalist called the university "one of the final homes of the Puritan code."

Universities had devised a "veritable straitjacket of petty rules in which to confine their young charges," wrote one scholar. "Every possible aspect of student life was regulated—promptness, attendance, dressing, idling, fishing, gunning, dancing, drinking, fighting, gaming, swearing, and so on ad infinitum." Most colleges prohibited smoking, "parking," and had dress codes that banned males from wearing T-shirts and jeans, and girls from wearing pants or shorts. University of Houston females had to cover their shorts while walking to an athletic field: "In other areas, lingering in sports attire (even though covered by a coat) is not permissible." Religious colleges were more strict: when two students at St. John's University were married in a civil ceremony, they were expelled for violating Roman Catholic law.

Furthermore, students had virtually no say at the university they supported with tuition. Administrators dictated course offerings, degree curriculums, and everything else on campus—speakers, types of intramural sports, news in student papers—and at most public institutions males had to participate in military training, Reserve Officer Training (ROTC). Campus life was a "barracks culture," activist Tom Hayden recalled of the University of Michigan, "thirteen hundred young men were cramped into my sterile quad, arbitrarily assigned to roommates, whether we preferred each other's company or not."

Why the rise of student power? The main reason for the campus revolt in the mid-sixties was printed in capital letters in an underground student paper at the University of Florida: NO RESTRICTION MAY BE PLACED ON STUDENT DRINKING, GAMBLING, SEXUAL ACTIVITY, OR ANY SUCH PRIVATE MORAL DECISION. In loco parentis meant that unlike regular citizens, then, collegiates between freshmen and graduate students could be tried by civil and university officials. Thus an underaged student who drank beer could be found guilty of state law and university regulation—jailed by the judge and expelled by the dean. Campus activists began to ask: Are students full citizens protected by the Constitution?

No. That became obvious when students returned for 1964 fall semester at the University of California, Berkeley. A dean simply informed all student organizations that from now on they were no longer permitted to set up tables on campus to promote "off-campus" causes such as civil rights or politics.

The regulation restricted freedom of speech, and it sparked a stunning response: students violated the ban. After all, it was an election year, and many students were concerned about civil rights and Vietnam. In September, Jack Weinberg and others set up political tables, resulting in President Clark Kerr suspending eight activists. That did not thwart activism, and on October 1, Weinberg and others handed out political flyers outside the administration building on Sproul Plaza. Officials and police approached, arrested them, and put Weinberg in a police car. Suddenly, someone yelled, "Sit down!" and within minutes hundreds of students surrounded and basically impounded the car. All afternoon students stood on top of the car and gave speeches, and thousands stayed all night, singing civil rights songs and sleeping on the plaza.

The Free Speech Movement (FSM), activists called it, and officials eventually agreed to hold discussions with the students. But in November President Kerr reneged on his agreement, declared the students were influenced by the "Castro-Mao-Tse-tung line" of communism, and pressed new charges against FSM activists. That provoked a massive demonstration. Thousands of students appeared on Sproul Plaza, where activist Mario Savio proclaimed, "There is a time when the operation of the machine becomes so odious, makes you so sick at heart, that you can't take part . . . you've got to put your bodies upon the gears, upon the levers . . . and you've got to make it stop." The crowd sang along with Joan Baez, "We Shall Overcome,"

Free speech movement, Berkeley, 1964.

and then they made the machine stop—they marched in and occupied Sproul Hall. They shut down the university administration building.

"We're not going to have anarchy in California," declared the governor, Edmund "Pat" Brown, and at 4 A.M. some 600 policemen entered Sproul Hall and began arresting students, eventually about 770, in the largest mass arrest in California history. Some 7,000 students remained on the plaza and handed out flyers. President Kerr met with faculty, who mostly supported the students, and discussed the situation with the regents. After a semester of turmoil, he abrogated the rule, and the Free Speech Movement held its first legal rally on Sproul Plaza. The FSM was a success, said Savio, because "it was so obvious to everybody that it was right."

Berkeley during fall semester 1964 was the first major student revolt of the sixties. Campus newspapers followed the events closely, and students made demands for more freedom and fewer rules at other universities, including Brandeis, Harvard, Indiana, Syracuse, and Texas. Yet Berkeley also stimulated another response from the older generation. The "UC Rebels" were "intolerable and insufferable," declared the *San Francisco Examiner,* they should be expelled, and the *Oakland Tribune* proclaimed that activists really wanted to turn Berkeley into a training ground for revolutionaries like the University of Havana. Many agreed with future gubernatorial candidate Ronald Reagan, when he declared, "Observe the rules or get out!"

Tonkin Gulf and the 1964 Election

Students and parents divided over Berkeley, but they united over another event off the coast of Vietnam. North Vietnamese patrol boats attacked an American destroyer, the USS *Maddox*, in the Tonkin Gulf. The *Maddox* was helping the South Vietnamese Army, ARVN, conduct sabotage missions in the north, but LBJ kept that from the public. Instead, the president declared that the American ship had been attacked in international waters and he was retaliating by ordering air strikes on naval installations in North Vietnam. The president then asked Congress to pass the Gulf of Tonkin Resolution, a vague charter that apparently gave him constitutional authority to help the South Vietnam ally. "It's like Grandmother's shirt," press secretary George Reedy said privately, "it covers everything."

The nation rallied around the flag. The *New York Times* declared the attack on the *Maddox* was the "beginning of a mad adventure by the North Vietnamese Communists," that the United States must "assure the independence of South Vietnam," and the *Washington Post* applauded LBJ's "careful and effective handling of the Viet-Nam crisis." The president's approval rating soared to over 70 percent, and Congress passed the resolution overwhelmingly. Two-thirds of the public supported the resolution, including at least that percentage of college students. The editors of *Michigan State News* were happy that LBJ had not "patted North Vietnam's leaders on the head for launching an unprovoked attack on our ships."

LBJ assured the public that he had no intention of expanding America's role in the war. It "ought to be fought by the boys of Asia to help protect their own land," he said, continuing that the issue for the presidential campaign was "who can keep the peace." Johnson pledged moderation, and if Americans ever desired to become involved in a major war in Southeast Asia—or to declare war on North Vietnam— then they had a clear choice at the polls that November: Republican Party nominee Senator Barry Goldwater.

Goldwater had published a book that became a best-seller in 1960, *The Conscience of a Conservative*. It sold 3 million copies and shortly thereafter he was writing articles that were syndicated to over 160 newspapers. He advocated limiting the role of government; in fact, he never had authored a bill and declared, "My aim is not to pass laws but to repeal them." He wanted to end most government regulations, along with social security, and wrote that federal grants to states not only infringe on states' rights but are a "mixture of blackmail and bribery." He had opposed the *Brown* decision, writing that "integrated schools are not required" by the Constitution. In foreign policy, Goldwater opposed containment as too defensive, "Like the boxer who refuses to throw a punch." American "strategy must be primarily offensive," he said. "We should encourage the South Koreans and the South Vietnamese to join Free Chinese Forces in a combined effort to liberate the enslaved peoples of Asia." As for Vietnam, "I'd drop a low-yield atomic bomb on the Chinese supply lines in North Vietnam or maybe shell 'em with the Seventh Fleet."

This handsome senator from Arizona was very popular with conservative students, and in 1960 he suggested that they should form a national organization. Journalist William F. Buckley agreed, and he held a conference at his estate in Sharon, Connecticut, which established the Young Americans for Freedom (YAF). The Sharon Statement and the YAF magazine, *New Guard*, noted that the greatest threat to America was communism. Conservative activists held a rally at Madison Square Garden in 1962, and thousands applauded as Brent Bozell, editor of the *National Review*, called on the United States to tear down the Berlin Wall and immediately invade Cuba. They opposed the Peace Corps and U.S. participation in the United Nations, and supported fighting communism in Vietnam. Goldwater, of course, was one of their sponsors, as were John Wayne and Ronald Reagan.

Americans today look back at the sixties as a radical era but often forget that there was activism on both sides of the political spectrum. The sixties generation was not a monolith. During cold war America, the left naturally generated more media interest and received more press. The youthful revolt against the establishment—at lunch counters, on campuses, or in the streets—was dramatic, perfect for television news.

And there were many liberal organizations, such as the National Student Association, but the one that eventually became the most influential was the Students for a Democratic Society (SDS). Al Haber formed SDS at the University of Michigan in 1960, and during the next two years some members had worked with SNCC in the civil rights movement. In 1962 about 50 of them met and discussed a manifesto written by Tom Hayden, which became known as *The Port Huron Statement*. It began ominously: "We are people of this generation, bred in at least modest comfort, housed now in universities, looking uncomfortably to the world we inherit."

Like black activists in the South, these and many other young intellectuals were uneasy because of the paradoxes in America, the inconsistencies between ideals and realities: racial bigotry while the nation proclaimed equality; growing affluence while millions remained impoverished; declarations of peaceful intentions while politicians voted for expanding military budgets. SDS proposed a new ideology for the sixties—the new left—which advocated civil rights, equal opportunity, and personal liberties. These activists called on citizens to wake from the fifties slumber, were appalled by most students who "don't even give a damn about apathy," and advocated that all should get involved in "participatory democracy." They felt politics affected everything, or as member Greg Calvert wrote, "The *personal* and the *political* could not be divorced. . . . The revolution is about our lives."

Although SDS and YAF later became influential on some campuses, their national influence has been overstated by historians, and they never played a significant role in elections. That was the case in autumn 1964. Conservative Goldwater won the Republican nomination after a bruising convention against the moderate New York governor, Nelson Rockefeller. But Goldwater faced an uphill battle against liberal LBJ, and the senator did not help himself on the campaign trail. His staff was disorganized and his speeches were confusing or inappropriate. Although he had voted against the Johnson tax cut because he labeled it fiscally irresponsible, he suddenly advocated an even larger reduction to conservatives in Los Angeles. In Tennessee he alarmed workers by calling for the sale of the large federal employer, the TVA. In North Dakota he shocked farmers by calling for "prompt and final termination of the farm subsidy program," and in Florida he astonished elderly listeners by attacking social security and LBJ's idea of Medicare. Furthermore, Goldwater made nuclear war an issue. The Russians had the atomic bomb, of course, but in 1964 the Chinese also exploded their first one. Goldwater had opposed JFK's popular Test Ban Treaty, and he declared that U.S. military commanders should be given the power to decide if and when to use tactical nuclear weapons. American missiles were so good, "we could lob one into the men's room at the Kremlin." He frightened many during a national speech when he declared, "Extremism in the defense of liberty is no vice . . . Moderation in the pursuit of justice is no virtue." Democrats used atomic fear to their advantage, placing a TV ad with a girl in the foreground and the bomb mushrooming in the background. Meanwhile, the president talked moderation and campaigned tirelessly. As Press Secretary Reedy commented, "LBJ campaigned as if he had an extra pair of glands."

On Election Day Johnson crushed Goldwater in one of the greatest landslides in American history. LBJ won 61 percent of the vote and 44 states. Goldwater won southern states that opposed civil rights. As LBJ told an aide when he signed the Civil Rights Act, "We delivered the South to the Republican Party for your lifetime and mine." Yet the defeat also smashed the conservative wing of the Republican Party, resulting in more moderate Republicans in elections until 1980. The Democrats increased their strong majorities in the Senate and the House. It was clear: Americans favored LBJ's liberalism of civil rights, social programs, and moderate foreign policy. Citizens wanted to stop communism but were not eager for a war in Southeast Asia, and they felt government had a role to play in responding to—and solving—national problems.

In the conservative era later, many citizens came to believe, as President Ronald Reagan said, "Government is not the solution to our problem; government *is* the problem." But we must remember that negative feelings about the federal government were a result of three major events that stunned citizens between 1968 and 1974: the Tet Offensive and a seemingly endless war in Vietnam, the Pentagon Papers, and the Watergate scandals. Before that, the majority of citizens had faith in a federal government that had fought the Great Depression, won World War II, and helped spread affluence to a growing suburban middle class.

Launching the Great Society

LBJ also had faith, a Texas-size faith that he and the government could solve problems facing the nation in the sixties. "I'm sick of all the people who talk about the things we can't do," he told an aide. "Hell, we're the richest country in the world, the most powerful. We can do it all." What problems confronted Americans then, and how did liberals address them?

The president had declared in 1964 that he was assembling various experts to participate in White House conferences "on the cities, on natural beauty, on the quality of education, and on other emerging challenges. And from these meetings and from this inspiration and from these studies we will begin to set our course toward the Great Society."

After his election, Johnson eventually established 135 task forces to develop plans and policies. Realizing the importance of the first months of any administration, the president bombarded Congress, sending 65 messages to Capitol Hill in just seven months. LBJ became "a great, hurtling locomotive," said friend Clark Clifford, "running down the track."

Johnson's top priority was health care, which was in crisis. Less than half of America's workers had health insurance. More significantly, fewer had coverage after retirement—the time most needed, when one illness could wipe out a lifetime of savings. Private hospitals often turned uninsured patients away, leaving care to overburdened public or charity clinics. To alleviate this situation, the federal government had made grants to the states that were supposed to share the cost of health care for the impoverished elderly. But the system had failed; in 1964 some 10 million people were eligible, but only 5 percent of them were covered.

Kennedy had proposed a health care bill, but the idea met immediate resistance from conservatives, the insurance industry, and the American Medical Association. This "socialized medicine," the AMA claimed, would "destroy the doctor–patient relationship" and decrease the nation's high standards of medical care. Johnson proposed Medicare for the elderly, and the AMA eventually spent $50 million opposing it in one of the costliest lobbying campaigns in history. Yet in spring 1965 the liberal congressional majority went on the attack, eventually passed Medicare, which provided health and hospital insurance for citizens over 65. The patient paid a deductible and a low premium and received up to 90 days hospitalization and other medical services. A small provision of the bill that attracted almost no attention was called Medicaid. All states eventually elected to participate in Medicaid, and since then they have shared the cost with the federal government to pay health bills for welfare recipients and those below the poverty line. Many liberals felt the nation was on its way toward a universal health care system, but the new program did not address most of the population—working Americans under 65.

The Johnson administration then attacked what were called the "three killers" (heart disease, cancer, and strokes), by greatly increasing federal funds for research. And after Dr. Oscar Auerbach's research linked smoking to lung cancer, the administration mandated the "warning" on cigarette packages.

Eventually, Johnson could boast more health legislation than all other presidents combined, but during spring 1965 he and his advisers again were interrupted by the civil rights movement and war in Vietnam.

LBJ Expands Civil Rights

Selma, Alabama, was a typical town in the Deep South. Although the Fifteenth Amendment guaranteed the right to vote, only 2 percent of blacks had been allowed to register. Although the Civil Rights Act guaranteed integration of public facilities, all remained strictly segregated. Thus in March, activists planned to help local blacks get the vote by joining with them for a 54-mile march: Selma to the state capital Montgomery. About 600 began their trek, moving across the Edmund Pettus Bridge, when 200 state troopers and deputies at the other end told them to halt. They did. A minute later the troopers charged: a cloud of tear gas, nightsticks swinging, bullwhips cracking. White spectators whooped approval as officers stormed defenseless blacks. Troopers knocked John Lewis to the ground and beat five women unconscious. "I saw a posse man raise his club," recalled a participant, "and smash it down on a woman's head as if he were splitting a watermelon."

"Bloody Sunday," activists called it, and that evening the nation saw it on television or read about it in the press. "The news from Selma," the *Washington Post* wrote, "will shock and alarm the whole nation." Liberals, ministers, professors, and students rushed to Selma and joined the march—and again the response was vicious. Four local whites attacked three activists, including Boston minister James

Bloody Sunday in Selma.

Reeb, whom they struck in the head with a large club, shattering his skull and killing him. Despite firm identification, the local white jury later acquitted the killer.

In fact, between the Greensboro sit-ins of 1960 and the Selma march of 1965, at least 26 civil rights activists were murdered, but only one of the killers went to prison. Local and state governments would not uphold the law. That is why activists and liberals called for federal intervention. "I don't see how President Johnson can send troops to Vietnam," declared John Lewis, "and can't send troops to Selma."

Johnson also was appalled by the killing, and so were citizens across the nation. Thousands marched in sympathy in many cities, including Boston, Chicago, Detroit, Los Angeles, and New York. Some 3,000 again began the journey from Selma to Montgomery; this time it was peaceful. President Johnson then addressed a joint session of Congress. An enormous TV audience of perhaps 70 million watched as LBJ spoke, recalling Lexington and Concord, Appomattox—and Selma. He called on Congress to pass a voting rights act. He beseeched Americans: "It's not just Negroes, really, it's all of us who must overcome the crippling legacy of bigotry and injustice. And we *shall* overcome."

Congress rose to a standing ovation. The media hailed the speech, even in most of the South, and months later LBJ signed the Voting Rights Act of 1965. The bill invalidated the use of any test or device to deny the vote, ending gimmicks such as literacy tests, and a constitutional amendment ended the poll tax. More important, the law meant federal examiners could register voters in states with a history of discrimination. South Carolina sued the federal government, and the Warren Court upheld the act. The result was dramatic: federal intervention ensured virtually no violence, and by the next summer half of southern adult blacks had registered to vote. In November 1966, for the first time since Reconstruction, African Americans lined up at the polls—and that changed politics in the South forever.

Johnson then attempted to increase employment opportunity for minorities by issuing an executive order stating that employers should take "affirmative action to ensure that applicants are employed . . . without regard to their race, color, religion, or national origin." As LBJ declared, "You do not take a person who for years has been hobbled by chains and liberate him, bring him up to the starting line of a race and then say, you're free to compete with all the others." Affirmative action was an interesting concept: federal, state, and local governments buy enormous amounts of goods and services, from navy ships to county roads, which cost taxpayers billions. Tax dollars thus employ millions of workers, usually about a quarter of the nation's work force. The idea behind affirmative action was that governments, agencies, and businesses funded by taxes should hire all taxpayers, not just white males. Recall, for example, that like many cities, Albany, Georgia, had a large number of black citizens whose taxes contributed to funding the local government, but not one ever had been hired by the city. To end that practice, the Johnson administration required contractors to develop affirmative action plans for hiring minorities; no quotas were mentioned.

Thus affirmative action and Title VII of the Civil Rights Act were aimed at changing the tradition of hiring mostly white men in the well-paying jobs of the nation, ending employment discrimination and opening positions to all taxpayers. The Johnson administration began the process that fundamentally altered employment practices in the nation, and most citizens either supported the changes or more likely were unaware of it because they were more concerned about South Vietnam.

LBJ Americanizes the Vietnam War

During spring 1965 the Vietcong attacked a small American base at Pleiku, and that angered Johnson. "I'm not going to be the first president to lose a war," said LBJ, and he changed U.S. policy by ordering Operation Rolling Thunder—air strikes against North Vietnam. He also decided that the only way to prevent defeat was to change policy again, and he sent a few thousand Marines. Previously, the U.S. troops there were to *advise* ARVN. Now, the commander in chief gave those 25,000 soldiers new orders: they could conduct combat missions with ARVN to search out and destroy the enemy. As one general proclaimed, "No one ever won a battle sitting on his ass."

Americans either rallied behind the president or knew little about the administration's policy. Opinion polls demonstrated that about 80 percent supported bombing the North, and the same percentage thought it was "very important" to prevent a communist South Vietnam. Earlier surveys also revealed that two-thirds of the public either had not followed or had no opinion of LBJ's policy, and a fourth did not even know U.S. troops were in Vietnam. Significantly, the administration attempted to conceal the escalation and downplay involvement. LBJ was more concerned with civil rights and his Great Society, and he did not want to provoke the Soviets, Chinese—or the Americans. A secret memorandum declared the "President desires that . . . publicity be avoided by all possible precautions" and that subordinates should minimize any appearance that the United States was enlarging its commitment. The president, said one adviser, wanted to "go to war without arousing the public ire."

Yet the bombing provoked some peace organizations and a few professors and students to question American policy during spring semester 1965. The first significant campus antiwar movement received attention when almost 50 professors decided to hold a "teach-in" at the University of Michigan. Inspired by civil rights sit-ins, and just days after the Selma march, 200 professors took out an ad in the *Michigan Daily* appealing to students to join them in a teach-in, an attempt to "search for a better policy." Throughout the night of March 24–25 more than 3,000 students and faculty participated in lectures, debates, and discussions. As a professor described it, "One honors student later told me that this was her first educational experience provided by the university during four years' attendance," and that spirit spread to other campuses. Teach-ins were held at about 35 universities, including

Columbia, Illinois, Rutgers, Wisconsin, and at usually sedate campuses such as Carleton in Minnesota. Berkeley held the largest and longest teach-in: some 20,000 participated for 36 hours. At Oregon, 3,000 students jammed into Union Hall and listened to speakers, poets, and folksingers. One pretty female wore a homemade card pinned to her sweater: "Let's make love, not war."

In April, the budding peace movement arrived in the nation's capital. Bused in from campuses all over the country, some 20,000 appeared on a warm, beautiful Sunday. They picketed the White House and then began marching to the Washington Monument. "The times they are a-changin'" the students sang with folksingers Judy Collins, Joan Baez, and Phil Ochs. Many gave speeches. SDS president Paul Potter called for a "massive social movement" to change America while activists waved signs: GET OUT OF SAIGON AND INTO SELMA. FREEDOM NOW IN VIETNAM. WAR ON POVERTY NOT ON PEOPLE. The crowd sang "We Shall Overcome" as it walked down the Mall and to the Capitol where it presented Congress with a petition: "The problems of America cry out for attention, and our entanglement in South Vietnam postpones the confrontation of these issues. . . . We call on you to end, not extend, the war in Vietnam."

A surge of energy appeared on campuses during spring semester. At Michigan State, activists confronted the administration's in loco parentis regulations, which not only included dress codes, but also administrative approval to distribute printed material on campus. Over 4,200 students signed an 80-foot petition, and by April the president gave in and agreed to end most regulations. At Ohio State, free speech was the issue. Students filed a suit against the university's fifties gag rule, which resulted in censoring all so-called unpatriotic speakers. Almost 300 activists held a sit-in at the administration building, the first one in OSU history, and they invited a communist philosopher to campus who sat silently on the stage in a "nonspeech," which gained national press coverage that ridiculed censorship. The administration abolished the gag rule. At Kansas, the day after Bloody Sunday in Selma, activists marched into the administration building and demanded that the university hire its first black faculty member and integrate fraternities, sororities, and dorms. By autumn semester, the chancellor prohibited all forms of discrimination at KU.

"The times must be a-changing," wrote *Michigan State News,* and they were as students took final exams and headed for summer jobs. A survey of 850 colleges revealed increasing activism, and that students felt the most important issues on campus were in loco parentis rules followed by free speech and a usual concern of young adults, food service. Like their parents, students stated the most important national issue was civil rights—there was little concern about Vietnam.

Thus the emerging antiwar movement had little or no impact on the Johnson administration, and the president did not change his policy in Vietnam. In fact, most Americans considered peace marchers as beatniks, kooks, or communists, and the demonstrators received little press. Americans supported LBJ, and that included most students. When 30 activists at Kent State protested the war, an angry crowd five times larger pelted them with rocks. A teach-in at Wisconsin resulted in 6,000 students signing a letter supporting the president's policy, and a fourth of the student body did the same thing at Yale. A survey of student opinion demonstrated that only a quarter supported negotiations or withdrawal from Vietnam.

In July the president announced he was increasing the number of U.S. troops to 125,000. Significantly, he did not admit he already had authorized a higher escalation to 200,000 and had given the field commander, General William Westmoreland, permission to conduct independent combat missions against the enemy—clearing the way for the U.S. Army to replace ARVN as the primary combat organization and thus Americanize the war. When a reporter asked if the buildup signaled a new policy, the president lied, stating it "does not imply any change in policy whatsoever." Citizens and the press cheered. *Life* proclaimed that it was wise and moral to "fulfill a promise to defend a victim of attack," South Vietnam, and *Time* editorialized that the conflict was the "crucial test of American policy and will. . . . The Right War at the Right Time."

Great Society

With popular support secure for his foreign policy during 1965, LBJ returned his attention to his Great Society and to his aim of eliminating discrimination, this time in immigration. American law then was the National Origins Act of 1924, which was based on the 1890 census. The result was to limit immigration from all nations except the United Kingdom and Ireland. Thus the annual British quota was 65,000, but just 5,666 for Italy, 308 for Greece, and only 105 for China. During the war and cold war the United States passed some temporary measures for refugees, and generally quotas were not applied to Canada and Mexico.

President Kennedy proposed abolishing quotas in 1963, but a new act was left to the Johnson administration. The president considered the old law a "very deep and painful flaw in the fabric of American justice," and he signed the 1965 Immigration Act. The law eventually abolished the old quotas and established a preference system based on family relations and occupational qualifications, thus opening the "golden door" to all cultures—regardless of national origins.

Johnsonian liberalism then turned to a topic of growing concern, the environment, which the president had addressed in 1964:

> We have always prided ourselves on being not only America the strong and America the free, but America the beautiful. Today that beauty is threatened. The water we drink, the food we eat, the very air that we breathe, are threatened with pollution. Our parks are overcrowded, our seashores overburdened. Green fields and dense forests are disappearing.

The president ordered Interior Secretary Stuart Udall to lead the charge, and in 1964 Congress passed two important bills, the Land and Water Conservation Fund

The Cuyahoga River on fire. Such pollution provoked
LBJ to advocate and then sign clean water acts.

and the Wilderness Act. The former established user fees at national parks and forests, generating revenue for establishing new areas, and the latter resulted in changing over 9 million acres of federal lands into wilderness areas void of roads or commercial activities. LBJ established 46 new federal areas, including the first new national parks in a generation—Canyonlands in Utah, Redwoods in California, North Cascades in Washington, and he authorized Guadalupe Mountains in Texas. Furthermore, the administration created novel areas that differed from traditional parks, such as Ozark National Scenic Riverways, Fire Island National Seashore, 20 historical parks and sites, and the Appalachian scenic trail, a hiking path from Maine to Georgia. Thirty-five new recreational areas were established, more than during the Teddy Roosevelt and Franklin Roosevelt eras, and Udall called it the "third wave of conservation."

The administration also confronted pollution, and that campaign was led by Democratic Senator Edmund Muskie of Maine, who became known as "Mr. Clean." The problem was alarming. Without enforced federal standards, cities often dumped their sewage and factories discharged industrial chemicals into waterways. The lower Great Lakes—Michigan, Erie, Ontario—were cesspools, and Erie was "dead," too polluted for fish. Udall labeled the Hudson River a "floating garbage heap," and when a man tossed a lit cigar into the Cuyahoga River in Cleveland, the river burned for eight days.

The Water Quality Act of 1965 passed both the Senate and House overwhelmingly, beginning federal supervision of water quality standards. Muskie and Udall then turned their energies toward America's plummeting air quality. Again, few states enforced their standards, if they had any at all. Industry and power plants pumped oxides and sulfur into the atmosphere. Half of the emission problem was caused by vehicles, none of which had pollution control devices. As a result, in many industrial cities people drove with their headlights on at noon. Brown, smelly air was the norm in all major cities, and that contributed to soaring rates of lung disease, emphysema, and bronchitis.

Kennedy had proposed and Johnson had signed the Clean Air Act of 1963, but it was a weak bill that lacked strict enforcement clauses and auto pollution provisions. In 1965 Muskie introduced Title II to the act, and it was passed, eventually mandating pollution control devices on all automobiles. But on the next Thanksgiving, New

"Smog Here Nears the Danger Point," declared the *New York Times*.
Eventually, the pollution was blamed for at least 80 deaths
in one week—a reason for LBJ's Air Quality Act.

York City experienced an ecological catastrophe, an air inversion that bombarded New Yorkers with almost two pounds of soot and gases for each person—sending hundreds to hospitals and killing 80.

The disaster provoked Congress and the president to get down to business, and the Senate approved the bill 88 to 0; not to be outdone, the House voted 362 to 0. LBJ signed the Air Quality Act of 1967, which basically allowed the federal government to fix national standards for industrial air pollution and resulted in unleaded gasoline—and much cleaner air.

Johnson later boasted that during his administration he had signed almost 300 conservation measures, more than during the first 187 years of the Republic. His wife Lady Bird also contributed by her campaign against highway billboards and for beautification of the nation's capital, resulting in the planting of hundreds of dogwood and cherry blossom trees on the Washington Mall. The Johnson administration also passed the first Endangered Species Act, boosted historic preservation, and shifted the focus from conservation of land to what became known as *environmentalism:* "The quality of life," wrote Udall in 1968, "is now the perspective and purpose of the new conservation."

Meanwhile, another Johnson task force was involved in solving the education crisis, caused by baby boomers flooding classrooms and bursting local school board budgets. Inner-city high school dropout rates were exploding, and almost 70 percent of the nation's elementary schools did not have libraries. Wealthy states spent twice as much on their students as poor ones, and in the latter, schools averaged less than half a textbook per child. JFK had tried but failed to pass an education act; he was a Catholic and the debate became mired in the church–school debate: should public funds be used to help parochial education? Another education issue then was access. Millions of students were denied a good education because they lived in states or urban areas too poor to provide one, or they had physical or mental handicaps in districts that did not provide special education, or they simply could not afford college tuition.

LBJ knew poor schools. He had attended them in the Texas hill country, and after attending Southwest Texas Teachers College, he had taught impoverished Mexican children at Welhausen Elementary School in Cotulla, Texas, before his political career. In 1965 the president was obsessed with passing an act, and he told his commissioner of education, "I want to see this coonskin on the wall."

Again, the church–state issue threatened to stall LBJ's education act, but his advisers arrived at a unique solution: the federal government would provide aid to *pupils,* not to *schools.* In essence, then, federal funds would go to public or state agencies, which could share services with private schools, and thus aid students in all schools—as long as they accepted integration. Congress embraced this "child benefit" idea, and they greatly boosted federal funding to local school districts by passing the Elementary and Secondary Education Act.

The administration quickly proposed a second bill, the Higher Education Act of 1965. In essence, this was to boost research at universities and develop a federal college student loan program. Earlier, after the Russians launched *Sputnik*, the Eisenhower administration signed an act that provided some loans for defense-related majors, such as science and engineering, and a dozen states began their own small loan programs. Yet LBJ advocated a federal program—one for most students. In 1960 median family income was $6,000. Almost 80 percent of high school graduates with a family income twice that attended college, but only a third did if their family income was half of the median. Furthermore, the primary reason for dropping out of college was financial difficulty. The question was, Who should be able to attend college? Only the fortunate from wealthy families who could afford tuition, or anyone who had the intelligence and drive to earn a degree? Johnson answered the question when he signed the Higher Education Act, which provided federal scholarships for needy students and government-insured private loans for students whose families made less than $10,000. He recalled teaching at a "little Welhausen Mexican school" and remembered "the pain of . . . knowing then that college was closed to practically every one of those children because they were too poor."

Johnson's education acts were unsurpassed in history, boosting college enrollment and eventually tripling the percentage of federal funds that financed local education. School boards began building programs and buying library resources and textbooks; they also initiated new teaching programs in the languages, music, advanced science, and special education. Universities expanded research facilities and had more funds for graduate studies. College students applied for low-interest guaranteed loans. For the first time, some public money funded parochial schools, but not for "religious worship or instruction." The acts boosted integration, because funds could not be appropriated for segregated schools. The president also announced that the Office of Economic Opportunity would begin a preschool program for needy children, Head Start, and to promote the arts, LBJ established the National Endowments for the Humanities and the Arts.

The passage of Great Society legislation, along with the rulings of the Warren Court, demonstrated that during 1965 the nation reached the pinnacle of liberalism. In less than two years, LBJ had signed bills that concerned virtually all major aspects of daily life—health care, education, air and water quality, recreational lands, voting and civil rights, taxes and poverty.

By 1966 the Great Society was winding down, the president and nation were becoming more focused on Vietnam, but LBJ pressed on. Johnson attempted to alleviate poverty in slums by establishing a federal program of urban renewal with his Model Cities Act, coordinated by a new Department of Housing and Urban Development, and he aimed to end housing discrimination by proposing an "open housing act." Because the three networks then provided no educational programming, LBJ signed a bill establishing the Public Broadcasting System (PBS), and that eventually led to National Public Radio (NPR). He also signed consumer protection legislation mandating that lending institutions be truthful with clients concerning interest rates and food companies state the nutritional values of their products. After Ralph Nader provoked the public with his book *Unsafe at Any Speed*, the president signed bills that resulted in seat belts and other safety devices in automobiles. Finally, the president continued his attempts to control pollution, and along with Lady Bird, beautify America.

Johnson was destined to leave an unparalleled legacy, signing more bills than any other president; early in 1965 he submitted 87 bills to Congress, and nine months later he had signed 84 into law. A "legislative grand slam," *Congressional Quarterly* declared, and columnist James Reston quipped that LBJ was "getting everything through the Congress but the abolition of the Republican party, and he hasn't tried that yet." His big Texas ego grew to epic proportions, and he joked, "Gentlemen, when you dig my grave, don't dig it too deep because I'll be up in three days."

Yet the question remains: Were Johnson's domestic programs successful? The answer has been debated ever since. Conclusions are complicated because each program must be evaluated on its own merits or demerits, and answers often depend on what citizens think is the role of government—and if they benefited from LBJ's programs.

Whatever we think now, during 1965 Americans applauded Johnson's liberalism. His approval rating was about 70 percent. Most felt the nation was moving forward, that LBJ was fulfilling Kennedy's idealism—and more. The mood was glowing in August when Johnson called civil rights leaders together and signed the Voting Rights Act. Martin Luther King Jr. spoke of the president's "amazing sensitivity to the difficult problems that Negro Americans face in the stride toward freedom," and the leaders proclaimed LBJ the "greatest president" for blacks, surpassing Lincoln. African Americans were making legal, and also social, progress. Actor Sidney Poitier became the first black to win an Academy Award for his leading role in *Lilies of the Field*, and Bill Cosby became the first TV star by appearing on the popular sitcom *I Spy*. Muhammad Ali proved he was "the greatest" by winning the heavyweight boxing title while an all-black Texas Western basketball team beat all-white Kentucky and won the 1966 NCAA championship. That year LBJ appointed the first black to the cabinet, Robert C. Weaver, and the next year to the Supreme Court, Thurgood Marshall. Massachusetts voters sent Edward Brooke to the U.S. Senate and those in Cleveland elected the great-grandson of a slave, Carl Stokes, as the nation's first black mayor of a major city.

On campus, students also were optimistic. They had challenged in loco parentis, and throughout the mid-sixties university administrators were either liberalizing or ending most regulations. True, some youth were concerned about Vietnam; yet no one thought the war would continue for more than a year. Besides, the sixties generation was having too much fun testing its new moral limits, bundling on the beach, taking "the pill," or gyrating in miniskirts to the Frug and Watusi at new disco clubs.

Newsweek surveyed students at numerous universities and found that over 90 percent expressed confidence in higher education, big corporations, and the federal government, and over 80 percent were satisfied with college and had positive views about organized religion and the armed forces. "Flaming Moderates," a journalist labeled youth in 1965, and no one would have predicted that in just two years hippies would be smoking marijuana publicly during the Summer of Love and angry students would be marching on the Pentagon. Campus life at mid-decade was cool, the good life. As the student body president of the University of Texas said, "We haven't really been tested by war or depression. We live very much in the present because we don't have to be overly concerned about the future."

During the next two years Americans would be tested, as the nation tumbled from the pinnacle of liberalism into the days of decision.

Chapter 3

Days of Decision, 1965–1967

What *Life* called the "Decade of Tumult and Change" began after Lyndon Johnson signed the Voting Rights Act. A "growing swell of demands for extreme and immediate change" emerged, most of it caused by the nation's two most pressing problems between autumn 1965 and the end of 1967—*race* and *war*. These issues forced citizens to make decisions about the course of the nation, even about their culture, because at the same time a youthful counterculture emerged to confront the values of mainstream society.

The "days of decision," folksinger Phil Ochs called these difficult years, a time when the sixties experienced "a change in the wind, a split in the road." Those days first appeared with two events during the remaining months of 1965—one in a ghetto at home and another in a valley in South Vietnam.

"A Time Bomb of Black Rage"

In August a riot erupted in Watts, the black ghetto of Los Angeles. It began simply enough. A white policeman stopped a young black driver and began to arrest him for speeding and possible intoxication. A crowd assembled, and the officer radioed for reinforcements. Other cars arrived, and when the police attempted to force the suspect into a car, he struggled. "We've got no rights at all," shouted an onlooker. "It's just like Selma!" Bystanders began pelting police with rocks and bottles, and within two hours an angry mob was attacking white drivers and setting cars aflame. Some began looting, a few began shooting, which forced the police to call for the National Guard.

The riot raged on. Fires burned out of control. Shots were exchanged. Eventually, authorities called in over 15,000 troops and police. Troops grew tense, shooting wildly. A presidential commission later reported, "Several persons were killed by mistake. Many more were injured." Authorities restored law and order after six days, but at a high price: almost 4,000 arrested, over 1,000 injured, and 34 dead.

"If a single event can be picked to mark the dividing line" of the sixties, *Life* editorialized, "it was Watts," because that "sudden and violent" episode "ripped the fabric of lawful democratic society and set the tone of confrontation and open revolt."

Watts did incalculable harm to the civil rights movement. Many white Americans agreed with former President Eisenhower, who blamed the riot on "an increased lack of respect for law and order throughout the country." The "white backlash" emerged, whites who resented the civil rights movement and felt that the federal government was concerned only about minorities, not about the white majority. Conservatives who had advocated "states' rights" over "federal interference," who had supported only local police protection for southern blacks, now demanded "whatever force is necessary" to stop the riot. To restore law and order the *Oakland Tribune* advocated employing the "full power of the Federal Government."

The Johnson administration responded to Watts by sending officials to discover the reasons for the riot, which revealed the plight of urban blacks. Outside of the South, most whites thought African Americans had better opportunities. In fact, a decade after the *Brown* case, educational facilities remained segregated because white officials drew school district lines. The Civil Rights Commission found that between 1950 and 1965 segregation in 15 large northern cities actually "rose sharply," and that in those cities black unemployment was double that of whites, even during the booming economy of the sixties. In Watts, the black unemployment rate was 30 percent, and nationally, the majority of blacks were underemployed in unskilled and service jobs, the prescription for poverty. Over 40 percent of nonwhites were below the poverty line, and another study demonstrated that the average combined underemployed and unemployed rate for blacks was almost nine times that of whites. The contrast with white America was startling. A black Watts resident told a white from Los Angeles, "You've got it made. Some nights on the roof of our rotten falling-down buildings we can actually see your lights shining in the distance. So near and yet so far. We want to reach out and grab it and punch it on the nose."

Even if a black had graduated from high school, attended college, and acquired a good job, few could escape the ghetto. All major cities had housing restrictions: the better areas and the suburbs were restricted for "whites only," the rundown districts for "coloreds." Thus 95 percent of suburban residents were white, and 80 percent of northern blacks lived in segregated ghettos. Unlike white America, then, the key to success—hard work—had little meaning for urban minorities. They were trapped in slums.

Nor did urban minorities have any political clout. Many city officials were racists, or they simply were not concerned about their black constituents. When those residents asked that war on poverty funds be spent in Watts, Los Angeles Mayor Sam Yorty said that such demands were caused by "Communist agitation." When King complained about housing restrictions, the mayor responded, "That's no indication of prejudice. That's personal choice." It was, but only for whites. When King asked the police chief why he referred to black rioters as "the criminal element" and as "monkeys," the chief declared, "That's the only language Negroes understand." City police forces were notorious; before affirmative action programs began later in the decade almost all police officers were white men, only high school graduates, and in the ghetto cops were known for racism and brutality. L.A. policemen called their billy clubs "nigger knockers."

Racial attitudes were demonstrated vividly as President Johnson's two trusted assistants arrived in Watts. One was white, and the other was Roger Wilkins, a black assistant attorney general. As the two drove into Watts, two white cops immediately stopped them. While one cop asked the white official some questions and for identification, the other policeman pulled Wilkins from the car, frisked him roughly, drew his pistol, jammed the barrel into his stomach, and began asking questions to find out "why a nigger was riding with a white," Wilkins recalled. "My blood was boiling, and I came within an inch of exploding—and losing my life—until the other policeman told his companion, 'Well, well, we've made a hell of a mistake.'"

Rage, frustration. As Wilkins walked down the filthy streets, past the shabby bars and gutted stores of Watts, he saw another culture: the ghetto. He reported these were "the poor people, the voiceless people, the invisible people," that they *"had* been ignored, and they were enraged." A local black minister explained during the riot, "Here's the man who doesn't have any identity. But *tonight* he has the Los Angeles Police Department and the Los Angeles Fire Department upset. He has the National Guard called out. Tonight he is somebody."

That was the level of hopelessness and frustration, and that was the reason for the urban riots of the mid-sixties. As *Life* noted, "A time bomb of black rage exploded in the ghettos."

The president responded to the rage by asking Congress to pass a Model Cities Act for urban renewal and an Open Housing Act to end restrictions, but the first was not effective and the latter was debated for years in the Senate. The real problem was cultural: decades of segregation had led to two different perspectives. Blacks saw an America filled with discrimination. Passage of the civil and voting rights acts did not immediately decrease the racism or open many doors of opportunity, and that was frustrating. Whites saw an America finally trying to live up to its dream by passing social programs aimed at helping minorities; they could not understand why ghettos were burning. "What do they want?" LBJ asked. "I'm giving them boom times and more good legislation than anybody else did, and what do they do—attack and sneer. Could FDR do better? Could anybody do better? What do they want?"

"We'll Lick Them"

Watts faded the glow of LBJ liberalism that autumn, and so did Vietnam. Some began wondering about the war, especially about Johnson's escalation of American involvement. On the weekend of October 15–16, 1965, activists held the International Days of Protest. The protest was minor, with the largest demonstrations on the coasts. In New York, 20,000 participated in a peace parade to the UN Plaza, and 300 gathered for a "speak-out" at the armed forces induction center on Whitehall Street. At dusk, David Miller declared that "napalming of villages is an immoral act," and he lit his draft card and lifted the flame over his head. Television broadcast the event, and Miller became the first citizen indicted and imprisoned in the decade for violating the Selective Service Act. In Berkeley, students held a teach-in on Friday, and that evening a crowd of over 10,000 left the campus on a "peace invasion" of the Oakland Army Base. The local district attorney declared the march treasonous, and the Oakland mayor refused to issue a parade permit. Consequently, when the activists reached city limits they were confronted with a wall of 300 policemen. They returned to the campus, but the next afternoon activists attempted another march to the army base where they were confronted by another wall of police, and a number of Hell's Angels who suddenly attacked the protesters, ripped up banners, one yelling, "Go back to Russia, you fucking Communists!" The bikers beat the activists. The police attacked the Hell's Angels. Order was restored.

Commenting on the demonstrations, Republican gubernatorial candidate Ronald Reagan declared, "If you ask me, the activities of those Vietnam Day teach-in people can be summed up in three words: Sex, Drugs, and Treason."

Most Americans agreed, especially a few days later as U.S. troops engaged the enemy in the first major battle of the war—and the second event that initiated the days of decision—the Ia Drang Valley. Vietcong and North Vietnamese troops launched an offensive in what appeared to be a plan to cut South Vietnam in half, and General Westmoreland met the challenge by sending his troops to stop the advance in the valley. American soldiers confronted three regiments of the North Vietnamese Army (NVA), and for three days just one U.S. battalion, outnumbered seven to one, withstood a dozen enemy human-wave attacks. U.S. officers called in massive air strikes, and artillerymen fired so fast that at times their barrels glowed red. Reinforcements arrived, and brief but violent engagements continued for five weeks. During the last fray at landing zone Albany, U.S. units suffered 60 percent casualties. A survivor recalled dead enemy snipers hanging from trees, piles of tangled bodies, the ground sticky with blood, and labeled the scene the "devil's butcher shop." The enemy retreated, and both sides counted bodies: at least 2,000 and perhaps 3,000 enemy died and almost 240 Americans.

The Ia Drang battle had an impact on the belligerents. The NVA avoided engaging U.S. troops in conventional warfare for over two years, until January 1968 in the Tet Offensive. The enemy, realizing American soldiers were well trained and had massive firepower, shifted back to guerrilla warfare and employed tactics of ambush, hit and run, before vanishing into the jungle. The enemy rarely would stand a fight and take a licking; John Wayne was an American show. For U.S. policymakers, Ia Drang somewhat ironically confirmed the search-and-destroy strategy of General Westmoreland. He cabled the president that he now faced conventional war, and the way to win was to search out and then destroy the enemy with additional U.S. troops. A "policy of attrition," the general called it, "bleeding them until Hanoi wakes up to the fact that they have bled their country to the point of national disaster." Then, supposedly, they would give up. In South Vietnam, meanwhile, American officials would try to "Win the Hearts and Minds" (WHAM) of the Vietnamese people by building public projects such as irrigation canals that would improve the standard of living. LBJ sent more funds for projects, and he quietly raised the ceiling of U.S. troops in Vietnam to 375,000 as Pentagon officials proclaimed Ia Drang a "resounding military success."

Ia Drang also was important at home, for it rallied the American people. "Fury at Ia Drang," *Newsweek* declared, and the magazine pictured two soldiers helping a wounded man with the caption "Red Badge of Courage." Journalist Joseph Alsop called Ia Drang a series of "remarkable victories," and *U.S. News* boasted about America's tenacious fighters who beat the "best the Communists could throw at them." Pollster Louis Harris reported a dramatic shift in favor of administration policy with about 65 percent approving of LBJ's handling of the war, only 11 percent favoring negotiations or withdrawal. Harris reported that the "most hotly debated issue among Americans was whether they should first carry the ground war North or destroy the Vietcong in the South."

"We'll lick them," declared Secretary of State Dean Rusk, and given the popular mood, antiwar demonstrators provoked resentment. War supporters in Washington, D.C., held signs, "Burn the Teach-in Professors," and over 25,000 prowar New Yorkers marched behind five winners of the Medal of Honor while a World War II veteran carried a sign, "Support our men in Vietnam—Don't stab them in the back."

During that first autumn of the war, less than one-tenth of 1 percent of the population participated in an antiwar demonstration, and on campus students favored the war at higher rates than their parents; a remarkable 75 percent of 20-something youth favored sending troops to Southeast Asia. Prowar students held marches at Purdue, Cornell, Pittsburgh, and Brigham Young, and they lined up to sign petitions supporting LBJ's policy: approximately 16,000 at Michigan State; 9,000 at Minnesota; 6,000 at Wisconsin and at Boston; and 4,000 at Texas and at Rutgers. Stanford and Ohio State students held "bleed-ins," donating blood for casualties in Vietnam; in Ann Arbor, over 2,000 students sent LBJ a 30-foot telegram supporting his efforts; not to be outdone, Texas A & M students sent one twice that long.

Yet even the small number of protesters concerned the government. In the mid-sixties, it was one thing to demonstrate for civil rights or student power, issues moderates and liberals could support, but it was another thing to question American foreign

U.S. Marines on a search-and-destroy mission
often made easy targets for enemy snipers.

policy during the cold war. Who were these dissidents? Attorney General Nicholas Katzenbach stated there were "some Communists involved," and FBI director Hoover declared that subversives participated in the demonstrations. The Senate Internal Security Subcommittee held hearings and then proclaimed that the control of the antiwar movement had passed from the liberals to the "Communists and extremists who favor the victory of the Vietcong and are openly hostile to the United States."

Nonsense. Moderates, liberals, radicals, all were involved, and as historian Charles DeBenedetti demonstrated, "no one was in control of the antiwar movement." No one ever was in control, certainly not the communists. Antiwar activists were concerned citizens who raised important questions: Was a war in Vietnam in the national interest, and did fighting on the other side of the world have anything to do with American security? Was this undeclared war legal, and was the way the nation raised an army—the draft—fair? Moreover, the United States had not been attacked, no Pearl Harbor, so pacifists wondered if youth should put their lives in harm's way for what they considered a dubious cause, a military government in Saigon led by generals Nguyen Van Thieu and Nguyen Cao Ky. Was the Thieu–Ky regime any better or worse than that of Ho Chi Minh? Many liberals were angry that they voted for peace candidate Johnson in 1964, only to get the war policy of Goldwater.

Such questions would be debated endlessly for the next eight years. To influence Americans to oppose the conflict, moderate dissidents wrote letters or editorials advocating negotiations with the enemy or held peaceful marches urging eventual withdrawal. The few radicals protested by holding rambunctious marches, burning their draft cards, or shouting their demand: "Out Now!"

Radical tactics proved counterproductive, for during the days of decision uncivil behavior only appalled the public. Most citizens then accepted the notion that activists were beatniks, subversives, even communists. Sitting in their suburbs they understood little about the war and had no idea how to win it. Few Americans felt that Vietcong peasants or the North Vietnamese Army would be a match for the "greatest nation on earth." Faced with an army of John Waynes, the enemy would give up quickly. How could America lose? Furthermore, Americans trusted the president and his "best and brightest" advisers; they did not accept failure. LBJ had assured the nation that he was prepared to "go anywhere at any time" to talk peace, that he supported "unconditional negotiations" with Hanoi. His subordinates added that although the administration shared the same goals as the dissidents, they had "secret information" that justified their policy.

Thus Johnson continued what citizens eventually learned were a long string of lies concerning Vietnam. The president had no secret information nor any knowledge about the Vietnamese people. The Texan once said that Vietnam was "just like the Alamo." On another occasion, LBJ tried to "cut a deal" with Ho Chi Minh. As if he was using the "Johnson treatment" on U.S. senators, the president proposed to provide massive public works for North Vietnam (a Vietnamese Great Society) if Ho would withdraw his troops and stop fighting in the South. Ho and his followers had been fighting the French and now the Americans for 20 years, not for public works, but for independence—for a unified nation. As far as war was concerned, Ho told a Western reporter, "The Americans greatly underestimate the determination of the Vietnamese people."

Johnson did not understand, but soldiered on, "We're not going to tuck our tails and run home." Yet behind the bravado he had doubts, as he later admitted to Doris Kearns:

> I knew from the start that I was bound to be crucified either way I moved. If I left the woman I really loved—the Great Society—in order to get involved with that bitch of a war on the other side of the world, then I would lose everything at home. All my programs. All my hopes. . . . But if I left that war and let the Communists take over South Vietnam, then I would be seen as a coward and my nation would be seen as an appeaser.

Like Kennedy, Johnson feared that conservatives would blame him for "losing Vietnam," as they had blamed Truman for "losing China." In fact, stated LBJ, Truman's problems over China were "chickenshit compared with what might happen if we lost Vietnam." There would be an "endless national debate—a mean and destructive debate—that would shatter my presidency, kill my administration, and damage our democracy."

So throughout 1966 America sunk deeper into the Vietnam quagmire. Justified by the vague aim of "stopping communism," citizens watched and waited, hoping for some sign of victory. In September, three-fourths supported and only a quarter opposed the war; about the same percentage wanted to expand the war and attack North Vietnam as wanted to withdraw the troops. That same month *Time* summarized the national mood: "Along with most other people, the politicians are letting Lyndon Johnson take the responsibility, and waiting for something to happen."

Black Power!

Civil rights activists also were waiting for something to happen in 1966, debating about tactics and location—should they continue concentrating on the rural south, or after Watts, shift efforts to northern ghettos?

Suddenly, an individual made something happen: James Meredith. Four years earlier Meredith had been the first black to attend the University of Mississippi. By June he had graduated and decided to begin a "walk against fear" in his state, declaring that the 225-mile trek from Memphis to Jackson would demonstrate that a black man could walk on the highways without being harmed: "Nothing can be more enslaving than fear." With only 30 percent of eligible black Mississippians registered to vote, Meredith aimed to encourage black citizens to take advantage of the new Voting Rights Act and register before the November elections. He began the march with only two companions, a minister and a journalist, for the major civil rights organizations had shied away from the walk—until the second day. Then, when he had hiked only ten miles into his home state, a white man stepped out of the bushes, shouting, "James Meredith! I want only James Meredith!" He fired his shotgun three times, and Meredith, screaming, fell to the pavement. He was rushed to a hospital in Memphis where doctors extracted a hundred pellets in his legs, back, and head.

Activists rushed to Memphis. Roy Wilkins of the NAACP, Whitney Young of the Urban League, Floyd McKissick of CORE, Stokely Carmichael of SNCC, and King and his SCLC aides began discussions on continuing the March Against Fear. But this march would be different from the last major event, Selma in 1965. Since then young blacks in CORE and SNCC had elected new leadership. Members of SNCC had replaced John Lewis with Carmichael, and CORE had replaced James Farmer with Floyd McKissick. The veterans had been voted out, and the new leadership reflected militant attitudes that had been emerging since the 1964 Mississippi Democratic Freedom Party and the Democratic Convention.

The Meredith March would mark the emergence of black power, and the reasons for that phenomenon had been developing for a couple of years. Since the Democratic Convention many activists had become disillusioned with white liberals, impatient with moderate black civil rights leaders, and by 1966 they were resentful that the Johnson administration seemed more interested in Vietnam than enforcing racial justice in America. Most activists had tired of the violence, of taking the beatings and turning the other cheek. Moreover, change seemed so slow; in January, a year and a half after Congress passed the Civil Rights Act, black activist Sammy Younge demanded to use an illegal "white only" rest room in Alabama—and he was shot in the head.

Other activists had been questioning their identity: "blackness or black consciousness." Some felt if SNCC or CORE excluded whites then they would also be eliminating those cultural values and beginning the search for their own African roots. "If we are to proceed toward true liberation, we must cut ourselves off from white people. We must form our own institutions, credit unions, co-ops, political parties, write our own histories." That year SNCC and CORE expelled all white members.

Another reason for the rise of black power was Malcolm X, who had been outspoken throughout the early sixties. He felt Christianity was hypocritical, so he condemned segregated churches, converted to Islam, and became a leader of the Black Muslims in Harlem. After centuries of slavery and segregation, he argued that blacks had no future in the United States. "I don't see any American dream; I see an American nightmare." He enraged whites by labeling them "blue-eyed devils," and he demanded that because the United States was corrupt with racism, the United Nations should intervene and create separate black states, the only way they could obtain racial justice. "Separatism" naturally angered moderate blacks who had worked hard for integration, but to Malcolm, Martin Luther King was "just a twentieth-century Uncle Tom." Furthermore, King's tactic of nonviolent activism was absurd. Don't turn the other cheek, Malcolm declared, stand tall: "We're nonviolent with people who are nonviolent with us. But we are not nonviolent with anyone who is violent with us."

The idea was not original, not novel with the emergence of black power; such thinking came right out of frontier America. For centuries Anglos had treated everyone else on the continent by standing up and swinging back, often by swinging first. If such views had been stated by a white citizen, there would have been no interest, no media coverage, because whites felt it was their "right" to arm and defend themselves. But Malcolm was not white; he was not a typical black politely asking for his rights. He was the first of a new phenomenon—a bold black man demanding self-determination and if necessary self-defense. That shocked white America. *Newsweek* called him a "spiritual desperado . . . a demagogue who titillated slum Negroes and frightened whites."

Whites had little to worry about in the first half of the decade for few blacks were listening to Malcolm X. A *Newsweek* poll in 1963 found that blacks ranked

King first and Malcolm last in popularity and effectiveness, but that changed in mid-decade. In 1964 Malcolm was becoming famous in Africa, touring and urging the development of a Pan-Africa movement. Then, the next February, Black Muslims assassinated Malcolm X. The killing shocked many young blacks, and later that year, with the publication of his fascinating autobiography, Malcolm X became more famous in death than he had been in life. To many, he was a martyr, even a hero—a black militant, a teacher of African heritage, an avatar of black pride. "I never knew I was black," stated Denise Nicholas, "until I read Malcolm."

At the same time a very different man was preaching black pride, Muhammad Ali, who had won the heavyweight boxing championship. Unlike all other black athletes then, Ali boasted he was not only "the greatest" but also the "best looking" champ. Few whites had ever considered that African Americans could be good looking, because they rarely appeared in films or on TV. Ali challenged society, and soon his young fans were saying, "black is beautiful" and singing along with James Brown's hit, "Say It Loud—I'm Black and I'm Proud."

Armed with such ideas, young activists arrived in Memphis to continue Meredith's March Against Fear. As they negotiated the terms of the march with older leaders, it became apparent that the civil rights movement was in disarray. The older moderates wanted another Selma, a call to white liberals to join them in a drive for voter registration and support for another civil rights bill, but the militants advocated a march of blacks only, urged condemning liberals and LBJ, and wanted to employ a black Louisiana group, Deacons for Defense, as an armed protection force. Moderates Roy Wilkins and Whitney Young were appalled, refused to participate, and left Memphis.

The civil rights movement continued melting in the hot summer sun of Mississippi. King, Carmichael, and McKissick led the march, but for the first time very few whites participated. Along the route, King was warmly received by local residents, and he continued to preach nonviolence and love. But within the ranks the mood had changed. "I'm not for that nonviolence stuff anymore," declared a young marcher. "If one of those damn white Mississippi crackers touches me, I'm gonna knock the hell out of him." Carmichael, McKissick, and King discussed ideas, and although they grew fond of each other, they also disagreed. "I'm not going to beg the white man for anything I deserve," declared Carmichael. "I'm going to take it."

Each night the marchers pitched camp and held a rally. King preached nonviolence and brotherhood, but when SCLC members attempted to sing "We Shall Overcome," militants sang a new version: "We Shall Overrun." When the crowd reached Greenwood, Carmichael violated police orders and pitched a tent on the grounds of a black high school. State troopers arrested him. After he was released, he held a large rally, where he jumped on a platform, shot his arm into the sky with a clenched fist, and shouted, "This is the twenty-seventh time I have been arrested—and I ain't going to jail no more! The only way we gonna stop them white men from whuppin' us is to take over. We been saying freedom for six years and we ain't got nothin'. What we gonna start saying now is Black Power!"

The crowd roared back, "Black Power!" Another activist, Willie Ricks, jumped on the platform, and yelled, "What do you want?" "Black Power!" they shouted, and then Carmichael yelled, "You know what to tell them. What do you want?" And they continued, "Black Power! Black Power!! Black Power!!!"

"Everything that happened afterward was a response to that moment," wrote participant Cleveland Sellers. "More than anything, it assured that the Meredith March Against Fear would go down in history as one of the major turning points in the black liberation struggle."

Black power was on television, made national headlines the next day, but what did it mean? "We must come together around the issue that oppresses us—our blackness," stated Carmichael. "It doesn't mean that you take over the country. Black power is the coming together of black people in the struggle for their liberation." Civil rights moderates were upset. A. Philip Randolph saw the new creed as dangerous to integration, promoting separatism, and "a menace to racial peace" that only would result in more black deaths. "It is the father of hatred and the mother of violence," claimed NAACP's Roy Wilkins, "a reverse Ku Klux Klan." Many white liberals agreed. "We must reject calls for racism," declared Vice President Humphrey, "whether they come from a throat that is white or one that is black." Carmichael countered: the movement needed "a rallying cry . . . a new slogan with 'black' in it."

The debate would have no victors, but a few days later the movement would have more victims. Southern whites again boosted the black militants' position, this time in Neshoba County where two years earlier racists had murdered Chaney, Schwerner, and Goodman. King attempted to hold a memorial service, but whites encircled the activists, taunted them, and then charged, clubbing them with ax handles. Police stood by. Young blacks began swinging back, and only then did law enforcement officers intervene, stopping the clash. That evening whites and blacks exchanged gunfire. The situation continued to deteriorate as the marchers entered Canton. In a driving rain, they tried to set up camp in a black school yard, but police refused permission. Soaked and tired, the marchers continued pitching tents in the darkness. The police fired tear gas, and then charged, whipping and clubbing.

The brutal episode alienated young marchers and boosted black power. On the last day of the march, when 15,000 rallied in Jackson, the crowd needed no coaching. The chant of "Freedom Now!" had been replaced with "Black Power!" McKissick ended the final rally with the declaration, "1966 shall be remembered as the year we left our imposed status as Negroes and became *Black Men* . . . 1966 is the year of the concept of Black Power."

Riots, Rebellion, and Responses

Yet calls for black power had little to do with the summer riots of 1966. Like Watts the year before, the cause was years of discrimination, smoldering frustration, usually sparked by white police behavior. Ghetto dwellers rioted in Cleveland, Dayton,

Milwaukee, and San Francisco, resulting in 3,000 arrests, 400 injured, and at least 7 dead. The sight of fires in the streets, broken store windows, and looters running into the darkness became common on the TV evening news.

These were the days of decision concerning the future of civil rights. Perhaps conservative critics were right, many thought, civil rights had gone too far, had led to "crime in the streets." Republican Gerald Ford asked what many city dwellers wanted to know: "How long are we going to abdicate law and order—the backbone of civilization?" Polls that autumn found that at least 75 percent of whites now felt that civil rights was being harmed by marches and calls for black power.

Many whites recoiled, and the white backlash received more adherents, many who began demanding law and order while some even advocated "white power." A vivid example occurred in Chicago, where throughout the sixties activists had been attempting to desegregate schools and end housing restrictions. King decided to lend his support, and with Jesse Jackson and many local activists, they promoted an "open housing campaign" to provoke Congress to pass the federal act. The activists staged numerous marches into white neighborhoods, and the response was vicious. Scores of locals threw bottles and bricks, holding signs: "Nigger Go Home" and "White Power." In August, violence reached its peak as King and followers walked to Marquette Park. Whites waved Confederate flags, shouted, "We Hate Niggers!" "Martin Luther Coon!" And they hurled bottles and rocks, hitting King and knocking him to his knees. He called off further demonstrations, commenting, "I have never seen such hate, not in Mississippi or Alabama as I see here in Chicago."

King left Chicago, but young militants continued the desegregation campaign by announcing a march through working-class Cicero. Not one black lived there, and the county sheriff called the plan "suicidal." Fearful of certain violence, only 200 blacks participated, and on the short route they had to be protected by 700 police officers and almost 3,000 National Guardsmen. Whites pursued the procession, throwing bottles and rocks, and the demonstration degenerated into street fighting. This three-mile walk against fear in Chicago resulted in almost 40 arrests and a dozen injuries.

How to respond to the violence and to the burning ghettos? LBJ and his advisers felt one answer was for companies to employ more African Americans, and in cities with high minority populations, to get them jobs as police officers, firefighters, and officials. "The more educated, the more experienced, and the more integrated the Negro labor force becomes," one expert remarked, "the less tension and the fewer problems we'll have in this country." The Equal Employment Opportunity Commission began pushing this idea, many corporations began hiring and training programs, and the EEOC began receiving thousands of complaints about job discrimination.

Surprisingly, over a third of those complaints came from women charging sex discrimination, yet an EEOC official recommended that "less time be devoted to sex cases since . . . they deserve a lower priority than discrimination because of race." The only female commissioner on the five-member EEOC was African American Aileen Hernandez. "The message came through clearly that the Commission's priority was race discrimination," she recalled, "and apparently only as it related to Black *men.*" Hernandez only was stating the usual response in the era before the women's liberation movement, for in 1966 the idea of sex discrimination disturbed corporate bosses. "We're not worried about the racial discrimination ban," an airline executive told the *Wall Street Journal.* "What's unnerving us is the section on sex. . . . What are we going to do now when a gal walks into our office, demands a job as an airline pilot and has the credentials to qualify? Or what will we do when some guy comes in and wants to be a stewardess?"

"De-Sexing the Job Market" the *New York Times* called it, and whimsically labeled it the "Bunny Problem," referring to the popular Playboy Clubs. What would happen, asked the paper, when a man applied to become a Playboy Bunny or a woman to be an attendant in a male bathhouse? And the language has to be neuterized, the *Times* claimed, "Handyman must disappear . . . he was pretty much a goner anyway, if you ever started looking for one in desperation. No more milkman, iceman, serviceman, foreman. . . . Girl Friday is an intolerable offense." It might be better, the paper added, if Congress "just abolished sex itself. . . . Bunny problem, indeed! This is revolution, chaos. You can't even safely advertise for a wife anymore."

Something seemed funny, at least to many men: women asking to be treated equally? At EEOC meetings the male commissioners refused to take women's complaints seriously, and that provoked a few women to action, including Betty Friedan, African American law professor Pauli Murray, and Mary Eastwood of the Justice Department, all who attended a national conference on the status of women in Washington. At one session, the women attempted to present a resolution mandating that the EEOC enforce laws against sex discrimination, but were told that they were not permitted to recommend policy, a rebuke that made them "fighting mad." Time for a little rebellion; Kathryn Clarenbach declared that they must "stop being afraid to rock the boat," and Murray advocated a women's march on Washington. But instead, all of them agreed it was time to organize, and they formed NOW, the National Organization for Women, with the purpose "to bring women into full participation in the mainstream of American society *now.*" Friedan became the first president, and the executive vice president was Aileen Hernandez, who resigned from the EEOC.

Although this was the nascent phase of the women's liberation movement, a few officials began to listen, including President Johnson. His wife, Lady Bird, had quietly let key congressmen know in 1964 that she supported the addition of the word *sex* to Title VII of the Civil Rights Act, and that year LBJ had told his cabinet to start looking for females, "this untapped resource," for executive positions in the federal government; it was time to end "stag government." In 1967 the president signed an executive order that amended his 1965 order on affirmative action, which did not mention gender, and charged the government "to provide equal opportunity in Federal employment and in employment by Federal contractors" without discrimination because of "race, color, religion, sex or national origin," which has been the rule ever since.

Thus the Johnson administration's response to a small number of early women's liberationists and to massive urban riots was similar—a significant attempt to open up the workplace to all Americans. That also resulted in resentment from many white men and fueled the white backlash that appeared at the November 1966 elections. Employment opportunities and the war were not yet an important issue at the ballot box, but race certainly was. A Chicago congressman noted that his constituents were "talking about Martin Luther King and how they are moving in on us and what's going to happen to our neighborhoods." Analysts stated that the white backlash was a prominent factor in the defeat of liberal Illinois senator Paul Douglas and the election of Republican Ronald Reagan in California. Polls demonstrated that in two years the percentage of citizens doubled to over half who felt LBJ was pushing too hard for civil rights, a mood apparent at the voting booth as the Republicans picked up almost 50 seats in the House of Representatives.

The sixties continued to move away from liberalism. Urban riots and calls for black power divided the civil rights movement and hurt King, who never regained the position of leadership that the media granted to him in the early sixties. Moreover, by the beginning of 1967 the nation's focus was shifting away from civil rights—and toward Vietnam.

My Country, Right or Wrong?

There were some obvious connections between race and war. Some blacks were upset as federal funds staggered for poverty programs and soared for the war, and others saw the irony in blacks fighting for the rights of the South Vietnamese. A leaflet in McComb, Mississippi, urged African-American mothers to encourage their sons to avoid the draft: "Our Fight Is Here at Home!" Carmichael blasted selective service as nothing more than "white people sending black people to make war on yellow people in order to defend the land they stole from red people."

The draft was unfair. Blacks were the poorest and least educated sector of the society, and like poor whites, few were attending college during draft age, from registration for the draft after the 18th birthday to turning 26. Local draft boards across the nation were composed of the so-called upstanding citizens, meaning 99 percent of their members were white. In the South, local boards were notorious. After civil rights activists Bennie Tucker and Hubert Davis filed to run for city offices in Mississippi, they received their induction notices, and after Willie Jordan reported for his physical a few minutes late he was sentenced to five years in prison. Meanwhile, draft boards arbitrarily granted deferments to some fathers, for certain hardship cases, and to all those affluent enough to attend college. Until the summer of 1968 student deferments could be extended for graduate or professional school, and educational deferments could be granted to graduate teaching assistants and public school teachers. Professors did not like to flunk students because that grade might send the kid to Vietnam. With degree in hand, the graduate would be offered a job, often with defense contractors, engineering firms, and many other corporations that guaranteed an employment deferment. Selective service considered most jobs at Lockheed, Dow Chemical, even at Honeywell designing thermostats as in the national interest. Or, if that was not possible, the graduate might continue his education or travel in another nation because the law stipulated that an American living outside his country could not be drafted. Young men from wealthy families were particularly immune to military service. In three upscale New Jersey suburban towns, not one of their high school graduates died in Vietnam (whereas ghettoized Newark lost 111), and of the 30,000 male graduates from Harvard, Princeton, and MIT in the decade following 1962, only 20 died in the war. As columnist James Reston wrote, selective service was "a system whereby poor boys are selected to go to Vietnam and rich boys are selected to go to college."

Furthermore, because most blacks and poor whites did not have a skill or could not type upon induction, they were perfect candidates for infantry training and then for Vietnam. Once sent to the war zone, there was additional discrimination. A much higher proportion of whites held rear support positions while blacks were stationed in the front lines. The United States had 12 percent black citizens, but the army in Vietnam was a quarter black and many front-line units were 50 percent. At times, forward bases were called "soulvilles," and so those troops took a disproportionate percentage of casualties. In 1966 the government reported that black soldiers suffered a quarter of casualties while fighting the Vietcong.

"I got no quarrel with them Vietcong," declared Muhammad Ali, who refused to register for the draft and was stripped of his heavyweight crown. By spring 1967 a growing number of blacks agreed. Martin Luther King watched the horrors of war on the evening news and admitted to aides, "I can't be silent. Never again will I be silent." In February he spoke out, calling on all "creative dissenters to combine the *fervor* of the civil rights movement with the peace movement . . . until the very foundations of our nation are shaken." A month later he led a procession of over 8,000 in Chicago, and in April he gave a memorable address. The "Great Society has been shot down on the battlefields of Vietnam," and he stunned many listeners by declaring America "the greatest purveyor of violence in the world today." The Nobel Prize winner then appealed, "We are at a moment when our lives must be placed on the line if our nation is to survive. Every man of humane convictions must decide on the protest that best suits his convictions—but we must all protest."

Many more *were* protesting in 1967, especially on campuses where students were winning the battle over in loco parentis and were turning their attention toward the Vietnam War. "I didn't go to college in 1965 expecting to become a radical," recalled Judy Smith, "but I didn't expect the Vietnam War to develop the way it did either. My friends and I became committed to *no life as usual.* For us it would have been immoral to just go on with college and career plans when the war was still going on. If you weren't part of the solution, you were part of the problem."

Smith and thousands of other students began to consider the relationship of their university to the war, and they were asking questions: Should male students have to participate in Reserve Officer Training Corps? Should university administrations cooperate with draft boards and release student grades to selective service officials, meaning that if grades were substandard then the board might reclassify the student from 2-S, student deferment, to 1-A, ready for military induction? Should those conducting the war—the military, defense contractors, or the CIA—be able to hold job interviews on campus?

Although most students still supported the war effort, a vocal minority began shouting "No!" When administrators divulged grades to draft boards at the University of Chicago, some 400 students took over the administration building and held it for three days. At other colleges, students picketed against defense companies conducting job interviews on their campuses, such as Honeywell, Lockheed, and General Dynamics, but the primary target was Dow Chemical, the largest manufacturer of napalm. A mixture of gasoline with naphthenic acid and palm oil, napalm stuck to whatever it contacted, burning or suffocating a victim. American military forces employed the weapon in massive quantities in Vietnam, and as napalm became a symbol of the war

Down with Dow protest at the University of Wisconsin, 1967.

Dow became the symbol for "war profiteer." The most rambunctious demonstrations took place at the University of Wisconsin, where hundreds obstructed interviews while chanting "Down with Dow." After talks between officials and activists failed, the university called in police equipped with riot gear, tear gas, and billy clubs. "Girls began to scream," reported the campus paper, "and both men and women students staggered sobbing from the building, many with blood dripping from head wounds." The demonstration tore the community apart. Thousands of students and 300 faculty members condemned the "animalistic brutality" of police and boycotted classes, while state assembly legislators passed a resolution 94 to 5 demanding the university expel protesters. One assemblyman called activists "longhaired, greasy pigs," and another yelled, "Shoot them if necessary. I would . . . it's insurrection."

University officials across the nation were caught in the middle by angry students and angry parents, but during 1967 even moderate students were becoming involved. College newspaper editors and student body presidents at 100 universities sent a letter to LBJ informing him that their colleagues were deeply troubled about a war "whose toll in property and life keeps escalating, but about whose purpose and value to the United States remain unclear." The campus leaders warned that unless this "conflict can be eased, the United States will continue to find some of her most loyal and courageous young people choosing to go to jail rather than bear their country's arms."

Other Americans also were becoming perplexed with the war by 1967, and that certainly was true of those conducting it in Washington, D.C. The United States had almost a half million troops in South Vietnam. A massive American military machine that supposedly had superiority on land, in the air, and offshore had been conducting combat operations for two years, yet victory remained illusive. In May, General Westmoreland stunned the Johnson administration by privately requesting an additional 200,000 troops.

The request ignited a fire of dissent within the Pentagon and White House. Secretary McNamara had become disillusioned, and when he heard of the request he leveled with the president, writing that the war was "becoming increasingly unpopular as it escalates. . . . Most Americans do not know how we got where we are, and most, without knowing why . . . are convinced that somehow we should not have gotten this deeply in. All want the war ended and expect their President to end it. Successfully. Or else." McNamara was more blunt with his staff, declaring, "Ho Chi Minh is a tough old S.O.B. And he won't quit no matter how much bombing we do."

The war managers were confused. In June, McNamara handed an assistant a list of 100 questions and ordered him to establish a task force to answer them: How confident can we be about body counts of the enemy? Were programs to pacify the countryside working? Was Ho Chi Minh a Soviet puppet or an independent nationalist? It was a clear indication that the blind in Washington were leading the blind in Saigon—a deadly policy for soldiers in the rice paddies. The subsequent report was leaked to the press in 1971 and became known as the Pentagon Papers.

Whereas U.S. policymakers were perplexed in 1967, the enemy knew what to do. They continued to avoid conventional battles and used guerrilla warfare in an attempt to prolong the war until the Americans tired and left Vietnam. Then the north and their Vietcong allies could defeat the regime in Saigon. That meant LBJ again faced the classic dilemma of the Vietnam War. He had had the same choices in 1965; so did Kennedy earlier and so would Nixon later. The commander in chief could enlarge the war by increasing troop strength and by attacking enemy positions in Laos, Cambodia, even North Vietnam. That policy might bring China into the conflict, certainly would damage American–Soviet relations, and would provoke more domestic demonstrations. Secondly, he could limit troop size, stabilize the commitment, and hope the South Vietnamese Army could be trained to assume more of the burden of fighting the enemy. That would mean a long conflict, with a limited chance of success. Or he could demobilize the war. The killing would stop, but that would be political suicide because of the eventual collapse of South Vietnam. The third choice was possible but unthinkable. From Kennedy to Ford, no president would be able to overcome his own cold war mentality.

All the while, the war was beginning to take its toll. In 1965 fewer than 1,400 Americans died in Vietnam, but the next year that number soared to over 5,000, and in 1967 to over 9,000 for a total of about 16,000. Draft calls again increased, and the president decided to expand troop strength to over 525,000. The war also resulted in massive federal expenditures, deficits, and inflationary pressures. "We must finance this war," LBJ said to his advisers, and he advocated a 10 percent surtax. Tax increases had been passed to pay for World War II and the Korean conflict, but in a stark demonstration of how much Americans would sacrifice to stop communism in South Vietnam, the surtax was very unpopular and Congress delayed passage for a year. In 1967 South Vietnam was not worth a 10 percent tax hike.

These were becoming the days of decision over Vietnam, days that eventually would expand into years. The public had been waiting for victory, but the war dragged on, prompting many to wonder what to do. Prowar hawks said expand the war; some said invade North Vietnam. Antiwar doves said de-escalate; negotiate with the enemy. But if there was a bird that symbolized the growing disenchantment with the war in 1967 it was the albatross. As opinion analyst Samuel Lubell noted, Americans shared a "fervent drive to shake free of an unwanted burden." Citizens were confused, frustrated, and impatient. As one housewife commented, "I want to get out but I don't want to give in."

A growing number simply wanted to get out. The antiwar movement blossomed in spring 1967. In April the nation witnessed the largest demonstration until that time. Coretta Scott King addressed 50,000 in San Francisco, and her husband, along with Stokely Carmichael and folksinger Pete Seeger, marched with 200,000 in New York City. The movement was expanding, including students and professionals, blacks and whites, ministers and rabbis, children and grandparents, even some from the new Vietnam Veterans Against the War. A few former career officers began dissenting

The first antiwar march in Washington, D.C., April 1965.

against the war, such as retired Marine Corps General David M. Shoup, who declared all of Southeast Asia was not "worth the life or limb of a single American." Women Strike for Peace marched on the Pentagon demanding to see "the generals who send our sons to Vietnam," and Another Mother for Peace began printing up posters, buttons, and T-shirts with what became one of the most popular slogans of the era: "War Is Not Healthy for Children and Other Living Things." Some students declared Vietnam Summer, in which collegiate volunteers would go out into their communities and hold "teach-outs" to convince their neighbors to oppose the war.

A few young protesters were more radical, employing shocking behavior, especially after the regimented and polite fifties. Some Harvard activists confronted Secretary McNamara, surrounding his car, chanting, "Bullshit." At Howard University, students jeered the director of selective service, General Lewis Hershey, and burned his effigy; at Indiana, some students booed for so long when Secretary of State Rusk appeared at the podium that he left without making his speech. Whenever the president went out in public he was greeted with, "Hey, Hey, LBJ, How Many Kids Did You Kill Today?" At Sheep's Meadow in Central Park about 175 young men burned their draft cards while protesters chanted, "We Won't Go!" A couple of demonstrators carried Vietcong flags—and one burned the Stars and Stripes.

"The American people are not going to let this go on," declared Congressman L. Mendel Rivers. "They want this treason stopped." Was it treason? Many of the sixties generation asked, What is patriotism? General Westmoreland returned to Washington in April and announced his dismay "by recent unpatriotic acts here at home," and the president stated later that the nation must unite behind his policy as a "family of patriots." Dissidents disagreed. Arkansas Democratic Senator J. William Fulbright,who was publicly questioning the war, stated that dissent "is more than a right; it is an act of patriotism, a higher form of patriotism." Clergyman Robert McAfee Brown agreed: "The question is not what right have we to be speaking, but what right have we to be silent."

Patriotism would be debated for the remainder of the era, but in 1967 most politicians still desired cold war obedience. A hint of disloyalty was outrageous, and Congress overwhelmingly passed a bill making desecrating the flag a federal crime (later found unconstitutional by the Supreme Court). Millions of Americans bought a record number of flags, many putting flag decals on their car bumpers. Prowar posters appeared: "My Country, Right or Wrong." "Love It or Leave It." "One Country, One Flag." Old Glory was becoming a symbol of the sixties.

Summer of Discontent

Then in the summer of 1967, race again became the issue. In May, the *Los Angeles Times* declared "one of the most amazing incidents in legislative history." Thirty members of the new Black Panther Party for Self-Defense, 20 of them *armed* with rifles and shotguns, arrived at the capitol building in Sacramento to protest a bill restricting citizens from carrying loaded weapons in city limits, which was legal then in California. Huey Newton and Bobby Seale had formed the Black Panthers in Oakland earlier in the year, and the group quickly attracted young blacks. They wore black leather and saluted by raising their right hand stiff above their head, fist clenched, with black glove. Because the U.S. Army elites wore green berets, the Panthers donned black berets. They published a paper and a ten-point program that for that time made startling demands—education that "teaches us our true history," black offenders tried by black juries, black men exempt from military service—and to ensure racial justice they even called on the United Nations to intervene in America. They established breakfast programs and self-defense groups to combat police, or "pig," brutality. They held watch in their neighborhoods—armed. "So we floated around the streets," wrote Seale, "and we patrolled pigs."

They also confronted authorities. Seale, Bobby Hutton, Eldridge Cleaver, and the others marched into the capitol building, and with a mob of journalists following and cameras flashing, Seale read Mandate Number One: As "the aggression of the racist American government escalates in Vietnam, the police agencies of America escalate the repression of black people throughout the ghettos." Consequently, "the time has come for black people to arm themselves against this terror before it is too late." As the Panthers left, clamoring about repression, genocide, terror, some stunned whites mumbled the feared words "Niggers with guns, niggers with guns."

The Panthers represented a growing militancy among a tiny number of young African Americans, and so did Stokely Carmichael and his successor as SNCC chairman, H. Rap Brown. "Violence is necessary," Brown exclaimed to a stunned group of reporters. "Violence is as American as cherry pie." He told a black crowd in Cambridge, Maryland, to "get some guns," and to another group in Washington, D.C., he exclaimed, "The honkey don't respect nothing but guns." During the next years these militants shouted a new idea: armed self-defense.

The civil rights movement continued to divide into moderate and militant camps, but while the small group of militants attracted television cameras and scared whites, they did not have much influence in the black community. A 1967 survey of Detroit African Americans found that 86 percent favored integration and only 1 percent favored separatism. In Chicago, 57 percent felt that Martin Luther King best represented their position; only 3 percent chose Carmichael. Militant rhetoric, therefore, had little impact on what transpired that summer in over 100 cities: America's ghettos again became battlefields.

For the third time in three years, riots erupted. From Boston to Tampa, Buffalo to Wilmington, fires burned wildly in the streets. Then Newark exploded, a city with the nation's highest black unemployment rate and perhaps the most corrupt white city government. Rumor of white police beating a black taxi driver was all it took to spark anarchy. The governor declared the city in "open rebellion" and ordered in the National Guard. The troops unloaded, firing 13,000 rounds of ammunition, wounding 1,200 and killing 25 African Americans. A week later Detroit exploded. The ghetto quickly turned into an inferno. The governor mobilized the National Guard, who fired wildly, over 150,000 rounds of ammunition. LBJ sent the U.S. Army, which arrived with tanks, machine guns, helicopters, and better leadership. The army cooled tensions and ended the upheaval: 4,000 arrests, 2,000 injuries, and 43 dead. Detroit, *Newsweek* wrote, was "An American Tragedy." Throughout the nation, the 1967 urban riots resulted in 4,000 injured and at least 90 killed in action. At home and abroad, America was at war.

The riots clearly demonstrated that LBJ's guns-and-butter policy, fighting a war abroad and poverty at home, was a failure. While the administration spent over $300,000 to kill one Vietcong in 1967, it spent about $50 to help one American out of poverty. The War in Vietnam killed the War on Poverty, and it wounded attempts to continue the Great Society.

To investigate the reasons for the urban upheavals, Johnson appointed Illinois Governor Otto Kerner to lead a commission of moderates from both political parties. After surveying 20 cities, the commission found that the primary grievances rioters stated were a combination of police brutality, unemployment or underemployment, and discrimination in housing and education. To "many Negroes police

The Black Panther Party emerges and becomes more evident in 1968
when they protest the arrest and trial of one of their leaders, Huey Newton.

have come to symbolize white power, white racism and white repression. And the
fact is that many police do reflect and express these white attitudes." The Kerner
Report summarized, "What white Americans have never fully understood—but
what the Negro can never forget—is that white society is deeply implicated in the
ghetto. White institutions created it, white institutions maintain it, and white society
condones it." The commission concluded, "Our nation is moving toward two soci-
eties, one black, one white—separate and unequal."

By summer 1967, then, the sixties were becoming what *Life* called the Decade
of Tumult and Change. The glow of liberalism had been snuffed out during the days
of decision as citizens argued over race and war. Urban blacks demanded the end of
police brutality: suburban whites called for law and order. Doves shouted, "Peace
Now!" Hawks roared, "Bomb Hanoi!" All the while the older generation who had
won World War II were outraged by the sixties generation, some of whom criticized
the nation or tried to avoid the draft. "Here were those kids, rich kids who could go
to college, didn't have to fight," a worker fumed. "They are telling you your son died
in vain. It makes you feel your whole life is shit, just nothing." *Newsweek* declared
the "Summer of Discontent."

Summer of Love

Others announced the Summer of Love. A growing number of young people were "dropping out," rejecting war, racism, and indeed, the entire American way of life.

In July *Time* published a cover story that introduced "The Hippies." Actually, the editors admitted, hippies had been emerging on the U.S. scene since the last months of 1965 as "a wholly new subculture, a bizarre permutation of the middle-class American ethos." A few had gravitated toward the Haight, the Haight-Ashbury district of San Francisco, near the Panhandle of Golden Gate Park. Dressed in anything unusual—granny gowns, pirate or Old West costumes, Victorian suits, British mod fashions with black boots—they attended "happenings" at the Fillmore Auditorium and danced to groups called the Great Society, Jefferson Airplane, Quicksilver Messenger Service, Grateful Dead, Moby Grape, and Big Brother and the Holding Company. Throughout 1966 more came to the Haight, smoking and selling marijuana, and joining in with Ken Kesey's group of Merry Pranksters and dropping LSD or, as they joked, participating in the Trips Festival and taking Acid Tests. They blew bubbles, wore beads and bells, looked into distorted mirrors, and chalked colorful designs on the sidewalks. Some adopted new names—Apache, Coyote, Superspade, White Rabbit, Blue Flash. A mailman was known as Admiral Love, a cop went by Sergeant Sunshine, and Ulysses S. Grant wore his dress uniform. They bought groceries at Far Fetched Foods, posters at the Blushing Peony, Zig Zag paper at the Psychedelic Shop, and drank coffee at I/Thou while reading "underground newspapers," such as the *Oracle*. They ate free food collected by older bohemians, the Diggers, who held a Full Moon Public Celebration (Halloween), where a few hundred feasted in a garage known as the Free Frame of Reference. Haight had energy, vibrations, and for many questioning youth it became a spawning bed.

During 1966 most San Francisco newspapers referred to these people as *beatniks*, and in New York City author John Gruen labeled them "new bohemians" as he described their spawning bed, the East Village. Longhaired girls, bearded guys, and interracial couples wore boots and bell-bottom pants, went to poetry readings or experimental theater at Cafe La Mama, browsed at boutiques such as The Queen of Diamonds, or read a growing number of underground publications such as *Nadada, Fuck You/A Magazine of the Arts*, or *The East Village Other*. The East Village was experiencing a Renaissance. Allen Ginsberg read poetry, LeRoi Jones wrote plays, Yoko Ono composed her "insound music," The Fugs played their sexual tunes, "What Are You Doing After the Orgy?" Jim Dine, Red Grooms, and many others painted. Dick Higgins, Claes Oldenburg, and Robert Rauschenberg put on "happenings," art in action. Andy Warhol pioneered "pop art," painting American popular culture with portraits of Campbell's soup cans, the electric chair, and Marilyn Monroe. Ed Sanders hung signs in his Peace Eye Book Store that read "POT is FUN" and "Legalize Cunnilingus Now." "It can truly be said," reported Gruen, "that for New Bohemians every day is Independence Day."

Some of the sixties generation were beginning to feel alienated, part of a different society, a strange underground movement outside or below the Establishment. "Who is the Underground?" asked *Avatar.* "You are, if you think, dream, work, and build towards the improvements and changes in your life, your social and personal environments, towards the expectations of a better existence. . . . Think—look around—maybe in a mirror, maybe inside."

Looking different, behaving differently, even hair length after the crew cut fifties, provoked an incredible backlash. In San Francisco, the police routinely stopped anyone with long hair and harassed them. *Life* ran a cover story claiming LSD was the "Exploding Threat" to the nation, and in autumn 1966 California passed a law that made LSD illegal. The next year a writer for the *San Francisco Chronicle* informed citizens that smoking marijuana frequently caused "delirious rage which sometimes leads to serious crime." That's why, he claimed, marijuana is called the "killer drug."

Until the *Time* article, most citizens had no idea what these young people thought, just that they looked weird. To its credit, the magazine attempted to describe the behavior and philosophy, the "Highs & Lows of Hippiedom," from Acid to Zen. *Time* in 1967 concluded, "It could be argued that in their independence of material possessions and their emphasis on peacefulness and honesty, hippies lead considerably more virtuous lives than the great majority of their fellow citizens. . . . In the end it may be that the hippies have not so much dropped out of American society as given it something to think about."

That was one of the last times that hippies received favorable press. But that didn't matter to them; they were interested in meeting others with similar values. Thus in January 1967 the Diggers called for a "gathering of the tribes," a "human be-in," and the *Oracle* declared a "Renaissance of compassion, awareness and love." Thousands appeared on a sunny Saturday, streaming into Golden Gate Park. Activist Jerry Rubin advocated peace, Allen Ginsberg chanted mantras, LSD guru Tim Leary told the gentle crowd, "Turn on, tune in, drop out." But the people themselves were the main event at the human be-in. They came in all shades, all colors, all costumes, "a polyglot mixture of Mod, Paladin, Ringling Brothers, Cochise, and Hells Angels' Formal . . . from Velvet Lotta Crabtree to Mining Camp Desperado." Some held "gorgeous flowing sheets of color, on the green as though knights were assembling on the Camelot plain," and others watched a parachutist float to the ground through rising yellow incense. The Diggers handed out thousands of turkey sandwiches, made from dozens of birds donated by LSD chemist Augustus Owsley Stanley III, who also donated ample amounts of his homemade White Lightning LSD. Music flowed all afternoon. People smiled.

That spring more youth hitchhiked to San Francisco where the hippies announced a Summer of Love. Authorities were alarmed, and the *San Francisco Chronicle* ran the headlines, "Mayor Warns Hippies to Stay Out of Town" and "Supervisors Back War on Hippies." But warnings made no difference. Hippies did not listen to the Establishment—that was the point—and by spring they were flooding into the Haight. "If you go to San Francisco," sang Scott McKenzie in a popular song, "wear a flower in your hair."

The Haight was blooming, and more than ever music was becoming the message. During the summer of 1967 the sixties generation was buying more than romance or dance tunes. The top five albums on the charts included the Beatles, Rolling Stones, Jefferson Airplane, and the Doors: "Break On Through to the Other Side." Between 1964 and 1966 the Beatles had grown from "She Loves You" to "Yellow Submarine," and to tracing the alienation of the younger generation in "Nowhere Man" and "Eleanor Rigby." They continued the theme in 1967 by producing one of the most significant albums of rock, *Sgt. Pepper's Lonely Hearts Club Band.* "It's getting better all the time," they sang, and that was because of generational unity, "A little help from my friends," and because of other help, "<u>L</u>ucy in the <u>S</u>ky with <u>D</u>iamonds." So if you were still part of the Establishment, they continued, it was rather hopeless, just "A day in the life." Give the new generation a chance, experiment: "I'd love to turn you on."

So would others, and they did in June at the first major music festival of the sixties, Monterey Pop. At the venue, the organizers provided a playground, projection room, shops and booths, a guitar workshop, and a Buddha. A producer filmed the event for a television special, which became a popular movie on campuses, and the crowd of about 30,000 for Friday evening swelled to 60,000 by Sunday. They came in peasant dresses, in bell-bottoms, leather vests, in colors: mellow yellow, panama red, moby grape, deacon blue, acapulco gold. Stanley supplied a new batch of LSD called Monterey Purple, dubbed Purple Haze, and the bands merged the San Francisco sounds with American pop, rock, blues, soul, folk rock, and the British Invasion. Groups for the three-day event included Eric Burdon and the Animals, Simon and Garfunkel, Otis Redding, Ravi Shankar, The Byrds, Country Joe, Steve Miller, Grateful Dead, Jefferson Airplane, The Who, The Mamas and the Papas, Janis Joplin and Big Brother and the Holding Company, and a U.S. Army veteran making his first important American appearance, Jimi Hendrix.

By all accounts, Monterey Pop was a success. "It was one of the first times that we all felt together, interconnected," recalled a participant. "So innocent, we all touched each other. It was magical." Considering its size, the largest festival up to that time, it also was incredibly peaceful. The local police chief reported on Sunday that he had sent half his force home, and many other officers got in the spirit, draping their motorcycles with flowers.

Yet back in the Haight, the vibes were turning negative by the end of the Summer of Love. The area was flooded, overwhelmed with youth, prompting the *Oracle* to write that if one comes to San Francisco "in addition to flowers" bring clothing, sleeping bags, food, even money. New drugs were introduced, some dangerous, and with drug dealers competing for profits, violence mounted. In August, two drug dealers were found dead, and hippie Charles Perry wondered, "Acid dealers *killing* each other? This was what the New Age promised?"

Many wondered. Although hippies in 1967 were just a tiny fraction of the sixties generation, the 75,000 who visited the Haight that summer returned home or to their campuses with different values. With the help of the Establishment's media coverage, the anti-Establishment spread. *Time* declared in July, "Today hippie enclaves are blooming in every major U.S. city from Boston to Seattle, from Detroit to New Orleans; there is a 50-member cabal in, of all places, Austin, Texas." The magazine noted that there might be 300,000 hippies, and "by all estimates the cult is a growing phenomenon that has not yet reached its peak—and may not do so for years to come." How prophetic.

"Vietnam Is Here"

For the nation, however, the Summer of Love soon became the autumn of anguish, and again, the cause was Vietnam. Activists announced Stop the Draft Week for October. Instead of "warmed-over speeches," their new method was more militant—to "confront the warmakers," to "disrupt the war machine." As activist Dave McReynolds declared, "Vietnam is here."

Vietnam certainly was here. While students held demonstrations across the nation on numerous campuses—from Harvard to Wisconsin to Berkeley—antiwar fever in 1967 reached its peak on Saturday, October 21, when Stop the Draft Week climaxed with the March on the Pentagon. This event stunned the public, for unlike any previous march this one demonstrated that the movement now included a mixture of middle-class liberals, students and hippies, civil rights moderates and black power advocates, even some Vietnam veterans, federal government workers, and business executives. The war continued to expand the movement. While some radicals proclaimed that they now were ready to fight, those of the counterculture joked that they planned to exorcise demons from the military control center by chanting "om" and levitating the Pentagon. About 50,000 assembled on the sunny Saturday in front of the Lincoln Memorial listening to Peter, Paul, and Mary, followed by Phil Ochs singing "Days of Decision." David Dellinger announced that the march was the end of peaceful protest: "This is the beginning of a new stage in the American peace movement in which the cutting edge becomes active resistance."

Across the nation, 1,400 young men returned their draft cards as the crowd in Washington began walking across the Arlington Bridge and toward the Pentagon. The federal government was prepared; for the first time since the Bonus March of 1932, it ordered its armed forces to protect the nation's capital against Americans. Upon arriving at the Pentagon, a few dozen radicals attacked; the military easily repulsed them and won the first battle. At the same time, a few hundred others began a sit-down in the Pentagon parking lot. "Soon diggers started bringing in food

March on the Pentagon, 1967.

and joints," wrote a participant. "A real festival atmosphere was in the air. People laughed and hugged." Many talked to other troops, chanting "join us," singing, "we'd love to turn you on." A few put flowers in the troop's rifle barrels—flower power. Some smoked dope into the evening; others sipped wine and built campfires. A few sang "Silent Night." Others sat in the lotus position and hummed "om." By most reports, the Pentagon did not levitate.

"Near midnight," reported a young activist, "paratroopers of the 82nd Division replaced the MPs. With the marshals at the rear they began massing at the center of the sit-in preparing to attack. . . . The brutality was horrible. Nonresisting girls were kicked and clubbed by U.S. marshals old enough to be their fathers . . . cracking heads, bashing skulls."

Stop the Draft Week was a prologue to the explosions of 1968, and it also had an impact on the administration. LBJ believed the peace movement was turning citizens against the war. That probably was not true—the frustrating war was turning Americans against the frustrating war. The president responded by announcing to his cabinet, "It is time that the administration stopped sitting back and taking it from the Vietnam critics." LBJ took the offensive, publicly labeling dissidents "bearded oafs," and privately instructing the FBI to watch antiwar leaders and conduct investigations. The CIA began Operation Chaos, which violated federal law excluding that agency from domestic investigations. Agents infiltrated groups such as SANE, CORE, even Women Strike for Peace in an attempt to find proof that they were controlled by foreign governments or communists. When the administration found no such evidence, the president ordered more studies while he and his aides leaked fabrications to hawkish politicians. House Democratic Leader Carl Albert declared the march on the Pentagon was "basically organized by International Communism," and House Republican Leader Gerald Ford added it was "cranked up" in Hanoi.

Johnson, therefore, attempted to change opinion in America instead of changing policy in Vietnam. Time to rally the nation. The president had not wanted the war, but once committed he could not back away. He would shoulder the burden. The president continued the same policy in 1967, historian George Herring has written, "for the same reasons he had gone to war in the first place—because he saw no alternative that did not require him to admit failure or defeat." For the Texan, the war had become a matter of pride.

The president flew to South Vietnam, shook hands with the troops, declaring, "We are not going to yield. We are not going to shimmy." Back home, LBJ privately told his advisers "to sell our product to the American people." Officials became salesmen. With great fanfare, Johnson replaced the best and brightest with another group of experts, the "wise men," who like the former knew little about Vietnamese culture or nationalism. They held many publicized discussions while others began the second phase of its policy: predicting victory. "We're winning the war," declared the army chief of staff, and the president told congressmen, "Westmoreland has turned defeat into what we believe will be a victory. It's only a matter now of will."

America could will a victory—or at least fake one. The administration intensified the charade. During autumn U.S. officials began to fudge the numbers. Generals wanted results and lieutenants sent privates back out to recount the enemy dead. Enormous pro-American kill ratios and body counts appeared on television, and few realized that they were meaningless because to be victorious the enemy would—and did—sacrifice many times more than the United States. In November, LBJ reminded his advisers, "The clock is ticking . . . the main front of the war is here in the United States." Accordingly, Ambassador Ellsworth Bunker left Saigon and returned home to proclaim, "We are making steady progress in Vietnam. . . . There is every prospect, too, that the progress will accelerate." The president stated he was "pleased with the results" and Westmoreland declared, "It is significant that the enemy has not won a major battle in more than a year." The general and ambassador appeared on *Meet the Press* and gave another premature victory speech: The United States now was "winning a war of attrition," the conflict had entered a phase "when the end begins to come into view." The administration could see "the light at the end of the tunnel."

The first casualty in war is truth. We were not winning, simply sinking deeper into the quagmire. Yet most citizens wanted to believe their government. Throughout 1967 popular approval for the war and for Johnson had been declining. In July, a Harris poll found that 72 percent of citizens supported the war, which slid to a new low of 58 percent by October. The war—and the urban riots—resulted in LBJ's approval rating declining to 39 percent in August and plummeting to just 28 percent in October, the lowest since Truman's stalemate in Korea. By November, those thinking the war was a mistake equaled those who did not. But victory speeches again rallied most citizens, and in December polls demonstrated that more approved than disapproved of the president's handling of the war. Almost 70 percent approved of General Westmoreland, and almost 60 percent favored increasing military pressure against the enemy. Significantly, the public also disliked antiwar demonstrations, 70 percent feeling they were acts of disloyalty and three-quarters stating that protests only encouraged the communists.

Yet the polls also demonstrated confusion. At a time when a half million American sons were killing and being killed on the other side of the world, a *New York Times* poll discovered nearly half of the respondents had no clear idea why their nation was fighting a war in Vietnam.

These were the days of decision for the sixties. By the end of the year, a citizen looking back to the summer of 1965, an era of liberalism and hope, would have been amazed at how far the nation had traveled in just over two years. The escalation of the war, civil rights marches, shouts for black power, endless urban riots, angry white backlash, mounting campus protests, weird kids flaunting mainstream values, and always the television visions—fires in the streets, napalm in Vietnam—all blended together by the end of 1967. *Time* noted a "noxious atmosphere" in the country, *Newsweek* smelled "a sharp scent of crisis in the American air," and in the last week of December the *Nation* suggested, "almost anything *might* happen in 1968."

It did. On January 30 enemy troops launched a ferocious attack—the Tet Offensive—and that began one of the most incredible years in American history: 1968.

Chapter 4

1968

On January 27, 1968, General Westmoreland told the nation the enemy has "experienced only failure," and he expressed optimism for success in 1968. Three days later, on Tet, the Buddhist lunar new year, enemy troops launched their most massive offensive of the war. The Vietcong and North Vietnamese regulars attacked most towns and villages controlled by the South Vietnamese government. In Saigon, some 4,000 Vietcong stormed into the city, blasted government positions, and broke into the symbols of security—the airport, national radio station, presidential palace, even the courtyard of the U.S. Embassy. In Hue, more than 7,000 troops overran the city and hoisted their flag above the Citadel, the historic capital of the Annam emperors. Fighting was brutal, door to door, and after three weeks the beautiful city was left a "shattered, stinking hulk, its streets choked with rubble and rotting bodies." All the while the onslaught continued at Khe Sanh, an American outpost near the Laotian border. Since the end of 1967, crack units of the North Vietnamese Army had been assaulting the hill, conducting a diversion for Tet, and during February they intensified their attack. American forces prevailed by employing massive B-52 strikes, perhaps the heaviest air raids in the history of warfare. Air power shell-shocked the enemy and saved Khe Sanh.

Tet was the first event of 1968 that demonstrated the sixties had become the "Decade of Tumult and Change." This one year was as significant as any during the twentieth century, for it radically altered social, cultural, and political realities, and that was demonstrated as 1968 exploded "over race, youth, violence, lifestyles, and, above all, over the Vietnam War."

Significantly, those explosions would be on television, and the first show was Tet, which produced sensational visions: U.S. officials defending themselves, shooting out of windows at the embassy. Marines in Hue ducking for cover, firing at the enemy hiding behind scarred, ancient walls. American planes strafing villages, dropping napalm canisters that burst into rolling fireballs. A U.S. officer standing on the outskirts of what remained of a Mekong Delta village stating, "We had to destroy it, in order to save it." The haggard faces, the haunted eyes of defenders at Khe Sanh. The South Vietnam national police chief walking down the street with a ragged Vietcong suspect, stopping in front of reporters, nonchalantly lifting his pistol, pointing it at the man's temple—pulling the trigger.

WHAM! "Winning Hearts and Minds," the U.S. Army called America's pacification policy in Vietnam, which now seemed ludicrous. Televisions zoomed in and showed helicopters machine-gunning peasants running below in rice paddies. "If he's running," said a helicopter crewman, "he must be a Vietcong." These scenes, these statements, became symbolic for the war. Many Americans wondered if all the brutality would bring victory or if it was just pointless. Editors of the *Christian Century* lectured, "This is the genius of our war effort—to destroy Vietnam in order to save it."

During Tet, General Westmoreland appeared on television and assured Americans that the enemy suffered heavy casualties and had been defeated. Although about 1,100 U.S. and 2,300 ARVN troops died, the enemy sacrificed as many as 40,000. Remnants of the enemy retreated back to the jungle and resumed guerrilla tactics for the next four years. But the sacrifice was irrelevant. Tet really demonstrated that Westmoreland's search-and-destroy strategy had failed. U.S. forces were no closer to victory in 1968 than in 1965, before a half million American forces entered Vietnam. Thus Tet was a shocking psychological defeat. It shattered the illusion of progress in Vietnam, and it forced the public to consider the agonizing possibility that the war might go on for many more years. The question haunted the public: Is South Vietnam worth the price?

More citizens also began to wonder about the Johnson administration. "What's going on here?" CBS anchorman Walter Cronkite asked millions of viewers. "I thought we were winning the war." Had the government been telling the truth? "The American people have been pushed beyond the limits of gullibility," declared the *New York Times*. The credibility gap became a canyon, and the press—who like most citizens had been supporting the administration's policy—now began questioning the war. The "U.S. must accept the fact that it will never be able to achieve decisive military superiority in Vietnam," declared *Newsweek,* and even conservative editors at the *Wall Street Journal* warned that "everyone had better be prepared for the bitter taste of a defeat." Late in February, Cronkite summarized the gloomy mood: "To say that we are mired in stalemate seems the only reasonable, yet unsatisfactory conclusion."

"If I've lost Cronkite," LBJ said to an aide, "I've lost the country." Indeed; disillusionment soared in the weeks after Tet. Polls from January to March recorded one of the most profound opinion shifts in history. Earlier, hawks had outnumbered doves 60 to 24 percent; a month later doves led hawks 42 to 41 percent. Furthermore, those approving LBJ's handling of the war plummeted to a record low, only

Police chief executing a Vietcong suspect in Saigon during Tet;
the picture horrified most Americans.

26 percent. Before Tet, a majority of citizens supported the administration's policy; after, a majority opposed it.

The swing in opinion also was apparent in Congress. After the *New York Times* reported on March 10 that the administration was considering a request from General Westmoreland for an additional 206,000 troops, both congressional hawks and doves demanded an explanation. Next day, senators grilled Secretary of State Dean Rusk on national television, demanding answers. "Can we afford the horrors which are being inflicted on the people of a poor and backward land to say nothing of our own people?" asked Senator Fulbright. "Can we afford the alienation of our allies, the neglect of our own deep domestic problems and the disillusionment of our youth?" And the senator asked the most important question: "Can we afford the sacrifice of American lives in so dubious a cause?"

Again: What to do in Vietnam? The issue continued to divide the nation. Hawks yelled, "Get tougher, stay the course, uphold our moral obligation to South Vietnam!" More military pressure on North Vietnam, demanded conservative papers, even if that meant calling up the reserves. Doves screamed, "Negotiate!" They urged the administration to talk peace with North Vietnam, consider withdrawing, and give much more of the war effort over to the South Vietnamese Army.

As for the president, he had become exasperated by the war. "I feel like a hitch-hiker caught in a hailstorm on a Texas highway," he said to aide Bill Moyers. "I can't run. I can't hide. And I can't make it stop."

LBJ's Decline and Fall

Tet also had an impact on the presidential primaries, for it provoked many activists to volunteer for the campaign of Senator Eugene McCarthy. The Minnesota Democrat had criticized LBJ's war in 1967, was saddened by the "deepening moral crisis in America—discontent, frustration," and in November he announced his intention to run for the nomination. Most citizens thought the bid was a joke, for the last time an incumbent president had been seriously challenged was in 1912. But these times were different, and after Tet an army of students headed to McCarthy's headquarters to help the senator in the New Hampshire primary. The students were idealistic and came from nearby Ivy League colleges, and eventually from over 100 universities, from Columbia to California. "They all are arriving sober," remarked one staffer, "an unprecedented phenomenon in students." Men with long hair or beards were asked to see the free barber, and the staff requested that females wearing stylish miniskirts search in their duffel bags for more traditional outfits, all in an attempt to quash any hint that these activists were radicals or hippies. "Clean for Gene" aimed to convince the state's moderate citizens that the volunteers were the boys and girls next door who wanted their neighbors to vote for peace.

"McCarthy's kids" spent long days ringing doorbells, making phone calls, and distributing campaign literature. Late in the evening they spread out their sleeping bags and crashed on the office floor or in church basements, empty gymnasiums, or at the homes of the candidate's supporters. With the exception of professional speechwriter Richard Goodwin, the effort was run by students. Harvard graduate student Sam Brown directed the campaign, the candidate's daughter Mary took leave from Radcliffe to help out, and returning Peace Corps veteran John Barbieri developed mass mailing. Dianne Dumonoski, who had taught black children in the South and participated in the March on the Pentagon, left campus with one suitcase and a sleeping bag and soon was assigning tasks to new volunteers. As Goodwin wrote, these activists went to New Hampshire because they believed in the "terrible wrong of Vietnam" and in the possibility that they and McCarthy "could use the political system to alter the course of American history."

The activists did alter history, and that was partly because of their hard work and because their campaign literature addressed a theme so relevant after urban riots and Tet: "In 1960 we started to get America moving again. Today, eight years later, the fabric of that great achievement is unraveling. . . . In 1963 our greatest cities were relatively tranquil. Today we look upon a period of virtual civil war. In 1963 we were at peace. Today we are at war."

Frustration during the days of decision had been mounting, and two candidates exploited that theme, both McCarthy and Richard M. Nixon. The former vice president also was in New Hampshire, running for the Republican nomination, and his message was simple: "Do you want four more years?" Nixon won the Republican primary overwhelmingly.

McCarthy's kids shifted into high gear to get out the vote on March 12. White House pollsters had predicted in January that McCarthy would win only 6 percent, compared to 76 percent for LBJ, but on Election Day the senator won an astonishing 42 percent, 20 of the state's 24 delegates, a showing that was interpreted as a defeat for Johnson. "Dove bites Hawk," a journalist wrote. The joke in January became the miracle of March.

Four days later Bobby Kennedy announced his candidacy for the Democratic nomination. RFK had said in 1967 that he hated the war. "We're killing South Vietnamese, we're killing women, we're killing innocent people because they're 12,000 miles away and they might get 11,000 miles away." But he hesitated, contemplating a run in 1972, which appeased party bosses but irritated many young supporters. When he arrived to give a talk at Brooklyn College he faced a sign: BOBBY KENNEDY: HAWK, DOVE, OR CHICKEN?

Kennedy's announcement annoyed many, especially McCarthy's kids. "We woke up after the New Hampshire primary like it was Christmas Day," one fumed. "And when we went down to the tree, we found Bobby Kennedy had stolen our Christmas presents." Johnson had feared a political challenge from the Kennedy family, and now wounded, he faced two Democratic opponents. LBJ hated Bobby, whom he called a "grandstanding little runt."

But the president had little time for domestic politics; he was preoccupied with Vietnam. In the weeks after Tet, LBJ replaced General Westmoreland as battlefield commander with General Creighton Abrams, Secretary of Defense McNamara resigned in a tearful press conference, and the president named a new secretary of defense, Clark Clifford. In March, opinion polls revealed that Johnson's popularity was slipping fast, and by the end of the month it had plummeted to a new low. In an attempt to develop a new plan for Vietnam, LBJ again called in the "wise men," only to discover that most of them had changed their position during the previous months and now believed the United States could not guarantee a noncommunist, independent South Vietnam. Concerning the military, former secretary of state Dean Acheson was blunt: "The Joint Chiefs don't know what they're talking about." Clifford added that the legal and business communities no longer supported the war, and the wise men suggested that the administration eventually should disengage. Johnson felt betrayed, bitterly complaining that the "establishment bastards have bailed out."

Yet by the end of the month he had arrived at similar conclusions. During a private conversation with Generals Abrams and Earle Wheeler, the president admitted, "The country is demoralized. . . . Most of the press is against us. . . . We have no

LBJ after Tet.

support for the war." Realizing "overwhelming disapproval in the polls," he predicted his fate in the upcoming election: "I will go down the drain."

On March 31, President Johnson addressed the nation on TV. He discussed the "divisiveness among all of us tonight," the Vietnam War, and at the end he became the most notable casualty by declaring, "I shall not seek, and I will not accept, the nomination of my party for another term as your president."

Americans were shocked. Just three years earlier LBJ had won an overwhelming electoral victory. In his first two years in office he had reached so far, achieved so much, and now everything was crumbling.

Looking back, if there ever was a time after escalation in 1965 that the United States might have disengaged from Vietnam it was after Johnson's speech. The president and his generals had no path to victory, and his retired secretary of defense, McNamara, later admitted that by late 1967 he knew "we were wrong, terribly wrong" being in Vietnam. The antiwar activists were right: the war was a mistake, a terrible mistake. Aware of that in spring 1968, the commander in chief could have ordered a withdrawal, one that could have been completed when he left office in January 1969. That decision would have caused more political turmoil, of course, but it would have saved lives. The Texan, and his war manager McNamara, did not have the foresight or the courage. Clark Clifford was correct when he recalled, "It was almost beyond human capacity to say at that time, 'We've been wrong.'" No American could die in vain. Instead, McNamara kept his mouth shut, and Johnson asked his Americans to "join us in a *total national effort* to win the war, to win the peace, and to complete the job." That job would mean another 20,500 Americans and about a million Vietnamese deaths during the Nixon years.

"I've Been to the Mountaintop"

Four days after LBJ's speech, the nation again was shocked. On April 4, a white petty crook, James Earl Ray, told his brother he was going to "get the big nigger," and that evening he assassinated Martin Luther King Jr.

King had traveled to Memphis to lend support to striking sanitation workers, almost all of them black. He also was publicizing his Poor People's Campaign, a forthcoming march on Washington by a coalition of poor from all races who would demand what he called the next phase of the civil rights struggle—Congress must pass an "Economic Bill of Rights" that would vigorously enforce integration, quickly end housing discrimination, and, most importantly, develop social programs that *guaranteed reasonable employment.* "It didn't cost the nation anything to guarantee the right to vote, or to guarantee access to public accommodations," said King, "but we are dealing with issues now that will cost the nation something."

King was somber in Memphis. He had been losing supporters and was being attacked by black power advocates and some moderates who were frustrated with his antiwar stance. He had been harassed continually by white conservatives and by FBI director Hoover, who wiretapped King's phones and spread malicious rumors. Moreover, by 1968 King had received 50 death threats, and as he told his audience on the night of April 3, "Well, I don't know what will happen now. But it really doesn't matter with me. Because I've been to the mountaintop. And I've seen the Promised Land. . . . Mine eyes have seen the glory of the coming of the Lord."

The next evening he was murdered, gunned down on the balcony of his motel. During the next few days, American restraint seemed to evaporate. Upon hearing the news, some Southerners were happy; some white students cheered in Arlington, Texas, and a delighted FBI agent in Atlanta declared, "They finally got the s.o.b.!" Yet most citizens were horrified, and activists were enraged. "When white America killed Dr. King," declared Stokely Carmichael, "she declared war on us."

Rioting swept the nation. Blacks poured out into the streets of over 100 cities, venting their frustration. Sections of Boston, Detroit, and Harlem sank into chaos, but the worst was Washington, D.C. Over 700 fires turned the sky dark; smoke obscured the Capitol. Nationwide, officials called out more than 75,000 troops to patrol the streets, to keep the peace. The final casualty count was 3,000 injured and 46 dead, all but 5 blacks. This because one violent white man slaughtered a nonviolent black man who had called on America to live up to its promise.

President Johnson declared a national day of mourning and on that Sunday hundreds of thousands of Americans, black and white, marched together in their cities, many singing freedom songs in honor of Martin Luther King Jr. The next day, the widow Coretta and her children conducted a silent memorial through the streets of Memphis with almost 20,000, and soon thereafter the city increased pay and benefits for sanitation workers, ending the strike. Tributes and condolences flowed in from all over the world, and on April 9 the funeral was held in Atlanta. Some 120 million Americans watched on television, saw the long lines of politicians, and witnessed the gentle weeping of average citizens, and of Mrs. John Fitzgerald Kennedy. A sea of humanity, perhaps 100,000 people, surrounded the Ebenezer Church. After the service, pallbearers placed the casket on a farm cart drawn by two mules, and a procession of 50,000 walked on Martin Luther King's last freedom march.

King's death marked another turning point in the civil rights movement. The assassination killed the phase of the civil rights struggle that began at Greensboro. More than any other person, King epitomized the dream of racial equality. He had inspired blacks and whites to become activists, to use nonviolent, dignified tactics to change the nation. Although he had been losing influence, he remained the only single focal point of the struggle, "the last black hope," wrote activist Todd Gitlin. King also had become a hope to other minorities. Mexican American organizer Cesar Chavez, who then was awakening the nation to the plight of farm workers in California, thanked Mrs. King for "the example set by your husband and by those multitudes who followed his nonviolent leadership . . . words alone cannot express our gratefulness." Throughout the year there would be new calls for "brown power" while at the same time the black civil rights movement became rudderless, adrift in a sea of bickering. By the end of 1968, SNCC was dead, CORE was dying, and SCLC was disintegrating.

Finally, King's assassination had a legislative impact. After stalling for more than two years on Johnson's proposed Fair Housing Act, Congress passed it. The act banned real estate agents from discriminating when they sold or rented property. Supported by blacks and Jews, both of whom had been kept out of many neighborhoods, the bill eventually cut restrictions based on race and opened suburbs and other areas to all citizens. Finally, eight years after the Greensboro 4 demanded a cup of coffee, the civil rights acts of 1964, 1965, and 1968, along with the Twenty-Fourth Amendment and numerous Supreme Court decisions, had ended the last vestiges of legal racism in the land of the free. The nation began living up to its promise and to King's dream.

Revolution?

Turbulence continued that spring, for just a week later some radicals staged a student revolt at Columbia University. To many students, the university was an appropriate target in 1968. The president, Grayson Kirk, sat on the board of directors of the university's Institute for Defense Analysis (IDA), which conducted weapons research and was funded partly by the Defense Department and the CIA. Antiwar students felt the IDA symbolized support for the Vietnam War, but Kirk possessed little understanding of this and other student concerns, simply stating the older generation's view that young people "reject authority, take refuge in turbulent, inchoate nihilism." Also, Kirk's administration was repressive. After activists confronted military recruiters in 1967, Kirk simply banned all indoor demonstrations, and the university refused to change many of its in loco parentis regulations. In March 1968 the university put a female student on trial for "living with a boyfriend," a hearing that prompted 60 other women to demand the same charge.

Columbia also had a problem with local black residents and its Student Afro-American Society. Throughout its long history, few blacks had been admitted, only 70 were enrolled then as undergraduates, and the university was located in crowded Morningside Heights, close to Harlem. It had been expanding by buying up old residential buildings and moving out tenants, almost all of them minorities, and now Columbia intended to build a new gym in Morningside Park. That raised additional issues: should the neighborhood or university decide how to use the park, and should private concerns be able to use public land in crowded Manhattan? To many activists the gym idea was racist—a rich, basically white corporation bullying poor, mostly black and Hispanic residents. The announcement prompted black students and neighbors to picket, some holding signs: "Gym Crow Must Go!"

Frustration and tension mounted during spring semester. Many of these activists had been demonstrating for years against racism, war, and campus regulations; they had conducted hundreds of meetings and debates and participated in dozens of marches. The result? Nationally, racism and war continued, yet locally many universities were changing policies, allowing more student participation in decision making at their university—but not Columbia. Kirk refused to budge. Thus, on April 23, approximately 500 activists, which included members from SDS and the Student Afro-American Society, held a rally at the campus sundial. The demonstrators marched to the proposed gym site, and some tore down a fence and briefly skirmished with police before they returned to the campus. The radicals then marched into Hamilton Hall. They took a dean hostage, proclaimed their demands, and prepared for the siege. In the middle of the night, black and white students argued, and black militants told white radicals to find their own building. The blacks remained in Hamilton and renamed it Malcolm X Hall. The disgruntled whites left and broke into Low Library where they occupied President Kirk's office, sat at his desk, and rifled through some of his files. When the working day began, the phone rang as usual. Student James Kunen answered, "We are sorry, but Dr. Kirk will not be in today because Columbia is under new management."

During the next two days 1,000 students joined the occupation, entered and "liberated" three more buildings, barricaded themselves inside, and created communes. "The administration," the *Columbia Daily Spectator* declared, is "faced with its greatest challenge from the voices of student power in the history of the school." Students discussed politics, society, ideology, and the role of the university. Sharing and brotherhood spread, and one couple even exchanged vows in a "movement marriage." Business as usual ceased at Columbia.

"If these students succeed in disrupting the disciplinary procedure," declared President Kirk, "then discipline at every university in America will be weakened. We are on trial here. Other universities will look to us for strength." Kirk had supporters, including a few thousand other students, conservatives who handed out flyers attacking the radicals' "tasteless, inconsiderate, and illegal" protest.

Meanwhile, a faculty group attempted to negotiate between the occupants and the administration. SDS members claimed to be spokesmen for the students, and they became as inflexible as Kirk. The radicals made demands, the most important that the university stop building the gym, sever ties with the Institute for Defense Analysis, establish an elected student-faculty disciplinary commission, and give amnesty for all those involved in the occupation. The faculty urged compromise. Kirk said no to amnesty, the regents said no to abandoning the gym, and SDS chairman Mark Rudd called faculty efforts to mediate "bullshit."

After countless meetings, President Kirk reached the end of his patience—he ordered in the police. In the early morning hours of April 30, 1,000 cops, armed with blackjacks, entered the occupied buildings. Some students gave up peacefully or climbed out of windows to safety, but others stood their ground, swearing, calling them "pigs." Police attacked. Student Dionision Pabon reported, "I was kicked in the head, face, back, stomach and groin. It felt like a herd of horses, instead of hooves—iron spikes."

The campus paper declared the cops conducted a "brutal bloody show." Heads pounding, faces bleeding, students were dragged or walked out to waiting paddy wagons or ambulances. A hundred were injured, and over 700 were arrested, a tenth of the student body.

By 1968 one might have thought a university president would have realized that relying on police force to resolve a student issue only resulted in violence and enraged the university community. If Berkeley's Free Speech Movement was too distant in the past, Wisconsin's Dow demonstration had been the previous semester. But somehow these and dozens of other campus confrontations escaped Kirk. He called the cops, who swung their nightsticks, and that played into the hands of the radicals and mobilized neutral professors and students who condemned the administration and police brutality. "Cops Out," declared the *Spectator*, and even many conservative students were appalled. "I had always respected the police," said one. "In this case the police action revolted me. I became a striker."

More students and many faculty joined the strike. Classes virtually ceased. The administration suspended radical leaders, which only resulted in a second occupation of Hamilton Hall in May. Some 250 participated, and again Kirk called in the police. Violence erupted, and the police arrested approximately 170, again uniting most students against the administration. Almost half the students and faculty signed a petition demanding Kirk's resignation, and they continued boycotting classes. The administration suspended over 70 students—and informed their draft boards that they had lost their deferments and were eligible for conscription. Meanwhile, the university canceled exams, and professors gave most students final grades of either pass or fail.

Tempers eventually cooled that summer. The students continued to press for their demands, and by the beginning of fall semester their efforts resulted in victory. Kirk resigned, and the new university administration asked the courts to dismiss criminal charges against building occupiers, pledged the gym would not be built without the community's consent, ended its affiliation with the IDA, and granted students a "voice and representation at the highest level of decision making."

The Columbia strike had national implications, for like so many of the shocking events of 1968 it contributed to the demise of the center of American political life. Many of the older generation took a step to the right. Richard Nixon declared that Columbia was the "first major skirmish in a revolutionary struggle to seize the universities," and Republican Congressman Robert H. Michel added that the radicals' next target could be "City Hall, the State Capitol, or even the White House." Many of the sixties generation took a step left. Campus and underground newspapers across the nation ran almost daily articles on "Berkeley East," accompanied by bloody photographs. To many students, Columbia again proved that the Establishment was repressive and corrupt, and thus, declared an activist, it was time for "revolutionary social change. . . . We, the youth, have no place but a revolutionary one in the present-day decaying America."

The idea spread that spring semester—*revolution!* Few stopped to define the term, for if you were young you understood what it meant. Activists hung pictures of their new heroes in dorm rooms and apartments: Malcolm X, Ho Chi Minh, Cuban revolutionary Che Guevara. Students dressed in work shirts and army surplus jackets read Mao Zedong's maxims in his *Little Red Book*. The sixties had moved from Greensboro and Thoreau to Columbia and Mao. Longhair students rapped about conflict and change, evolution and revolution, about creating "many Columbias," and they began using the Germanic, or Nazi, spelling for their nation: *Amerika*. A university's only function, proclaimed Mark Rudd, was "the creation and expansion of a revolutionary movement." Others rapped about radicalizing new students and used terms like *vanguard* and *cadre*.

The revolution fantasy seemed to inch closer as the youth revolt suddenly blossomed in numerous nations: 1968 became the year of the barricades. French students rebelled against their antiquated educational establishment, igniting an enormous strike that resulted in bloody clashes in the streets of Paris. English students held sit-ins, German radicals rebelled at the Free University of Berlin, and young Greeks fought with their military regime. Koreans threw firebombs at military police, and Japanese radicals performed snake dances at Tokyo University. Czechoslovakians confronted Russian tanks and their own Communist Party, demanding the end of the Soviet occupation during Prague Spring.

The revolution was coming, shouted radicals, as they shocked the older generation with absurd rhetoric. Tom Hayden declared that violence "could not be ignored as an option," and that students now would begin "permanent occupations" of universities that would force the government to change policy in Vietnam or send troops to occupy campuses. Jerry Rubin shouted, "Open the jails, let everybody out, and then put the pigs in," and young father Abbie Hoffman screamed "Kill your parents!" What was real? What was fantasy? A popular saying that year was "Be Realistic—Demand the Impossible." This was not revolution: this was 1968.

The outrageous rhetoric led many to assume, as one historian later wrote, that in 1968 the "goal of the movement became the seizure of power." No, the radicals called for revolution—but that was all. No students at Columbia picked up guns and shot at the cops, something true of virtually every student-police confrontation throughout the sixties. As the *Spectator* noted, "There is no question that the police are stronger and better-armed. . . . In any confrontation Columbia students can only lose." The student movement raised issues, created activity, but because it was so diverse it could not arrive at a common denominator, an answer for the nation's ills. "If there is a road to power," Todd Gitlin realized, "we have no map for it."

At Columbia, as at other universities, the vast majority of students in the occupation participated because they wanted to reform the university. The *Spectator* conducted a poll in which half the student body participated that revealed broad support for the aims of the occupation and broad opposition to the tactics of the radicals. When asked if Columbia was a good place to attend college, three-fourths said yes, and that response came from both strikers and nonstrikers. The upheaval was more radical in form because of mounting frustration and subsequent alienation, some caused by racism and urban riots but most of it caused by the endless war. A Columbia vice president said there were two wars, one in Vietnam and the other on campus, and a dean remarked, "If you could name a university where students aren't concerned with Vietnam and the cities, I'd be scared to death of the place."

That spring students again demonstrated their concern about the war by conducting a national strike. A million college and high school students, faculty and teachers, boycotted classes. In fact, the first six months of the year set records for antiwar activism: some 40,000 students participated in over 220 demonstrations at over 100 campuses.

Antiwar marches, student strikes, intemperate statements, urban riots—all created an uneasy atmosphere in the nation as politicians campaigned for the presidency. Almost everyone looked for someone, anyone, who could chart a path to domestic tranquility and out of Vietnam.

Gene and Bobby

Vice President Hubert Humphrey announced his candidacy in April, pledging an end to the war without "humiliation or defeat," calling for a return to "the politics of joy." He appealed to organized labor and to older, traditional Democrats. At that time, only 13 states had primaries, and so Humphrey began working behind the scene to gain the support of party regulars. Within weeks the vice president had the support of about 900 of the 1,300 delegates needed to secure the nomination.

To most of the sixties generation, the battle was between Eugene McCarthy and Bobby Kennedy. RFK seemed more concerned about poverty and minorities, declaring there were two parts of America, one of the comfortable middle class and the other of the "Negro, the Puerto Rican, and the Mexican American . . . a dark and hopeless place." Although both men condemned racism, McCarthy appealed more to white liberals and professionals. Concerning South Vietnam, the candidates called for a bombing halt, more determined negotiations, and granting the enemy some role in a future government in Saigon. McCarthy eventually went further, stating it was time for disengagement: "We shall take our steel out of the land of thatched huts." That was too extreme for RFK, who was not willing to abandon America's commitment.

The race was on. Bobby's advisers paved a colorful campaign trail into the ghettos and barrios and wrote speeches filled with rhetorical flourishes. Since the Nixon and Kennedy debate of 1960, these politicos were aware of the impact of television politics, the importance of image over issues. McCarthy was bland and lectured his audience, as Norman Mailer quipped, "like the dean of the finest English department in the land." McCarthy sounded like a philosopher; Kennedy appeared as an evangelist. RFK's relatively long hair, his boyish face, attracted many young Americans, not only scores of shrieking teenage girls, but New Left intellectuals and activists such as Tom Hayden, John Lewis, and Cesar Chavez. Both candidates hit the college circuit, both were popular, but to many students RFK sounded more hopeful: "Some men see things as they are and ask, why? I dream things that never were and say, why not?"

The spring primaries were inconclusive, setting the stage for a showdown in California. Kennedy called in all the family's political debts, and with a large staff of professionals he moved into the state and conducted a blitzkrieg, shaking hands and grinning from San Francisco to San Diego, from Watts to Hollywood. Along the campaign trail supporters waved placards: "Bobby is Groovy." "Go, Bobby, Go." Earlier in March, RFK had rushed to California to attend a large mass with Cesar Chavez, who had been organizing farmworkers and protesting wages and labor conditions by boycotts, strikes, even by fasting for 25 days. Upon the candidate's return, large Mexican American crowds cheered him enthusiastically. McCarthy also arrived in the golden state, and as bands played "When the Saints Come Marching In," students waved signs, including one of the senator's favorites: "We Believe You." Students and even flower children answered telephones and sent out campaign literature. "What I remember is bright young faces," wrote the senator, "homemade posters, peace beads, and amulets."

The race was tight, and early in June the people voted: 46 percent for Kennedy and 42 for McCarthy. A narrow victory, but enough for RFK to tell an adviser, "I'm the only candidate against the war that can beat Humphrey." RFK left his hotel suite and went to the ballroom where he took the podium and waved to the cheering crowd. He attacked Humphrey for avoiding the primaries, appealed to McCarthy's followers to join him, and called for an end to violence and division: "We can start to work together. We are a great country, an unselfish country, and a compassionate country."

"KENNEDY SHOT" declared the headlines of the *Los Angeles Times*. Sirhan Sirhan, a deranged Jordanian, pulled out a pistol and fired eight times, wounding three and shooting the candidate in the head. Kennedy died early the next morning. The body was put on a plane with his widow and two others—Jacqueline Kennedy and Coretta Scott King. Only eight weeks after the death of Martin Luther King, there were no riots, only a stunned, morbid silence. LBJ became the first president to call for federal gun control, and he proclaimed a day of mourning. The coffin rested at St. Patrick's Cathedral in New York City, where thousands waited for hours to pay their last respects, people of all races, all creeds, from the president to the poor. One black woman mumbled, "Seems like anybody speaks up for us, they get killed," and another wept, "Our friend is gone. Oh, Jesus, he is gone."

The next day the coffin was placed in the last car of a train. Filled with admirers, the train began the slow journey to Arlington Cemetery where Robert was buried next to his brother John. Along the way perhaps a million citizens waited. Arthur Schlesinger Jr. reported, "Some stood at rigid attention, hand over heart. Some waved. Some buried their faces in their hands. Some knelt. Some held up hand-printed signs—REST IN PEACE, ROBERT. . . . Many cried. Some threw roses at the last car. Some as if in a daze followed the train down the roadbed."

The killing raised agonizing questions: Why was America so violent? What type of people were we becoming? What was wrong with the nation? RFK in death became the great enigma of 1968: Would he have won the nomination in August, could he have won the presidency in November? If so, would he have ended the war honorably, and could he have ended the divisiveness and brought citizens together? Would he have fulfilled the dream?

Silent Majority, Wallace, and the New Nixon

Many citizens lost interest as the campaign continued on that summer. During the violence, many simply attempted to escape the sixties, which was possible even during the tumult of 1968. Although the war was on television every night and draft calls continued to increase, there still was no general mobilization as in World War II, no call-up of the reserves like during Korea. Moreover, a relatively small number of the sixties generation were asked to fight. Of approximately 27 million young men who came of draft age from 1964 to 1973, little more than 2 million were drafted while almost 9 million enlisted, and only 1.6 million saw combat in Southeast Asia. Surprisingly, only 6 percent of the sixties generation fought the war in Vietnam.

During America's longest war, then, most families were not directly affected, and they could and did tune out the war simply by changing the channel. This was demonstrated by a journalist in 1968 who wrote an article in the *Saturday Evening Post* on Millersburg, Pennsylvania. There, the majority of residents were "the indifferent" who thought little about Vietnam. "I really couldn't care less," one stated, but most citizens would not admit that and instead held fuzzy ideas about the conflict. "I like to think of my country as Number One," said one resident. "If we are in a thing of this sort, we have to win it." Their cars had bumper stickers: My Country Right or Wrong. Consequently, they detested critics who challenged the government. Indeed, they hated protesters more than the Vietcong, and many supported the war only because others were demonstrating against it. Residents in these Middletowns felt that a protester was a hippie, "a hairy youth with needle marks on his arm, wearing a blanket and flowers, who is more than likely also a Communist. A hippie does not believe in God, family, private property, good grooming, personal daintiness, Bing Crosby, Bart Starr or almost anything else that Millersburg believes in." Such feelings were supported by a Harris survey that found by three to one Americans felt protesters were not serious about ending the war but "hippies having a ball."

Millersburg citizens would become known the next year as the "great silent majority," and they were the majority of citizens—young and old—who spent the sixties, even 1968, on the sidelines, avoiding painful issues. On campus, these kids joined fraternities and sororities, went to football games, and watched demonstrations, eager to avoid anything that might hurt their future employment opportunities. "I never really knew what was going on," one later admitted, and another added, "I avoided the whole thing . . . too heavy." Their dads went to work every day, moms maybe part time at the mall, and came home to their new color televisions. Popular shows included *The Monkees* and *Mission Impossible*, which seemed the most appropriate program title for the year and perhaps for the decade. Bill Cosby of *I Spy* became the first black to win an Emmy award, and Don Adams received one for the best comedy show, *Get Smart,* another appropriate title. During the year, more citizens tuned into the last episode of *Howdy Doody* than to the war, and fans saw an incredible spring and summer of sports, including Lee Trevino, the first Hispanic to win golf's U.S. Open, Billy Jean King's third singles championship at Wimbledon, and Arthur Ashe, the first African American to win the tennis U.S. Open. All the while athletes from all over the world prepared for the autumn Olympics in Mexico City.

The silent majority also made money during the booming sixties, for the decade was one of the best in history. The 1964 tax cut gave the economy a tremendous boost, and the GNP that year soared an incredible 7 percent and over 9 percent in 1966. Profits rose, businesses paid more taxes, and the Johnson administration could boast a relatively small federal deficit and even a balanced budget his last fiscal year. Incomes rose, inflation was only about 2 percent, rising to over 4 percent in 1968, and jobs were plentiful. High school graduates could look forward to a union job with good wages, and a college grad would have many offers—another reason to avoid military service.

The silent majority generally supported conservative candidates, and in 1968 there were two vying for their vote: George Wallace and Richard Nixon. Wallace had been the Democratic governor of Alabama, and in that capacity was best known for standing up to the federal government in 1963 and attempting to stop the integration of the University of Alabama. In 1964 he took his message north, and during the Democratic presidential primaries in Wisconsin and Indiana he surprised pundits by winning more than a third of the vote against President Johnson. Wallace became the champion of states' rights and of the white backlash, all those who felt LBJ's social programs did not help them and who resented federal attempts to integrate schools: whites who prided themselves for being god fearing and law abiding, who practiced "traditional values" and the Puritan ethic.

The governor realized he never could win the Democratic nomination so he formed the American Independent Party, and shortly thereafter his numerous young conservative volunteers completed what they called "Mission Impossible"; they got their candidate on the ballot of all 50 states.

Wallace had many simple solutions to complex American problems. After Tet, all candidates shifted from escalation to deescalation in Vietnam—except Wallace. "I think we've got to pour it on," he proclaimed, and then for his running mate he picked tough-talking retired Air Force General Curtis LeMay, who advocated it would be "most efficient" to use nuclear weapons against the enemy and "bomb 'em back to the stone age." Wallace appealed to workers by attacking "briefcase totin' bureaucrats, ivory-tower guideline writers . . . and pointy-headed professors," who knew nothing; they "don't know how to park a bicycle straight." The Supreme Court should leave the states alone, he claimed, and Chief Justice Earl Warren wasn't smart enough "to try a chicken thief in my home county." To stop rioting, "We ought to turn this country over to the police for two or three years and everything would be all right." He lashed out at all those who demonstrated, "put a crease in their forehead," and as for campus protests: "Any Alabama student who takes the extreme line like sending blood and money to the Vietcong, or burning his draft card, or urging our troops not to fight—we'll expel the sons-of-bitches."

Like all third-party candidates in the twentieth century, from Teddy Roosevelt in 1912 to Ross Perot in 1992 and Ralph Nader in 2000, Wallace in 1968 never had a chance to win, but he could lose the election for Nixon. Thus the Republican's campaign stressed traditional values, but unlike Wallace, Nixon appeared "presidential," a trait he promoted throughout the nation. Most citizens felt he had grown beyond his earlier image of a rabid anticommunist who used any means to slay political opponents, "Tricky Dick," and that over the years he had become a moderate conservative, a mature leader who stood for law and order: the New Nixon.

In the first week of August the Republicans held their convention in Miami, or as a journalist labeled the affair, "a love-in on the beach." The nomination was over before the first delegate arrived because Nixon had won every primary; he easily fought off challenges from liberal New York Governor Nelson Rockefeller and conservative California Governor Ronald Reagan. After the first ballot, placards proclaimed, "Nixon's the One!"

The nominee's acceptance speech declared there was a "new voice" being heard across America, one different from "the voices of hatred, the voices of dissention, the voices of riot and revolution." This voice came from "those who did not break the law, people who pay their taxes and go to work, people who send their children to school, who go to their churches, people who are not haters, people who love this country." Nixon struck a chord, especially with those middle Americans who were becoming more conservative, tired of so much tumult and change.

For his running mate, Nixon picked a man who could help drain votes from Wallace, a Republican with a sharp tongue from a border state, Maryland Governor Spiro Agnew. The governor supported the war and had adopted a hard-line stance to squash rioting in Baltimore, which included ordering police to shoot looters. "If one wants to pinpoint the cause of the riots," he proclaimed, "it would be this permissive climate." When black students staged an orderly sit-in at the state house, the governor arrested over 200. "That guy Agnew is really an impressive fellow," said Nixon. "He's got guts."

The Republicans left Miami. Tanned and contented, they turned on their televisions to watch the Democratic delegates arrive at their convention in Chicago—and then destroy what remained of liberalism.

Chicago 1968

Four main characters acted in what became the Democratic tragedy at Chicago. The first was Senator McCarthy. He represented most activists and younger liberals, many students and professors, who supported a continuation of social programs and especially peace. The senator had won over 600 delegates in primaries, and so he and his supporters demanded an "open convention" with full discussion of the issues and some say in the party platform.

Humphrey was the second character at Chicago. Over the years he had been a solid liberal who staunchly supported social programs, civil rights, and he had been first to suggest ideas that became the Peace Corps, food stamps, and Medicare. "Most senators are minnows," said LBJ. "Hubert Humphrey is among the whales."

Although he had the support of traditional Democrats, many young activists disliked the vice president, feeling he was a compromiser who represented the machine politics of the Democratic establishment. Without winning one state primary he had worked behind the scenes and had won almost 1,500 delegates, securing the nomination. He also supported Johnson's war. "Nothing would bring the real peaceniks back to our side," stated an aide, "unless Hubert urinated on a portrait of Lyndon Johnson in Times Square before television—and then they'd say to him, why didn't you do it before?"

The third actor was the man who controlled the streets of Chicago, Democratic Mayor Richard Daley. The mayor played by the rules, his rules. During the riot following Martin Luther King's murder, he ordered his police to "shoot to kill any arsonist" and "shoot to maim or cripple anyone looting a store in our city." Police wounded 48 and killed 4 blacks. When students marched against the war in April, Daley dispatched his police, who attacked the peaceful crowd. The mayor's spokesman declared, "These people have no right to demonstrate or express their views." After the assassination of Bobby Kennedy, Daley was determined to maintain security at the convention and law and order in the streets. Consequently, he placed his 12,000-man police force on 12-hour shifts, stationed 6,000 Illinois National Guardsmen outside the city, and could call on the same number of regular army troops armed with rifles, bayonets, gas dispensers—even flamethrowers, grenade launchers, bazookas, and .30 caliber machine guns. A product of an older generation, Daley would "contain" the enemy, prevent young activists, the American Vietcong, from disrupting his convention or his Chicago.

The last characters were the 10,000 activists, the colorful mélange of young people who filtered into Chicago as the convention convened on August 26. They would make the 1968 Democratic Convention like no other in American history. Some supported McCarthy, others had worked for Bobby Kennedy, a few radicals had given up on liberal politics—all were against the war. Most felt it was appropriate to go to Chicago and confront Johnson's "war party," to hold a "People's Convention," and then march peacefully to the convention hall and proclaim their stand on the issues. "We are not going to storm the convention with tanks or Mace," said peacenik David Dellinger. "But we are going to storm the hearts and minds of the American people."

Most of these storm troopers were college kids, but the press zeroed in on a small number of the most outrageous—Yippies! Abbie Hoffman, Jerry Rubin, and their friends had created the Yippies earlier in 1968. "A political hippie. A flower child who's been busted. A stoned-out warrior of the Aquarian Age," explained Hoffman. Time for an alliance of activists and hippies, a "blending of pot and politics."

The Yippies were both protest and put on, political wisecrackers who loved attention. They dropped rumors: Yippie potheads in Chicago had been busy all spring growing marijuana in vacant lots for a giant August smoke-in; luscious Yippie females were going to pose as hookers and then kidnap Humphrey delegates; Yippies would put LSD in Chicago's water supply and storm the local Nabisco office and distribute free cookies; 100,000 Yippies would protest the war by floating nude in Lake Michigan during the day and at night they would burn draft cards in unison creating a flame spelling BEAT ARMY. They made up 20,000 buttons that read "Yippie Leader." Yippie proverbs: "Don't grow up. Growing up means *giving up your dreams.*" "Free Speech Is the Right to Shout 'Theater' in a Crowded Fire." Yippie slogans: "Amerika says: *Don't!* The Yippies say *Do It!*" Their "platform" advocated peace, freedom, free birth control and abortion, legalization of marijuana and psychedelics, and also that the police should disarm, that "people should fuck all the time, anytime, whomever they wish" and the government should abolish money and pay toilets. The final demand was blank: "You can fill in what you want."

Looking back, anyone listening or reading these remarks would have laughed, but the authorities knew nothing about their enemy—just like in Vietnam—and this was 1968. After the assassinations of King and Kennedy, few were interested in levity. The older generation reacted with force toward the activists. Daley ordered his plainclothes police to infiltrate movement organizations, and the federal government placed 1,000 agents in the city: for every six activists during the convention there was one undercover agent. The governor ordered troops to protect the water supply, and the *Chicago Tribune* published a series of alarmist articles about the "plans by Communists and left-wing agitators to disrupt the city," and how "Yippies Demand Cash from City" after Hoffman joked that if the city gave him $100,000 he would leave town. Pundits hinted the Yippies would attempt a coup against President Johnson. "We love LBJ," Rubin replied. "Where would we be without LBJ?"

The Establishment didn't get the joke. They were dead serious. Daley refused to issue parade permits to various movement organizations, refused to allow activists to use Soldier Field stadium for a rally, claiming it was "booked the entire week for Lyndon Johnson's Birthday Party." The mayor refused camping permits: against city regulations. Many radicals wondered why a citizen would need a permit to protest a war that was being fought without a permit, a declaration of war, and liberals agreed with McCarthy aide Allard Lowenstein, who concluded that the authorities "seem determined to have a confrontation that can only produce violence and bloodshed."

Inside the convention hall there was chaos. The Humphrey forces supported LBJ's policy in Vietnam, and McCarthy's delegates argued for a bombing halt and withdrawal. Unfortunately for the peace delegates, a few days earlier the Soviet Army had invaded Czechoslovakia, ending the reformist government that had been emerging since Prague Spring and boosting the hawk position that communism had to be contained. As for the doves' plank, hawk Congressman Wayne Hays declared, it would play into the hands of radicals who want "pot instead of patriotism, sideburns instead of solutions. They would substitute riots for reason." The delegates defeated the peace plank and continued quarreling as TV newscasters exposed the convention to the public that evening. As Americans watched, the convention floor became rowdy. Black northern delegates sneered at white Southerners, calling them racists, and when white Alabama delegates voted, other blacks marched out. A fistfight erupted between white and black delegates from Georgia, and tempers soared as conservatives and liberals shouted at each other and threw ice. More scuffles, a few more fights, and when CBS reporter Dan Rather rushed to the scene, a policeman slugged him, knocking him to the floor. Astonished, anchorman Walter Cronkite called the police "thugs."

So ended the first evening of the convention tragedy. The confusion and madness continued for three more days, all of it sending a signal into American households: the Democrats were out of control. The party became a mirror of the nation, cracking over the issues of race and war.

Outside the convention hall, the party platform made little difference—most activists were not listening. They had made up their minds during the last three years that civil rights were mandatory and the war was a disaster. About 1,000 of them were camping in Lincoln Park, and then at 11 P.M. the curfew passed. The police ordered them to leave. They stayed, and some taunted the cops. The authorities launched tear gas and charged into the park. As journalist Nicholas von Hoffman noted, the police had "taken off their badges, their nameplates, even the unit patches on their shoulders to become a mob of identical, unidentifiable club swingers." They chased kids through streets in Old Town, clubbing virtually anyone in the area, including onlookers, those going out to dinner, and two dozen reporters and cameramen. "The Chicago police force understands very little about civil liberty," wrote the *Washington Post,* "and apparently cares even less."

Finally, the last act. The antiwar forces declared they would assemble at Grant Park and march to the convention hall on the day of Humphrey's nomination. As expected, Daley refused the parade permit. As expected, about 10,000 people assembled at Grant Park, and as expected, they were met by the police and the Illinois National Guard. CBS later reported that some 200 undercover agents were in the crowd, and at least one of them was in a group of young men who approached the flagpole, took down Old Glory, and raised a red T-shirt. That prompted police to charge, clubs swinging. People scattered, and a few thousand gathered at twilight across the street from the Hilton hotel that housed the candidates. The authorities were prepared. Hotel and building lights lit up the sky as television cameras recorded the events. The marchers began down Michigan Avenue, chanting, "Peace now! Peace now!" "Dump the Hump." They approached the police line. Stop. A few began taunting police, throwing garbage, yelling, "Fuck you, LBJ," "Hell no, we won't go," "Fuck the pigs."

Bang! The police exploded into the crowd. Shouts, confusion, panic. Gas canisters exploded. Police clubbing. People screaming, bleeding. Some ran down streets, into hotel lobbies, back to the park. More cops arrived. Patrol wagons appeared. Police hit everyone. Tear gas floated into the Hilton, up the air vents, and into the suite of the vice president. On the street, kids chanting, "Sieg heil, Sieg heil, Sieg heil," and "The whole world is watching."

The "police riot" at the Democratic Convention in Chicago, Grant Park,
which was another event dividing the American people in 1968.

The world *was* watching, or at least an estimated 90 million Americans. NBC news commentator Chet Huntley declared to his viewers, the "news profession in this city is now under assault by the Chicago police." Those who did not have on their televisions read in newspapers that even "elderly bystanders were caught in the police onslaught," that the police chased and clubbed demonstrators, politicians, journalists, and any doctors or nurses who attempted to help the injured. "Some tried to surrender by putting their hands on their heads," wrote a journalist. "As they were marched to vans to be arrested, they were rapped in the genitals by the cops' swinging billies."

Meanwhile, at the convention hall, Democrats gave nomination speeches for Humphrey. But television cameras cut from the speeches and played footage from the chaotic street scene, prompting a senator to declare that Chicago's finest were outside using "Gestapo tactics." Enraged, Mayor Daley shook his fist, swearing at the senator. Later, Humphrey won the nomination and appointed Senator Edmund Muskie as his running mate. Although the candidate called on Americans to "Put aside recrimination and disunion," the most appropriate comment that evening was by activist Lowenstein: "This convention elected Richard Nixon President of the United States tonight."

Like so many events in 1968, Chicago divided the American people and demolished the political center. Liberals were discouraged, and during the next months McCarthy and his supporters refused to endorse Humphrey. Activists and many students were outraged, feeling that the Democratic Party had become a corrupt machine. Many youth began to believe that the U.S. government was no longer a democracy but had become an illegitimate institution led by "war criminals" and enforced by "the pigs." College polls revealed soaring alienation, and more kids were attracted to the counterculture—or to radicalism. Police brutality, in fact, created more radicals than all the pamphlets and books, all the speeches given by the New Left vanguard. Moreover, repression did not suppress radicalism; on the contrary, as Yippie Stew Albert said, Chicago was "a revolutionary wet dream come true."

Conservatives rallied behind the authorities, and so did a surprising number of ordinary citizens. "If other mayors followed Daley's action," a local man editorialized, "then we'd have a much better society." According to one poll, some 70 percent of citizens agreed, and George Wallace declared that the Chicago police "probably showed too much restraint." After a year of tumult, an increasing number of the older generation were calling for law and order, even if that meant bashing the heads and genitals of the sixties generation. The romantic dream that there would be a revolution in America was beaten senseless in Chicago.

1968 Finale

After the mayhem of the convention, many citizens hoped that the remainder of the year would quietly expire—but 1968 was unrelenting. In September, the Miss America Pageant began in Atlantic City, and it was the most unusual one in U.S. history. "Miss America Pageant Is Picketed by 100 Women," wrote journalist Charlotte Curtis. "Women armed with a giant bathing beauty puppet and a 'freedom trash can' in which they threw girdles, bras, hair curlers, false eyelashes, and anything else that smacked of 'enslavement' picketed the Miss America Pageant here today." The demonstrators marched around the convention hall, singing songs, carrying posters, and denouncing the all-white contest as racist. They insisted that women would not be free until they were "no longer enslaved by ludicrous beauty standards." No one burned a bra, but some carried signs: "Girls Crowned—Boys Killed!" "I Am a Woman—Not a Toy, a Pet, or Mascot!" Others ripped up a *Playboy,* dumped it into the can, and danced around shouting, "Liberation Now!" A few activists got into the convention hall during the telecast, one momentarily disrupting the event by throwing a stench bomb.

"The demonstrators," the *New York Times* wrote, "belonged to what they called the Women's Liberation Movement." Unknown to mainstream society, that movement had been developing throughout the decade, but this was the first time the term was used in the national press. *Women's liberation* would not become part of America's lexicon for another year, and the first major article hinting that women were forming their own movement did not appear until March 1968: Martha Weinman Lear's "The Second Feminist Wave" in the *New York Times Magazine*. The article asked, "What do these women *want*?" The answer, given by "theoretician" Betty Friedan and "analytic philosopher" Ti-Grace Atkinson, was a lot, including "wanting to be heard."

By autumn 1968 everyone wanted to be heard. In October some 500 uniformed servicemen stunned the nation: they marched against the war in San Francisco. Although some individual servicemen had spoken out against the conflict, and had been punished for stating their views, the nation never had witnessed hundreds marching against the war, against their commander in chief. The act of drafting civilians, sending them to boot camp to make them "military," no longer was purging young adults of their antiwar views.

The issues of war and race continued to explode, and the next venue was another unlikely place—the Olympics in Mexico City—where two black athletes on the U.S. team shocked the nation and the world. Tommie Smith wore a black glove on his right hand when he received his gold medal for breaking the world record and winning the 200-meter dash. John Carlos wore the glove on his left when he received the bronze medal. As "The Star-Spangled Banner" played, both men raised their hands in the clenched fist that symbolized black power. The Olympic committee immediately suspended them for boosting a political cause.

The episode again divided the nation. Many African Americans applauded, and the suspended athletes became martyrs, promoters of black pride. A "heroic demonstration," cheered a writer in *Ebony*, for the salute "forcefully thrust the black liberation movement into the international arena, and captured the admiration and support of black youth all over the country." Yet in 1968 the vast majority of white Americans knew little about black power, probably had never seen the salute, and agreed with a white Olympic swimmer who called the incident "a disgrace . . . an act like that in the medal ceremony defiles the American flag." A day later, at the compound housing the U.S. athletes, a sign hung from the dorm window of the rifle team: "Win the War in Vietnam: Wallace for President."

George Wallace was the unknown variable in the presidential campaign. How many votes would he win? Popular opinion polls predicted during the summer that he would win only 10 percent, but that figure quickly doubled after the chaos of the Democratic convention. If that trend continued he might have 30 percent by the election and force the decision into the House of Representatives. Accordingly, Wallace moved into the towns and suburbs, where he declared his opposition to school integration and the Fair Housing Act. He had predicted that white urbanites "will be so goddamned sick and tired of federal interference in their local schools, they'll be ready to vote for Wallace." He seemed correct, as crowds swelled for the "Wallace Whitelash." "I'm going to ask the Congress," he declared, "to repeal this law about the sale of your own property and let them know that a man's home is still his castle."

Olympics 1968: The first time
that most Americans saw
the black power salute.

Everyone wanted to know what the two main candidates would do about race and war. With a large lead, Nixon avoided controversy and remained vague, attacking Humphrey as a liberal big spender and blaming the Democrats for urban riots, crime in the streets, and student rebellion. The Republican emphasized law and order and declared it was time "to quit pouring billions of dollars into programs that have failed." Humphrey countered that the nation must continue social programs, civil rights, and integration. But Vietnam was the most important issue in 1968, and the media pressed the candidates. Both Nixon and Humphrey called for some sort of deescalation. The Democrat would continue Johnson's policy, which he said was winning the war. Nixon advocated "peace with honor," but when he refused to give details on how he would achieve that, critics labeled it a "secret plan." Actually, Nixon had no plan (which he admitted in 1985), and had no idea how to bring about peace—but neither did most voters—and neither did Humphrey. Citizens *hoped* the political leaders knew something, some secret, that would end the war honorably.

Humphrey went on the attack, challenging Nixon to a debate. The Republican refused, and Humphrey branded him "Richard the Chickenhearted." But the Democrat could not excite the nation, and by October it was obvious his only path toward victory was to distance himself from Johnson's policy in Vietnam. If elected, Humphrey declared, he would stop bombing North Vietnam and perhaps call on the United Nations to supervise the evacuation of all foreign troops from South Vietnam. He would begin the "de-Americanization of the war."

Humphrey leaned closer to the antiwar movement's position, and the tactic had an impact. Some students joined his campaign; so did older peace liberals. A week before the election Senator McCarthy endorsed the vice president: "I'm voting for Humphrey, and I think you should suffer with me." President Johnson announced a bombing halt on North Vietnam, and opinion polls called it a close race.

Nixon was the one, just barely. Winning a little over 43 percent of the electorate, he beat Humphrey by only a half million votes. Wallace won 13 percent, demonstrating the growing white backlash and that not many wanted to intensify the war.

Little was clear cut in 1968, including the election. The Old South continued its transition away from the Democrats and toward any conservative who would oppose civil rights, including a third-party candidate. Wallace won in Dixie. Nixon won the West, the southern border states, and many suburbs, demonstrating opposition to federal attempts to promote integration. In the rest of the nation, about 57 percent voted either for Nixon or Wallace and against the Democrats, suggesting the election was a repudiation of liberalism and signaled the rise of conservativism. Yet that is not clear. The voters elected more conservatives to the House and more liberals to the Senate. Liberals would control Congress throughout the next decade, when Americans again elected a Democratic president, Jimmy Carter. Actually, in 1968 the electorate voted for something different, something they felt had a better chance of ending the violence that had vexed the nation for three years. Because Wallace was an insult to thoughtful citizens, they had only one option: they voted for a "secret plan," hoping Nixon knew some way, any way to end the war at home and abroad. In a sense, then, the vote was a call for the return of the peaceful fifties and a rejection of The Decade of Tumult and Change. The silent majority voted for silence, for an end to the shouting.

Of course, the election did end Democratic control of the presidency, and that was a break with the past. Liberals and activists naturally were discouraged. "It's gray everywhere," commented Eugene McCarthy, "all over the land." Liberals knew

Nixon's policies would strive to contain communism abroad, meaning the war would continue for years, and that the new president would cut federal support for civil rights; the next agenda would be law and order.

The man who had stood tall for civil rights, Lyndon Johnson, retired to his Texas ranch. Just three years earlier LBJ had been compared to Abraham Lincoln and Franklin Roosevelt, but now he was tired, broken, and a few years later he died, age 64, a casualty of his own responses to the events and issues that overwhelmed America in 1968.

"What a Year!" declared *Time* in an essay, "one tragic, surprising and perplexing thing after another." After comparing 1968 with 1929 and 1941 as the most important years of the century, the editors asked why. "Americans failed to solve too many of the minor problems that eventually caused major explosions."

Those explosions would continue to sequester the nation. Not since the Civil War and Reconstruction had America been so divided: white versus black, hawks versus doves, liberals versus conservatives, culture versus counterculture, even families were sequestered. While Defense Secretary Robert McNamara was conducting the war, his son Craig was marching against it. The silent majority hated protesters: protesters could not understand how anyone could remain silent when a war was killing so many.

This was 1968. The election did not end the sixties or the shouting. There were more demonstrations after 1968 than before. More than politics, the sixties were defined by cultural and social activism, and that would continue to develop along two themes that were emerging during and especially after 1968—liberation and empowerment.

Chapter 5

From Counterculture to Sixties Culture

Liberation and empowerment were well under way by the end of 1968, and during the next few years the first would confront the culture, and the second would attack the Establishment. Both themes would merge to create a sixties culture, which would change the nation.

The *Establishment* was a vague term used by activists for the government, armed forces, institutions, and corporations. After 1968 the Establishment's trustee was Richard Nixon, who proclaimed he would return the nation to law and order and uphold the status quo for the "great silent majority." His vice president, Spiro Agnew, lashed out at those who did not support the administration, calling them "malcontents, radicals, incendiaries, civil and uncivil disobedients." Protesters supposedly were un-American, and they no longer were going to be tolerated. "If people demonstrate in a manner to interfere with others," declared Deputy Attorney General Richard Kleindienst, "they should be rounded up and put in a detention camp."

That would have been difficult to do, because by the late sixties the anti-Establishment had exploded over the issue of "lifestyles" and had become what *Time* called a "youthquake" shaking the moral foundations of America. This motley crew was composed of activists, some students and emerging feminists, and especially hippies. Although never organized, they created a great vocal minority that promoted liberation, challenged the great silent majority, and confronted and shocked mainstream culture—the counterculture.

The counterculture had been flourishing since the 1967 Summer of Love, even though after that event the culture declared war: "Trouble in Hippieland" wrote *Newsweek*, claiming that most flower children were "seriously disturbed youngsters" or "overprivileged products of the American dream." In 1968 *Reader's Digest* concluded for its 28 million readers that "Murder, rape, disease, suicide—the dark side of the hippie moon has become increasingly visible," and the next year a journalist summed up the older generations' knowledge of these cultural rebels when he gave his peers advice on how to spot one: "Well, hippies look like hippies."

The Establishment's interpretation of the counterculture had been written, and it became accepted creed. By the end of the decade an opinion poll asked citizens to identify the most harmful groups in the nation, and they listed "Communists, prostitutes, and hippies." Later historians and pundits of the era usually avoided writing about the hippies after discussing the Summer of Love, or they based their books on mainstream press sources as they wrote for the next generation of college students. In one popular text, a historian described hippies as "countless thousands of disturbed youngsters" whose experiences generally were "stupid, pointless, and self-defeating." Ever since, *hippie* has come to symbolize something negative, disliked, rather like *commie* in the fifties.

During the sixties, hippies recognized bias, of course; one youthful journalist, John Wilcock, quit the mainstream press and declared, "The newspaper owners are plain and simple liars." Wilcock began publishing an underground paper, *Other Scenes;* many others developed three national wire services and over 600 undergrounds that eventually had a circulation of about 5 million. Other cultural rebels composed music, drew posters, or wrote handouts, all of which declared their values and views. Writing history about the counterculture only using the Establishment's descriptions is tantamount to writing a history of the American Revolution and only examining the British documents, and not those of the rebels.

And hippies were rebels; they revolted from the norms, values, and morals of the established society. They were a minority counter to the majority culture, and they changed society, fundamentally altering America. That is why they must be examined, fairly, using their own documents.

The number of hippies soared after 1968. Although there were about 75,000 in autumn of 1967, by the end of the next year the press reported, somewhat ironically, that there were 200,000 "full-time hippies" and another 300,000 who shared the practices and beliefs, some 20,000 were dropping out each year, and "the number is accelerating geometrically." By the end of the decade, hippies had established thousands of communes, hip communities in almost every major city, and they were hitchhiking around the country and throughout the world—from Marrakech to Kathmandu. By the early seventies perhaps 3 million people identified with the counterculture. Although there always were many more conservative kids who were eager apprentices for the Establishment, it was the hippies who disturbed society, regardless of their numbers. "No one knows for sure just how large this massive generational upheaval really was," wrote a researcher. "We can only be sure that it took place on a scale *unprecedented in our history.*"

Indeed, yet the counterculture always was difficult to define, for it came in many shapes and colors, which resulted in many inconsistencies. Three researchers examining one form, the Jesus People, wrote that they discovered "some things to praise and some to criticize, but the balance shifts, sometimes drastically, from element to element within the movement." Moreover, the term *hippie* was invented, not by youth, but by a San Francisco journalist to mean a hip with-it kid who knew what was happening. Eventually, these youth called themselves hippies, or many other names, which changed over time and varied with location. Some were "seekers," searching for meaning, or "heads" because they used dope, or more often, "freak," a "far-out person" too odd, too abnormal to be part of society.

Freaks also were difficult to define because the counterculture included everyone and excluded no one. There were no hippie organizations, no membership cards, no meetings, no age limits, no prerequisites, no leaders. Being a hippie often was a very individualistic journey. One did not *have to* drop out for a semester, a year, or a decade to "qualify" as a hippie, or *have to* take drugs, participate in sex orgies, live in a commune, listen to rock, grow long hair. No minimum requirements. No *have to*. Some hippies might not be able to articulate their thoughts or define their existence, but most would agree that being part of the counterculture was a frame of mind. "Some of the most longhaired people I know are bald," laughed Jerry Rubin, and, when a University of Utah professor criticized the counterculture, a student responded, "The hippie movement is not a beard, it is not a weird, colorful costume, it is not marijuana. The hippie movement . . . is a philosophy, a way of life."

Some dropped out and became as apolitical as possible; others participated in various forms of cultural rebellion; some marched against the war. Perhaps the only constant was that they rejected some of the values of the culture and then developed and practiced different lifestyles.

"There Must Be Some Way Out of Here"

Commentators have discussed the origins of the counterculture. Most have mentioned that throughout American history there have been misfits, those who do not fit into the mainstream. In earlier times they might have been roamers, drifters, mountain men, or utopians at communities such as Oneida, New Harmony, or various Shaker or Hutterite settlements. As America urbanized they clustered in cities—bohemians after the First World War, student radicals during the depression, beatniks during the cold war. Because future hippies were being raised during the postwar era, some were influenced by contemporary intellectuals and poets. Paul Goodman discussed *Growing Up Absurd,* William Whyte challenged students to *"fight* The Organization," and beat poets ridiculed society and urged readers to get *On the Road.* Some writers emphasized the counterculture was a response to technology and the atomic age; others viewed the growth of hippiedom as a result of a massive sixties generation that came of age. More kids meant more dissension from social norms; throw in rock and roll, and presto: the Summer of Love.

Although those factors might be important before 1968, there was a much more significant reason for the *expansion* of the counterculture: alienation.

Alienation began early in the decade, during the civil rights movement. Those black and white youths who demonstrated in the South were startled to find the hatred and violence of racism. Being in the movement often meant being threatened or beaten simply for crusading for rights guaranteed by the U.S. Constitution. The activists also began to doubt the government and distrust the establishment. Not only did Kennedy and Johnson fail to give adequate protection to peaceful marchers, but FBI director J. Edgar Hoover called Martin Luther King "the most notorious liar in the country" and claimed SCLC was "spearheaded by Communists and moral degenerates." Such comments appalled young activists. "We didn't need a foreign ideology," wrote Mary King, "We owed no debt to any political theory other than Jeffersonian democracy." During Freedom Summer 1964 some young activists began to notice a change in their own behavior; they began to think of themselves as part of an alternative society, more flexible and experimental, an interracial "community" that shared everything from food to love. Some females became involved in interracial affairs, a taboo then; others began wondering why they were working so hard for civil rights when they did not have equality. Most began to abandon their collegiate dress for work shirts and blue jeans and to question their parents. "What would you do if a Negro moved in next door?" one asked his father and mother. "We don't mind," was the answer, but when he asked, "What would you do if I wanted to marry a Negro?" the answer was "No. You can't marry a Negro. No, no. You can't do that." The son couldn't understand why, because he had been "raised to believe Negroes were just like anyone else. Two and two just never made four," and that divided the generations.

Alienation also increased as students asked for their rights on campuses. In loco parentis regulations irritated students, but administrators expected obedience, or as a journalist wrote, "to show proper respect, to know their place and keep it." Yet students, tuition payers, demanded the end of puerile rules and often were confronted with endless delays. When student journalists asked too many questions, or were disrespectful, administrators fired or suspended them. Examples abound: *Florida Alligator* for writing editorials critical of state politicians; Johns Hopkins's *Newsletter* for writing a parody ballot for Man of the Year that included three serial killers with Lyndon Johnson; the University of Texas at El Paso's *El Burro* for a fictitious interview between John Lennon and Jesus. When two students at Monmouth College wrote that a regent was a "political hack," they were suspended from college, and when they returned, arrested for trespassing. Students felt powerless, and many dropped out in their own way. For 120 student government positions at the University of Minnesota, not even 100 ran for election in a university with 45,000 enrolled. Others moved off campus and established undergrounds without censors, or as hip writers for the Austin *Rag* proclaimed, "I'm not a student here, so you can go to hell."

Then there was 'Nam. Many younger Americans felt that the war against Vietnamese communism was illegal, inhumane, and immoral and the way to fight it, the draft, was unfair. A young man could either go along and join the military or fight the machine by protesting and resisting the draft. Neither had stopped the war, and after Nixon's election it was clear that the conflict would continue for years. What to do? Drop out. As musician Country Joe McDonald said, "You take drugs, you turn up the music very loud, you dance around, you build yourself a fantasy world where everything's beautiful."

Many kids blamed the war on the older generation. "What's happening," wrote an activist, "is that a whole generation is starting to say to its parents, 'You can no longer get us to kill and be killed for your uptight archaic beliefs.'" Many returning soldiers agreed. Unlike fathers coming home after World War II, Vietnam veterans rarely talked of heroism, duty, honor. Instead, the endless war became an endless barrage of horror stories and disillusionment. "I just lost respect for everything after Vietnam," Lieutenant Al Wilder commented. "Everything I learned as a kid turned out to be a damn lie." The agonizing onslaught of war tales and images repulsed more and more of the sixties generation. "From Vietnam," wrote Raymond Mungo, "I learned to despise my countrymen, my government, and the entire English-speaking world, with its history of genocide and international conquest. I was a normal kid."

Other kids felt the Establishment was hypocritical, and they blamed the inconsistencies, ironies, and contradictions on their elders. Young Americans were old enough, 18, to fight a war they did not create, but not old enough, 21 then, to vote for their commander in chief. Doctors wrote 150 million prescriptions a year for tranquilizers and amphetamines, parents consumed coffee (caffeine), cocktails (alcohol), and cigarettes (nicotine) while condemning youth for "using drugs." The federal government subsidized growing tobacco and at the same time paid for advertisements proclaiming cigarettes were harmful to health and told college students that if they smoked marijuana they would become addicted and "graduate to heroin." While some officials complained that a stamp picturing Henry David Thoreau made the author look too much like a hippie, President Nixon awarded Elvis Presley a citation for the singer's contribution in the "fight against drugs."

And the culture's response to the counterculture—or anything different—also created youthful alienation. When hippies first appeared at a restaurant near the University of Washington a waitress called police, who took them down to the station for no reason. When longhaired Protestants attended a Methodist service in St. Louis, the pastor stopped the proceedings and called the police, who apprehended all bearded youth and arrested 20 for "disrupting a religious ceremony." When Texas Southern University student activist Lee Otis Johnson gave an undercover officer one joint, he was charged with *selling* marijuana, tried, and given a 30-year sentence.

Near the University of Kansas, 150 armed officers raided a hippie house and arrested 30 laid-back kids for no reason; 200 cops stormed the sleeping campus of Stony Brook in New York, woke hundreds in dorm beds, and arrested 33, not for possessing illegal drugs, but for so-called evidence such as tobacco pipes and psychedelic posters. The governor of New Mexico advocated expelling all freaks, and his counterpart in Tennessee was more blunt, declaring, "It's war. We want every longhair in jail or out of the state."

The Nixon administration responded to the counterculture in a similar way, and that was demonstrated soon after the president's inauguration. In March 1969 the government began rounding up the so-called leaders of the demonstrations at the 1968 Democratic Convention, the Chicago 8, charging them with conspiring to travel across state lines "with the intent to incite, organize, promote, encourage, participate in, and carry on a riot." The federal judge, Julius Hoffman, represented the Establishment, and in opposition were the defendants: Dave Dillinger, Tom Hayden, Rennie Davis, Abbie Hoffman, Jerry Rubin, Lee Weiner, John Froines, and Bobby Seale. All were antiwar activists, except Seale, who was a Black Panther. After Seale called the judge "a blatant racist," he was shackled, gagged, and tried alone, leaving the Chicago 7, all who were found guilty of "conspiracy," even though some of them had never met. During the appeals, officials harassed the defendants, arresting them without cause, and kept them in and out of court for the next five years before a federal judge dismissed the case. The government's behavior appalled most youth, and a 1970 Harris poll found that only 30 percent of college students felt war protesters could get a fair trial. The forces of law and order left many to agree with activist David Harris: "If this is the law, then I want to be an outlaw."

By the end of the sixties, then, the smiling baby boomers who had entered college at mid-decade, had attended classes during the days of decision, graduated into a sea of frustration. "We do not feel like a cool, swinging generation," declared a Radcliffe senior. "We are eaten up inside by an intensity that we cannot name."

The name was alienation. "America," James Kunen jotted down. "Listen to it. *America.* I love the sound. I love what it could mean. I hate what it is." Many youth believed the nation had become a Steppenwolf, a berserk monster, a cruel society that made war on peasants abroad and at home beat up on minorities, dissidents, students, and hippies. America the Beautiful had become Amerika the Death Culture.

Opinion polls and surveys revealed a startling growth of alienation among college students during the late sixties and early seventies. By 1972 a third claimed marriage was obsolete, having children was not important, and those responding that religion, patriotism, and "living a clean, moral life" were important values plummeted 20 percentage points. Half held no living American in high regard, and over 40 percent thought America was a "sick society," did not think they shared the views of most citizens, and even considered moving to another country. As one thoughtful scholar noted, the "lesson to be learned from the turbulent youthquake is not that long hair or body odor or disrespect for traditional values are undermining the stability of America. The lesson for America is that *something is terribly wrong* with the systems that create such youthful unrest." During the entire American experience it would be difficult to find a more alienated youth than the sixties generation during the Nixon years.

It was no coincidence, then, that many youths no longer stood at sporting events as bands played the national anthem or that one of their favorite groups took the name the Grateful Dead, or that more kids were using drugs. "What is increasingly clear," wrote one participant, "is that drugs are not a dangerous shortcut to ecstasy so much as they are a device used for coping with modern society. Drugs are . . . a desperate, futile flailing at a society that increasingly rejects humanitarian values." Many agreed with Timothy Leary: "Your only hope is dope."

"There must be some way out of here," sang Jimi Hendrix. Alienation drove youth toward the counterculture, for a hippie creed was that institutions and experts had failed. The emperor had been losing his clothes throughout the decade, and after Tet, Columbia, and Chicago, he was stark raving naked. Bumper stickers appeared on colorful VW minivans: QUESTION AUTHORITY.

Thus the behavior of the dominant culture boosted the counterculture. Without racism, war, campus paternalism, police brutality, the size of hippiedom would have been proportionately about the same as the beatniks in the late fifties. There would have been more hippies, of course, because of the enormous number of baby boomers, but the counterculture would have been relatively small, confined to the usual bohemian enclaves of the East and West Coasts and a few college towns.

In fact, hippies were a strange sight in most cities before 1969. "To come to Chicago from New York," wrote an activist after the Democratic Convention, "is to come into a town where people still stare at you if you are longhaired." It was during and especially after 1968 that hip became a sign of the times. The sixties generation was graduating from crew cuts to long hair, from "Love me do" to "Why don't we do it in the road." Bell-bottoms, granny dresses, and paisley became fashion and eventually symbolized "the sixties." When students since think of the decade, they imagine people who look like hippies, when that occurred only in the last few years of the decade—and throughout the first half of the seventies.

Moreover, as baby boomers flooded campuses in the late sixties the earlier division between activists and hippies dissolved. Whereas youthful activists had called for social and political revolution earlier, after Nixon's election, "the talk . . . shifted to cultural revolution," noted a professor at Rutgers University. A University of Chicago student added that the "idea was to liberate yourself from the confining conventions of life and to celebrate the irrational side of your nature, kind of let yourself go." DO YOUR OWN THING.

What was their thing? What were their values and social thought, and what type of counterculture did they try to establish?

Values

The first value of the counter is that they rejected the values of mainstream culture. "The *first* revolution (but not of course the last) is in your own head," declared Tuli Kupferberg. "Dump out *their* irrational goals, desires, morality."

If the culture was racist, then hippies tried to be egalitarian. Young blacks and whites, of course, had been mingling throughout the decade, from civil rights marches to comrades in arms in Southeast Asia. "Our parents may have orchestrated Vietnam, but we played it, taking a curious dividend from that horror," recalled Toby Thompson. "We shook hands with black language, marijuana, G.I. hip." Black culture influenced many young whites; not only music and nonviolent activism, but sexual double standards did not seem as strict in the black community. Interracial dating became more commonplace, for civil rights workers and freaks both advocated a culture that discriminated against no one—a community of brothers and sisters.

When World War II veterans declared, "My country right or wrong," freaks shook their heads and said "Fuck the war." The Fugs sang "Kill for Peace"; the Doors, "Unknown Soldier"; and Country Joe and the Fish sang to the older generation, "You can be the first ones in your block/To have your boy come home in a box." Hippies ridiculed selective service, referring to the military as the "armed farces."

When the silent majority talked about "traditional values," freaks became the sixties generation's cultural shock troops, especially with their dress and language. Hair. "I never could tell where my husband's sideburns ended and his mustache began," said a baby boomer, "but he didn't care as long as it irritated his mother." Language. What could be more vulgar, more filthy, most hippies thought, than racial hatred and the war. "What is obscene?" one wrote. "Is it obscene to fuck, or Is it obscene to kill? . . . Why is free hate socially acceptable while free love is socially unacceptable? Which is really obscene?"

Because most citizens held dear the Establishment, hippies mocked them. "Institutions—schools, hospitals, courts," wrote a freak, "have become the ghouls, vampires, werewolves of our culture, the Frankensteins of our way of life." Hippies also blasted the church, an attack that had been initiated by many activist theologians such as James Groppi, Paul Moore, and Daniel and Philip Berrigan. The Reverend Malcolm Boyd spoke of a small but expanding group of committed men and women who were "forcing changes on the church from the middle and bottom," and he labeled it the Underground Church. Hippies joined the crusade. Arlo Guthrie sang "the streets of heaven have all been sold," and actors in the rock musical *Jesus Christ Superstar* asked Christ, "Who are you, what have you sacrificed?"

The counterculture aimed to sacrifice the society's cherished "bigger and better," "new and improved" way of life. What was progress? "At General Electric," the ad went, "progress is our most important product." Was new really improved, or was this progress simply the buy, buy ethic of the throwaway society? Hippies rejected the continual feast of consumption. They wanted to escape the suburban trap, the split-level house, the two kids and a dog, and they wanted to avoid becoming a "Nowhere Man," sang the Beatles, who "doesn't have a point of view, knows not where he's going to."

And because straights desired to make money, freaks scorned materialism, the 8-to-5 gray flannel day, the race for the almighty dollar. "All of us started to realize," wrote a hippie, "that the game of life played in school and the Supermarket U. leads only to Styrofoam coffins and oblivious servitude. . . . All are well trained towards indiscriminate consumption. Yet the feeling persists—there must be something greater than this!"

Hippies aimed to be "free from property hang-ups, free from success fixations, free from positions, titles, names, hierarchies, responsibilities, schedules, rules, routines, regular habits." Free. "I believe one of the major problems of our time is to teach people to do nothing," Lou Gottlieb noted. "Americans are all karma yogis, people who literally can't sit still." Sit back and relax, Gottlieb advised. Go with the flow: LET IT BE.

Instead of the normal life, musician Berry Melton recalled, "We were setting up a new world . . . that was going to run parallel to the old world but have as little to do with it as possible. We just weren't going to deal with straight people." Indeed, hippies considered the late sixties the dawning of the Age of Aquarius, a joyous, bright time, a new morning. "Here comes the sun," proclaimed the Beatles, and the musicians in *Hair* sang out, "Let the sun shine."

Sunlight flowed in, exposing *values* that hippies felt were positive, healthy—building a peaceful, gentle society that discriminated against no one and practiced love. "All you need is love," they sang. Another wrote, "Love is other, love is being and letting be, love is gentle, love is giving and love is dropping out, love is turning on, love is a trip, a flower, a smile, a bell." Other values were honesty, tolerance, personal freedom, and fun. Hugh Romney of the Hog Farm stated a hippie truism: "Do anything you want as long as nobody gets hurt." IF IT FEELS GOOD, DO IT.

Freaks did many things their parents had told them to reject, especially drugs and sex. Dope felt good. Dope was fun, and "dope" was the usual name, as a hippie explained in Atlanta's *Great Speckled Bird*:

> *Dope not Drugs—alcohol is a drug, pot is DOPE; nicotine is a DRUG, acid is DOPE; DRUGS turn you off, dull your senses, give you the strength to face another day in Death America, DOPE turns you on, heightens sensory awareness, sometimes twists them out of shape and you experience that too, gives you vision and clarity, necessary to create Life from Death.*

Dope helped hippies escape, of course, especially from the Establishment. "If it hadn't been for grass," said a freak, "I'd still be wearing a crew cut and saluting the flag." Dope also helped them expand or alter their own consciousness. Timothy Leary recalled his first LSD trip, the "most shattering experience of my life" for it "flipped my consciousness into a dance of energy, where nothing existed except whirring vibrations and each illusory form was simply a different frequency." While the Byrds soared "Eight Miles High," others declared their cosmic trips brought them closer to religion, or as an observer wrote, "a spiritual agility and a gracefulness which leads them to believe that they have achieved an unusual unification of the mind, the soul and the senses."

Thus, by taking dope, hippies felt different, Heads versus Straights, counter versus culture. "Grass opened up a new space for middle-class white kids," recalled Jay Stevens, "an inner space as well as outer space. It became a ritual—sitting around with your friends, passing a joint from person to person, listening to music, eating, talking, joking, maybe making out—all the senses heightened."

Generally, hippies used marijuana and its more potent form, hashish, which produced a quiet euphoria, or hallucinogens or psychedelics such as peyote or LSD, which expanded sensory perception. The idea was simple: dope that expanded psychological experience or felt good was fine; others that decreased perception, "downers," made one sick, or were physically addicting, "bummers." "I would like to suggest that you don't use speed, and here's why," cautioned musician Frank Zappa: "it is going to mess up your heart, mess up your liver, your kidneys, rot out your mind. In general, this drug will make you just like your mother and father."

Hippies made their own decisions, of course, and they violated these norms—even their own—because they enjoyed experimenting. Nevertheless, various surveys reported that at the beginning of the sixties only 4 percent of youth, 18 to 25, had tried marijuana, and that 12 years later that figure was almost 50 percent, 60 percent for college students, and much higher at some universities. Underground papers conducted their own unscientific surveys, and although unreliable, it appears that of those who responded usually 80 or 90 percent smoked marijuana, half to two-thirds had experimented with LSD, and perhaps 10 percent had tried hard drugs.

A majority of the sixties generation, then, tried marijuana, and many more attempted to liberate themselves from the older generation's sexual mores. Elders had taught children Puritan values that sex was reserved for married adults. Youth must avoid premarital sex and promiscuity, and rumors abounded that masturbation caused everything from blindness to hand warts. The sledgehammer to prevent such behavior was GUILT. Freaks rebelled, calling those ideas "hang-ups" and advocating "free love." They did not invent the idea, of course, for armed with birth control pills the sixties generation had been experimenting at college and sexual freedom leagues had been established earlier in the Bay Area and New York City. But freaks expanded the idea so sex seemed freer than at any time in memory. "Let's spend the night together" wailed the Rolling Stones as Janis Joplin advised her sisters to "get it while you can." As the airwaves became filled with blatant demands, freaks donned buttons: "Save Water: Shower with a Friend." Marriage was irrelevant, for as a hippie wrote, "A legal contract for a sexual relationship is, if not out of date, at least beside the point for most of us." This was different from a college kid "getting laid," they claimed. Free love meant a couple "making love," any time, any form, out of wedlock, and especially without guilt. "Make love," wrote a freak, "not to one guy or chick who you grab onto and possess out of fear and loneliness—but to all beautiful people, all sexes, all ages."

Hippie writings often were sexist by later standards because the counterculture developed before women's liberation. Sales of underground papers soared when they began publishing "personal" columns in which men would advertise for "groovy chicks who like to smoke weed and ball." In New York City, Underground Enterprises established a dating service called FUK: "For Turned-on people only. Heads Do the Matching." Guys could apply by sending five dollars, "girls apply free." By the end of the decade, however, freaks became aware of equality in free love and more tolerant of all forms of sexuality—masturbation, homosexuality, bisexuality. To them, sexual liberation meant all private acts between consenting people should be legal and probably attempted.

The counterculture also rejected the elders' fear of nudity, "dirty, shame," and underground papers were filled with nude couples skinny-dipping in ponds, sunbathing, and holding hands and singing. Beach areas near hippie enclaves suddenly witnessed a surprising number of topless young women, and some freaks even began protesting in the buff because, according to a San Francisco commune, disrobing prevented police from attacking demonstrators.

Yet sexual behavior and smoking dope usually was behavior conducted behind closed doors: dress was for the public, and it was a symbol. Hair represented rebellion from the crew cut cold war era, declared independence from Mom and Pop, and identified one with the counterculture. "Almost cut my hair," sang Crosby, Stills, and Nash, but instead they let their "freak flag fly," because, as Nash stated later, "If they had long hair you knew how they thought, that they were into good music, a reasonable life, that they probably hated the government." Hip men threw out sport coats and ties, and hip women abandoned cosmetics, girdles, and bras, and for the first time in memory revealed the soft contours of unbound bodies. "Long hair, beards, no bras and freaky clothes represent a break from Prison Amerika," declared Jerry Rubin, as clothes became costumes and costumes became clothes.

The older generation was appalled: "You can't tell the boys from the girls," during a time when even a beard on a businessman raised eyebrows. But freaks had different ideas about dress—and cleanliness. Although they did bathe, of course, they were not dismayed by the smell of the human body, for it was natural and a revolt against TV commercial values. They felt that deodorant, cosmetics, perfume, cologne were phony, Madison Avenue, and people should smell their bodies, for each individual's scent was different: "You're beautiful." If they desired a scent then they lit incense or wore musk oil, a secretion of the male musk deer. They abandoned synthetic clothing in favor of natural leather and cotton and ate fresh foods without preservatives and grown organically.

Hippies desired a "laid-back" lifestyle. Many critics labeled them "lazy," and parents complained, "You're throwing your life away. You don't know how hard it was for us." But that missed the point about hip values of work and play. "Life should be ecstasy," said Allen Ginsberg, and freaks *worked* to escape daily drudgery and to discover their own pleasureful existence. "What's your thing?" Many held jobs they liked, and others labored to build their vision of the future, either part or full time. Margy Kittredge asked, "Why should we work 12 or 16 hours a day now when we don't have to? For a color TV? For wall-to-wall carpeting? An automatic ice-cube maker?" And Tuli Kupferberg summarized, "Believe me when I say, if you enjoy it, it can still be good; it can still be 'work' (only we'll call it 'play'). Play is as good as work. Work has been defined as something you *dislike* doing. Fuck that. Do the Beatles *work*? Who cares."

Another counterculture value was brotherhood, which of course included everyone with similar lifestyles. "He ain't heavy, he's my brother," sang the Hollies, and the Beatles urged everyone to "Come together." The idea was simple, the *North Country News* editorialized. "You and I are part of the dawning of an age of sharing and cooperation. . . . LOVE ONE ANOTHER RIGHT NOW." Community: Help each other build the new culture.

Social Thought

Counterculture values continued developing during the Age of Aquarius. What resulted was a hippie social thought that never was static but always flowing and bubbling because one of their ideas was the continual need to experiment. "Change jobs, spouses, hairstyles, clothes; change religion, politics, values, even the personality; try everything, experiment constantly, accept nothing as given." An endless experiment: How? Search out, seek what had not been allowed, what was not real. As Tim Leary said, "It becomes necessary for us to go out of our minds in order to use our heads."

Far out. Hippies agreed with Plato's ancient maxim that a life unexamined is not worth living. Seek, look inside, demanded communards Ramon Sender and Alicia Bay Laurel, for your own wisdom "can rename you, reclothe you, give you dances, exercises and meditations, ceremonies and recognitions of divinity in everyday life that make your whole day an act of being radiantly blissful." Some hippies looked inside gently, conversations or meditations on a sunny afternoon; for others, the search was a continual excursion as they donned backpacks, put out their thumbs, and caught the disease—wanderlust. "If the vibes are good, I'll stay on," Joanie said about New Jerusalem commune; "if not, I've heard about a Zen group in the Sierras

I'd like to look into." Freaks hit the road, Keep on Truckin', and the quest did not end at U.S. borders. The demand for passports doubled, and by the end of the decade about 800,000 young Americans were traveling in Europe while over a million were thumbing throughout the nation. "We weren't fleeing home," said one, "we were seeking one."

Another hip social thought was humor, for because they grew up in the straight and narrow fifties, most hippies enjoyed making fun of society and celebrating the weird. Buttons: "Reality is a nice place to visit, but I wouldn't want to live there." "People who live in glass houses shouldn't get stoned." They delighted in making preposterous statements: "It will be an LSD country in fifteen years," claimed Tim Leary, and the "Supreme Court will be smoking marijuana." At Cornell they challenged the mayor of Ithaca to an arm-wrestling match because they believed in "armed struggle"; the "Manhattan Indians" at Columbia demanded return of the Indian head nickel, no classes on Sitting Bull's birthday, and a complete amnesty for Geronimo. Freaky students attended ROTC drills where they lampooned the cadets by playing leapfrog or blowing bubbles. New York hippies advocated a "loot-in" of Macy's department store, and the Berkeley *Barb* spread the Great Banana Conspiracy, claiming that kids could get a legal high by drying banana peels and smoking the inside scrapings. They had the government fooled; the Food and Drug Administration actually did experiments and declared the fruit was a "good source of potassium and fiber." Freaks laughed all the way to the Cheech and Chong movies.

Money usually wasn't such a laughing matter. How could hippies "afford" their lifestyle? Some freaks were employed, usually holding temporary jobs to earn "bread," saving up for a few weeks, then retiring, which became a familiar pattern. With the economy growing and jobs plentiful, it was easy to find temporary employment. Some collected food stamps; others lived off their savings, parents, or friends. Some sold dope, and many hippies established legal businesses, from underground newspapers, to "head shops," to whole food cooperatives, to FM radio stations, all of which were novel. The Yellow Submarine in Oregon made granola; Maharaj Ashram opened a whole-food restaurant in Santa Fe. Many rural communes produced food, livestock, and crafts, selling them at local markets. A few hippies actually became wealthy, including many musicians and rock promoters. Jann Wenner and Ralph Gleason founded one of the most successful undergrounds, *Rolling Stone,* and Stewart Brand published a how-to guide for the counterculture, *The Whole Earth Catalog,* which eventually sold a million copies. Britishers Tony and Maureen Wheeler produced the *Lonely Planet* guidebooks for hippies with international wanderlust, and a couple of Colorado freaks picked herbs for natural teas and then sold their company, Celestial Seasonings.

But most hippies just got by, and they did not need much money, which was part of their social thought: they desired a simple, antimaterialistic lifestyle. "It wasn't hard to drop out," one communard stated. "I had a lot of things to get rid of—a car, a hi-fi, a million useless things. . . . I got rid of it all. It was like getting a good load off." Living cheap became an art, and being poor was hip in America's throwaway society. Stores traditionally selling secondhand goods, Salvation Army and Goodwill Industries, witnessed scores of longhairs in their checkout lines. Freaks also scavenged, or as the Heathcote Community called it, "The Fine Art of Trashmongering." They reported the free plunder from just one evening in a junkyard: an elegant stuffed lion, only needing a wash; a pencil and a watering can; and a "blue blazer, nearly new condition, and emblazoned with the words 'College Bound,' which we removed."

Hippies debated about money and if their businesses should make a profit, but they did not debate nature: freaks were environmentalists. They did not invent the movement, of course, but hippies boosted ecology and spread the word. "Don't give me no hand me down world," The Guess Who demanded, and Joni Mitchell lamented, "They paved paradise and put up a parking lot." Instead, freaks tried to establish "people's parks" in the cities. "HEAD for the Park," wrote a Seattle kid, "a park is for living things, squirrels, children, growing things, turned-on things, people, love, food, lush green colors, laughter, kites, music, God, the smell of life." Some even attempted to organize and work with conservation groups; freaks in Eugene, Oregon, formed CRAP, Cyclists Revolting Against Pollution, "to show people there are ways to move other than foul automobiles spewing death." Others left the cities to grow organic food at their farms and communes, and some tried to develop an "Earth People's Park," a large ranch for their generation in New Mexico or Colorado.

Counterculture social thought also included a spiritual quest. As institutions and authorities appeared to be faltering, many asked, What is moral or amoral? Their answers and experiments took them on a voyage that ranged from astrology, to Hare Krishna, to LSD, to Taoism, to Zen—and back to Jesus. The idea of an underground church appealed to hippies. It was not that the new generation no longer believed in a supreme being, but they felt that answers to salvation no longer could be found at the established altars.

As early as the Summer of Love, Christian freaks opened a coffee shop in Haight-Ashbury to help kids on dope and talk about the Bible. The idea spread rapidly because some hippies identified with Christianity, especially the communal type practiced in the first century. In flyers they declared Jesus was the "notorious leader of an underground liberation movement" and his appearance was the "typical hippie type—long hair, beard, robe, sandals." To many youth, Jesus was a rebel, who, like them, challenged the Establishment. As a hippie wrote, "Did you ever happen to think what would happen if Jesus were to come down to earth again. What would the typical American think? He would probably be thinking, 'Look at that disgusting hippie. Probably high on something, preaching peace, happiness and goodwill.'"

Other hip religions flourished. Young Catholics began thinking about St. Francis of Assisi, who left a wealthy Italian family to live in poverty. Some Jewish youth began considering Hillel, the first century B.C. prophet who urged modesty and peace. Others joined the *havurot* movement, fellowships that emphasized experimental worship and communal living. Many other hippies developed an interest in Zen Buddhism, Hare Krishna, and the beliefs of Native Americans. "A day will come when a people with white skin will walk our lands," stated an Indian prophecy, "their hair and clothing will be as ours and they will adopt our customs. We will know them because even their name will sound like our name . . . Hopi." Most hip religions usually were tolerant of other creeds and did not have a rigid deity. They often emphasized the discovery of the inner self, helping one to "get it together," while seeking affirmation and individualism within a community of brothers and sisters.

Counterculture social thought generally paralleled two themes that often appeared in the lives of many hippies. Some rebelled and searched for personal liberation, and the freedom they practiced often was unstructured, libertarian, even anarchistic. Through experimentation, they often grew into what they felt was a more independent and holistic person. Others rebelled, tasted freedom, and rushed to a more authoritarian form of counterculture; they often joined spiritual retreats or ashrams, where leaders or gurus developed a more structured, disciplined day and members practiced religious beliefs aimed at personal growth or inner development. Both of these avenues aimed to balance self-realization and fulfillment with community, and the eventual results depended on each individual.

Builders of the Dawn

All the while, hippies developed their alternative society; they dropped out of society and became "builders of the dawn." Some trucked up to the country while a larger number remained in cities. Both built various types of hip enclaves they called communes, cooperatives, collectives, or communities, all difficult to define because freaks interchanged these names and because those living arrangements always were evolving. There probably were over 2,000 rural and at least 5,000 urban communes by 1970, housing some 2 to 3 million hippies, but no one knows the exact number because most residents or communards wanted to be left alone and would not reply to surveys.

Earlier, during the Summer of Love, pioneers established a few rural communes. Musician Lou Gottlieb founded Morning Star outside of San Francisco for anyone who wanted to practice "voluntary primitivism," and other colorful freaks established the Hog Farm, "an expanded family, a mobile hallucination, a sociological experiment, an army of clowns." But the stunning growth of communes appeared after turbulent 1968. "I had done the political trip for a while," wrote a communard, "but I got to the point where I couldn't just advocate social change, I had to live it."

Eventually, many different types of people joined the "back to the land" movement—artists, visionaries, ecologists, radicals, academics, vegetarians, gays, organic farmers, Vietnam veterans, urban professionals, along with some who left personal problems behind such as former drug abusers, people leaving bad marriages, women searching for more liberation. Many were students. At the end of the decade, a survey of college youth found a third were interested in spending time in a commune or collective and almost half wanted to live for a while in a rural setting. Consequently, most communards were in their twenties, middle class, and had attended some college. Almost everyone felt trapped in mainstream society, alienated from the policies of their government and from materialistic, violent America. They usually were searching for new values in their own community. "What they all had in common was the highest human aspiration," stated one observer: "to be free."

Communards naturally experimented with personal freedom and liberation. Some of the early communes advocated completely free love, where all members engaged in sexual encounters and where group sex or bisexuality might be accepted. Harrad West in Berkeley and Talsen in Oregon were "group marriages," spouses or singles who switched partners, and Bryn Athyn in Vermont practiced "sexual coziness" where members supposedly "played with each other's sexual parts without fear or guilt." But much more common were communes where hippies became partners, agreeing on various arrangements, and at some only monogamous couples could reside. Many communards used dope and perfected the idea "grow your own"; some later settlements abstained from using any drugs in an attempt to become completely natural. Daily routine varied from anarchy at Wheeler Ranch to structured schedules at Lama Foundation. Visitors were welcome anytime at some communes and they became little more than "crash pads" for hitchhiking freaks. To prevent that, other communes established visiting hours, some restricting guests to the weekends, and others allowed only those who adhered to their rules and beliefs.

Hippies developed many types of communes. Most were farms that aimed to become self-sufficient, such as Active Acres Co-operative in Wisconsin or Magic Forest Farm in Oregon. Some freaks took over an abandoned town in Minnesota and created Georgeville Trading Post, and hip architects in Colorado constructed Libre, futuristic homes located beneath the Rocky Mountains. Followers of psychologist B. F. Skinner built a society based on behavioral principles at Twin Oaks in Virginia. Hare Krishna disciples developed New Vrindabsn in West Virginia, and fundamentalist Christians established a Children of God settlement on a ranch near Brenham, Texas. Maharaj Ashram in New Mexico practiced yoga techniques and concepts, and The Farm in Tennessee blended Zen Buddhism with Hindu philosophy and a touch of Christianity.

Many more freaks resided in urban hip communities where a counter society flourished. Old Town in Chicago, Peach Street in Atlanta, West Bank in Minneapolis, Pearl Street in Austin, near Dupont Circle in Washington, D.C., and other areas in university towns like Ann Arbor, Boulder, Eugene, Isla Vista, Ithaca, Lawrence, and of course, Madison and Berkeley. "The frats are dying fast," said a hippie in Madison, "and some of them have been taken over by collectives—frats turning into communes!" These communities were easy to find. Ask any longhair, and soon one would be walking down a street where on the STOP sign was painted WAR, where someone was throwing a Frisbee for a dog, and where a few freaks would be talking, "rapping," on the porch of a brightly painted old house, American flag curtains floating in the breeze. Crosby, Stills, Nash, and Young melodies drifting out to the street, along with the smell of musk or grass.

Urban collectives came in many colors. Many were political, such as the Kate Richards O'Hare Collective near Cornell University, which was based on socialistic ideals, or the South End commune that had been formed by SDS members in Boston, or Reba Place, a Christian social action commune in Evanston. Members worked in their communities on various programs and at times formed umbrella groups such as the Seattle Liberation Front. Many freaky students developed college collectives, where some went to school and others worked, both usually part time, and religious adherents established numerous spiritual communes. Feminists eager to discuss new women's issues formed Bread and Roses Collective in Boston, and gay men established 95th Street Collective in New York. Soldiers returning from Vietnam organized the Veteran's Collective in San Francisco.

Psychedelic buses often carried hippies
to musical "happenings" and to their communes.

Tribal Gatherings

That was how hippies tried to live, but when we consider the counterculture few think about daily life in a commune; instead, we usually recall rock festivals. Music was important, for along with underground newspapers, music was a carrier of the counterculture. Both spread the word, spread the cultural movement. Music festivals were a "gathering of the tribe," freaks coming together to do their own thing—beyond the norms and laws of mainstream society.

By 1969 hippies had held festivals in numerous venues, from Monterey to Miami, from Seattle to New Orleans, and that year over 100,000 appeared at the Atlanta and Atlantic City pop festivals. But it was Woodstock that was destined to become the most famous of the era, to live on in mythology. Woodstock began as a commercial enterprise. The four producers offered Max Yasgur $50,000 to use his 1,000-acre farm near Bethel, New York. They hoped 50,000 people would come to "The Woodstock Music and Art Fair: An Aquarian Exposition" and pay $18 for three days to hear over two dozen bands, including Jimi Hendrix, Janis Joplin, Joan Baez, The Who, The Grateful Dead, Country Joe and the Fish, and Crosby, Stills, Nash, and Young.

Yet Woodstock became much, much more. Before the first band began to play, a pilgrimage of young people streamed toward Yasgur's farm in unprecedented numbers, clogging the roads for miles, creating the most massive traffic jam in New York history. The kids rarely honked, and instead they took out their guitars and tambourines and played songs, shared foods and drinks, passed joints in perhaps the most patient jam of the decade. By evening the colorful horde was flooding into the farm and pitching tents and tepees. Eventually 400,000 were camped, and one reported that as far as he could see there were young people "walking, lying down, drinking, eating, reading, singing. Kids were sleeping, making love, wading in the marshes, trying to milk the local cows and trying to cook the local corn."

"We were exhilarated," one participant recalled. "We felt as though we were in liberated territory." They were, and because their numbers overwhelmed local authorities, police made little attempt to enforce drug or nudity laws as the counterculture exposed its own values. "We used to think of ourselves as little clumps of weirdos," said Janis Joplin. "But now we're a whole new minority group."

The gathering of the tribe, however, also was ripe for disaster. Overcrowding created nightmares. Sanitation facilities were inadequate and some waited an hour to relieve themselves. Toilets overflowed. The hungry crowd consumed a half million hamburgers and hot dogs on the first day and food ran out, as did almost all drinkable water. Dope was sold and given away openly, and many consumed too much. Medical supplies became dangerously low, and the traffic jam meant that musicians, medicine, doctors, and food had to be flown in by helicopter at tremendous expense. Then the rains came, and came, and people huddled and slept in meadows that turned to mud.

Before the music began the first evening, a voice boomed out of the speakers: "We're going to need each other to help each other work this out, because we're taxing the systems that we've set up. We're going to be bringing the food in. But the one major thing that you have to remember tonight is that the man next to you is your brother." For many participants, the growing sense of community turned this rock festival into an unforgettable countercultural experience. "Everyone needed other people's help, and everyone was ready to share what he had as many ways as it could be split up. Everyone could feel the good vibrations."

Good vibes even affected many of the older generation. Bethel residents talked to the kids, and then opened soup and sandwich kitchens, and left their hoses running for drinking and bathing. The Establishment's press even praised the hippies: "For three days nearly half a million people lived elbow to elbow in the most exposed, crowded, rain-drenched, uncomfortable kind of community," *Life* exclaimed, "and there wasn't so much as a fist fight." The *New York Times* added, "Hippies have never been so successful."

Woodstock, of course, affected each participant differently, but in some way most leaving felt warm, and they sang along with Joni Mitchell:

> *We are stardust*
> *We are golden*
> *And we've got to get ourselves*
> *Back to the garden*

If hippies could stay in the garden, cultivating their culture, many thought it could happen—a cultural revolution. Many in the sixties generation began talking about the birth of a New America. The old nation had struggled with race and war, and the new one, they dreamt, would have a culture committed to peace and love, an idea popularized in numerous undergrounds and by Abbie Hoffman in *Woodstock Nation*.

The Empire Strikes Back

As this form of "the dream" began to emerge for the counterculture, the Establishment presented another interpretation; in autumn 1969 the press published a cold-blooded story from California: "Sharon Tate, Four Others Murdered," proclaimed the *Los Angeles Times:* RITUALISTIC SLAYINGS. To many in the Establishment, this was the beginning of the end of the hippies—and of the sixties.

During the next months police reported crimes committed "by a group of hippies known as 'The Family' under the leadership of Charles Manson." *Newsweek* labeled the trial the "Case of the Hypnotic Hippie." *Time* wrote about "a weird story of a mystical, semi-religious hippie drug-and-murder cult led by a bearded, demonic Mahdi," and ran an article about "Hippies and Violence," quoting a doctor that hippies "can be totally devoid of true compassion. That is the reason why they can kill so matter-of-factly." TV turned the trial into a spectacle. Presto: the silent majority was convinced. Manson was a hippie, and longhairs could be killers.

Actually, as a few journalists reported and court documents proved, Manson was insane. His mother was a prostitute and he never knew his father. During his first 35 years he spent more than 20 either in foster homes, juvenile detention centers, or in prison. By the time he was 20 a state psychiatrist labeled him a sociopathic personality. Nevertheless, he was paroled, and drifted to Haight-Ashbury, where he impressed some unstable teenage females, runaways whom he had sex with, sometimes three a day. In 1969 he had been arrested four times, and he often stopped priests and claimed he was Jesus Christ.

Hippies loathed Manson, for he gave people with long hair a bad name, and as one claimed, he represented a "social category, a demon hippie, a symbol of 'What can happen to your son or daughter.'" But he fascinated the silent majority, because his case raised a horrific possibility—hippies with guns—and it also had another stimulating ingredient—hippie sex. "The idea that communal life is a sexual smorgasbord is a myth created and sustained by the media," noted a social scientist. "Much of the media fascination with Charles Manson and his covey of willing women can be explained by the fact that he personally staged many men's fondest sexual fantasies." That seemed to be the case, for when a journalist went undercover and grew long hair and a beard to report on the counterculture, businessmen approached him and inquired about his "sexual habits. . . . These guys just seemed to assume that because I was hairy I was some kind of incredible stud, getting laid constantly." Richard Atcheson's experiences helped him understand why so many citizens loathed hippies: "They are presumed to be sexually free, and they have to be hated for that."

Manson remained in the headlines that December as the Rolling Stones announced a free concert at Altamont Speedway near Livermore, California, a festival that many older citizens felt was the second example that proved what they suspected all along—the counterculture was going mad.

Just four months after already famous Woodstock, hip Californians were eager to have "Woodstock West." Some 300,000 appeared at Altamont, most of them were good-natured, but close to the stage about 50 became violent, many drunk or stoned. In perhaps the most shortsighted move in the history of rock, the Stones gave $500 worth of beer to the Hell's Angels motorcycle gang with orders to guard the stage. When the crowd moved closer to the music, when some drugged kids began to dance wildly, the motorcycle thugs beat them, busting pool cues over heads. As Mick Jagger sang "Street Fighting Man," the Angels grabbed a young black, Meredith Hunter, stabbed him repeatedly and kicked in his face. Horrified and stunned, the crowd did nothing. Hunter died in a pool of blood.

Altamont disgusted hippies. "The Failure of the Counter Culture" wrote one, and a participant called it "Pearl Harbor to the Woodstock Nation" while another lamented, "It made you want to go home. It made you want to puke."

More important, Altamont gave mainstream society more ammunition for their attack on the counterculture. *Business Week* claimed that "Middle America has come to view festivals as harbingers of dope, debauchery, and destruction," and state and local officials drafted regulations aimed at preventing rock festivals. While businesses across the nation put up door signs, "No Shirt, No Shoes, No Service," police continued illegal harassment. In Charlotte, North Carolina, officers raided and searched hippie houses without warrants, Boston cops arrested 200 on the Commons for "idleness," and Nevada officers arrested three longhairs with money for vagrancy and held them for 50 days before trial. New Orleans police even arrested a hip female in jeans for "wearing the clothes of the opposite sex." Moreover, officials held countless raids, "drug busts," and trials that were of dubious legality. Two dozen policemen and narcotic agents invaded Wheeler Ranch in California without a search warrant, and later, 150 launched a predawn assault: "Many people were awakened staring up the barrel of a gun," Bill Wheeler reported, which led to the demise of the commune. In Michigan, officials arrested cultural activist John Sinclair, who gave two joints to an undercover agent in Detroit. The state judge sentenced Sinclair to ten years in prison, prompting John Lennon and Yoko Ono to participate in a rally that drew 15,000 people chanting, "Free John now." After he spent two years in jail, federal courts threw out the case.

But the most publicized case was in Berkeley. For years the University of California had owned a parcel of vacant land located a few blocks from the campus. In 1969 hippies began to plant trees, grass, and flowers; they set up camp and declared a "people's park." A festive mood prevailed, with daily happenings. But to university officials, the freaks were trespassing, and one daybreak they sent the police, who chased the kids out and built a fence. By noon, 1,000 hippies and students marched to take back the park. Street fighting erupted. Police shot buckshot into the crowd, hurting 30, and mortally wounding one. Although 80 percent of the faculty and students, along with the Berkeley City Council, voted to develop a park, Governor Reagan stated the Establishment's view of the counterculture: "No more appeasement." He sent the National Guard in full battle gear, and they installed martial law, made random arrests, and occupied the campus. Nevertheless, students still conducted rallies, and the governor responded with helicopters, which sprayed potent tear gas on campus. As students cried or vomited (many in class), the governor declared, "If it takes a bloodbath, let's get it over with."

The behavior of the culture did not stifle the counterculture; just the opposite, it stimulated more alienation and hippiedom blossomed from coast to coast. The political middle continued to collapse, and the generation gap expanded to its largest size since the twenties. Spiro Agnew's daughter was hanging out with hippies (often followed by cameramen and secret service agents), and one mom said about her hitchhiking son, "He's gone. Far away. Dead." The "war at home," one observer labeled it, who suggested the nation's greatest internal conflict was "not between the rich and the poor, or the black and the white, or even the young and the old, but the people with long hair and the people with short hair."

"America Will Never Be the Same Again"

By the end of the sixties the counter was already having a subversive impact on the culture. Hippies had infiltrated the very foundations of the Establishment—government, business, universities, religion, even the U.S. armed forces. "Everything is being attacked," said a government official late in 1969. "The values that we held so dear are being shot to hell." *Newsweek* agreed, writing that "middle-class values are under more obdurate attack today than ever before." During the early seventies cultural activists were running for office on campuses and for city councils, participating in "smoke-ins" and marching for the decriminalization of marijuana, developing people's parks and nude beaches, holding university conferences on their own lifestyles, even smoking dope and challenging military orders in Vietnam. Corporations noticed that youthful employees had long hair and were more interested in "corporate responsibility" and the "quality of life" than the profit motive. And the counterculture spread, as more hippies appeared with long gray braided hair. "Flower Power," wrote an observer, "is as revolutionary as Black Power, and after it America will never be the same again."

Nor would many Americans, for the counterculture often was a personal movement. Was it a success? Did they get back to the garden? Some times. Some places. Other times and other places they did not. As mundane as it sounds, hippies were simply people who possessed all the human frailties as those in the Establishment. For many of the sixties generation, the counterculture was just a lark, a time to smoke weed and get laid, a long party. The hippie lifestyle of dope, free love, music, and values of brotherhood and sharing invited phonies, freeloaders, runaways, drug dealers, and various self-appointed preachers and zealots. There were weak people who were lost, who could not think for themselves, those who would allow others to boss them, those who would join cults and submit to various hip heroes and gurus. A thousand rock stars, 100,000 lost groupies. And there were the criminals who grew long hair, the vicious drug runners who stalked teens searching for a free high and free love. Ed Sanders noted the counterculture was a noble experiment but that so many were vulnerable, "like a valley of thousands of plump white rabbits surrounded by wounded coyotes."

There were many casualties who never understood "freedom." "Freedom is a difficult thing to handle," wrote communard Richard Fairfield. "Give people freedom and they'll do all the things they thought they never had a chance to do. But that won't take very long. And after that? After that, my friend, it'll be time to make your life meaningful." Freedom was not free; it took responsibility to make a meaningful life. It was easy, even vogue, to revolt against authority, but then what? Many never answered, and to them freedom meant any behavior, no matter how self-destructive, rude, amoral, or crazy, leaving scores of strung-out kids and unwed mothers.

Hip behavior naturally caused problems. The emphasis on experimentation often meant pushing life to extremes. Eventually, most freaks realized dope had diminishing returns, was no longer an experiment. Others found the ultimate downer, as too many overdosed in too many ways, including Jim Morrison, Janis Joplin, Jimi Hendrix, Pigpen of the Grateful Dead. Untold numbers had bad trips, or worse. Problems also became apparent at communes and collectives. Many freaks admitted they had a difficult time sharing everything, overcoming jealousies and hatred, and at times stronger personalities often dominated the weaker as free-flowing anarchy slipped toward authoritarianism. Interpersonal relations strained quickly at free love communes where one shared soul and body. Talsen, for example, lasted only a year and eventually became a settlement of Jesus People. Freeloading forced many communes to build gates, even post guards. Musician Neil Young closed his open ranch because he had too many people hanging around who "lived off me, used my money to buy things, used my telephone to make their calls. General leeching."

Some communes lasted weeks, others lasted years, some probably still exist. At most of them, however, life was much more difficult than hippies had imagined when they left the city. "I remember having soybeans for breakfast, lunch, and dinner, and nothing else," recalled Cynthia Bates of The Farm. "Having kids made you more sensitive to the lack of necessities . . . how long could you live in a house with fifty other people?" Especially a house with no running water, no flush toilet, no electricity. After a while, many began to ask, What's the point?

Moreover, hip became fad, meaning more longhairs looked the part, preached counterculture values, but fewer practiced them. When businessmen marched to work in suits with flared trousers wearing paisley ties, when pickup drivers grew ponytails, the cultural revolution was in demise, and with it the community and its values. Communes and collectives locked doors as theft became too common in hip communities. After someone stole stereo equipment from Abbie Hoffman, he announced his "resignation" from the counterculture.

How can the counterculture be evaluated? Reliable surveys and statistics do not exist, so it is difficult to judge. Subsequently, most assessments have been personal and emotional. Many of the older generation loathed the children for rejecting traditional values, and many kids loathed the parents for holding on to what they considered archaic beliefs. To longhairs the question if the counterculture was a failure or success missed the point. Hippies were not taking a college course, trying to pass an exam, earn a grade, get ahead. The counterculture looked at it a different way. How good were communes? Compared to what, they asked, the best or the worst families in America? How good was living together versus marriage? Compared to what, the best or worst marriages? The fact that they experimented with their lifestyle was success enough for most of them, for they no longer were normal. They had been different; they had dropped out of mainstream culture, challenged their past. They had considered their existence on planet earth, and in some ways, many had changed their lives. As Richard Fairfield wrote, "If, through participation in the communal experience, individuals feel more alive and fulfilled (greater awareness of self and others, etc.), such a commune must be deemed a success."

For the most part, then, the counterculture was an individual experience, affecting each participant differently. Some like Richard Fairfield grew into a more aware, holistic person, and some like Jimi Hendrix overdosed on the experiment and committed the ultimate downer.

Whatever the case, the counter challenged and transformed the culture. Hippies sought liberation from established values, and as their numbers grew they altered the consensus that had dominated the nation throughout the cold war era. By 1969 a "sixties culture" was developing, one that included a mélange of hippies, activists, students, minorities, and feminists. Like the counterculture, they never were organized, but together they transformed the movement from social activism focused on civil rights, campus issues, and war to a sixties culture interested in liberation and empowerment.

In 1970 two very different people published similar books. Antiwar activist Mitchell Goodman produced *The Movement Toward a New America,* and Yale Professor Charles Reich wrote the best-seller *The Greening of America.* They both came to the same conclusion: "There is a revolution coming," declared Reich, one that Goodman proclaimed "penetrates the churches, the army, the theater, the high schools. . . . It is sexual, political, cultural." Reich added, "It promises a higher reason, a more human community, and a new and liberated individual."

The counterculture was having an impact, and Goodman and Reich were describing the emerging sixties culture. During the next few years it would transform America.

Chapter 6

Days of Discord, 1969–1970

"Bring Us Together" was Richard Nixon's campaign slogan, and by his inauguration in January 1969 most Americans desired just that: a time of national healing and unity.

Yet during that year and the next there was only one event that brought Americans together—the landing on the moon. In July, *Apollo 11* left earth and circled the moon. As lunar module *Eagle* descended, some 123 million Americans, and about a fourth of the people on earth, watched the event on TV. For a moment humanity stopped: stock markets were quiet, juries left courtrooms, classes recessed. Then, with a remarkably good picture broadcast from 250,000 miles, America won the space race: "Houston, Tranquility Base here. The *Eagle* has landed." Shortly thereafter, Neil Armstrong and then Edwin "Buzz" Aldrin Jr., walked on the lunar surface. They planted an American flag and left a plaque that said, "We came in peace for all mankind."

Unfortunately, that peace and unity lasted only a few days. Conflict emerged again, and by June 1970 a government commission wrote that division in the nation was "as deep as any since the Civil War." The president and the silent majority faced a vocal minority who were busy liberating themselves and demanding empowerment: the sixties culture confronted traditions, and the clash marked 1969 and 1970 as the days of discord.

Nixon

In the midst of this sat President Richard Nixon, a complex man who, one aide said, had a "light and a dark side." The private man was suspicious of virtually anyone who criticized his policies, and that would become his downfall. The public Nixon appeared as a statesman who had run for office on three themes: law and order, the New Federalism, and peace with honor in Vietnam.

After years of civil rights demonstrations and campus turmoil, law and order was popular with the suburban silent majority, the urban and rural white backlash, and with most Southerners. To these people, civil rights programs had gone too far, so had violence, and Nixon called for a "war on crime," doubling funds for local police forces. More importantly, the president and his attorney general, John Mitchell, felt that for the first time since the Democratic Party captured the South in the 1870s, the Republicans now had a chance to dominate Dixie. George Wallace had won 13 percent of the vote in 1968, and Nixon was determined to capture that vote in 1972.

The Mitchell–Nixon idea became known as the "southern strategy," which appeared as policy in 1969. The president opposed the extension of the Voting Rights Act, Congress passed it anyway, and the attorney general supported the state of Mississippi in arguing against integrating its school districts. The administration also opposed busing students to achieve school desegregation. A "new evil," Nixon called busing, "disrupting communities and imposing hardship on children—both black and white." Instead of busing, the president supported a "freedom of choice" plan. Students supposedly could choose which schools they wanted to attend, which resulted in very little desegregation, and was ruled unconstitutional by the Supreme Court. The Court also mandated school integration "at once" and ruled busing constitutional within a school district.

Like Eisenhower at Little Rock, Nixon grudgingly enforced the law, writing to assistant John Ehrlichman, "Do what the law requires and not *one bit* more." During 1970 most school districts finally integrated, 16 years after the *Brown* decision. Ironically, Nixon became the president identified with enforcing school integration, and as we shall see, enlarging affirmative action, both of which contributed to the days of discord. By eight to one whites opposed busing, and by two to one whites thought integration was going too fast while that same ratio of blacks thought too slow. But unlike previous attempts to challenge tradition, integration continued and did not result in major riots.

Southerners blamed the Supreme Court, not Nixon, for school integration and busing, as the president initiated another feature of his southern strategy, appointing conservative judges to the Court. But his first appointment was for chief justice, because Earl Warren resigned, and the president avoided a conflict with the Democratic Senate by nominating a popular moderate conservative, Warren Burger, who was quickly confirmed. Shortly thereafter, Abe Fortas resigned, and the president began his strategy, nominating Clement Haynsworth of South Carolina, a federal judge whose rulings had not supported integration. For the first time in 40 years, the Senate rejected a court nomination, with 17 Republicans voting against their president. Angry, Nixon then turned to Judge G. Harrold Carswell, who years before had publicly declared his "firm, vigorous belief in . . . white supremacy." Moreover, higher courts had reversed 60 percent of his rulings, raising questions of competency. The president's congressional liaison told Nixon that senators "think Carswell's a boob, a dummy. And what counter is there to that? He is." Again, the Senate rejected the nominee, this time with 13 Republicans voting against their president. Furious, Nixon proclaimed the Senate had made "vicious assaults" on his nominees because of "regional discrimination . . . they had the misfortune of being born in the South." That stance won political support in Dixie, but not in the Senate, so Nixon nominated moderate Harry Blackmun of Minnesota, who easily won confirmation.

Nixon also began his domestic response to LBJ's Great Society, the New Federalism, the idea of reducing federal programs and power and giving control and revenue back to the states. To help him, he asked Harvard professor and Democratic intellectual Daniel Patrick Moynihan. The results were intriguing. Moynihan proposed and Nixon accepted a poverty and welfare plan aimed at streamlining Democratic programs and cutting the federal bureaucracy, the Family Assistance Plan, which actually guaranteed an annual wage. Under the proposal, each impoverished family of four would receive at least $1,600 a year, plus food stamps, paid directly to the families. Eventually, the recipient would have to accept training or work, popularizing the idea of "workfare." Nixon was right in calling the plan "almost revolutionary," but Democrats thought the basic income was too low, Senator McCarthy labeling it the "Family Annihilation Plan." Conservatives were horrified. Governor Reagan called it a reward for the idle, and Nixon's young speechwriter Patrick Buchanan accused his boss of proposing a "liberal Democratic domestic program."

The Family Assistance Plan failed to pass in the Senate; yet it and other policies demonstrated that liberalism did not die with Richard Nixon's election. During his first two years in office the Republican president signed Democratic bills that increased federal regulations and irritated conservatives and some businesses. The Occupational Safety and Health Administration regulated corporations and aimed to reduce industrial accidents, and the Environmental Protection Agency (EPA) was destined to become the nation's largest regulatory agency. Nixon also expanded the federal government by creating the Drug Enforcement Agency and the Office of Management and Budget. He did not cut Great Society programs, and he continued the Model Cities program, increased funding for food stamps, Medicare, and Medicaid. Faced with a growing sixties culture, the Republican reformed the selective service system with its numerous deferments to a fairer lottery in which all 19-year-old males could be selected for military duty. Nixon also signed a bill that resulted in reducing the voting age to 18, which became the Twenty-Sixth Amendment to the Constitution.

Why did this Republican president sign so many Democratic ideas into law? In 1968 Nixon was elected with the smallest plurality since the 1912 election, only 43 percent, and he had no political coattails; the opposition party controlled both the House and the Senate. Thus Nixon knew it would be impossible to roll back LBJ's Great Society. Also, he realized that liberals and their activist allies were dominating domestic politics, and they were demanding more change. Although the president privately called one Democratic bill expanding women's rights a "monstrosity," he signed it anyway because it was "probably inevitable and not worth the flack to oppose it." As biographer Joan Hoff wrote, Nixon was an "a principled pragmatist." Moreover, he could compromise on domestic issues because he did not consider them as important as America's role in the world. "The president makes foreign policy," Nixon declared, and here there was no compromise.

The president's foreign policy was based on his cold war mentality, which was shared by his primary adviser and national security chief, Henry Kissinger, a former professor at Harvard. Yet these men would prove to be more flexible than their predecessors concerning relations with the two communist superpowers, the Soviet Union and China. "After a period of confrontation," Nixon said in his inaugural address, "we are entering a period of negotiation." The Soviets listened carefully, for during spring 1969 their relations with the Chinese had deteriorated to such an extent that the two nations were fighting on their mutual border; one armed clash left over 30 Russian troops dead. Nixon and Kissinger seized the initiative and established the policy of "détente." Accordingly, the administration would attempt to reduce world tensions with the USSR and China while creating a balance of power, with Washington holding the equilibrium between Moscow and Beijing. The United States publicly engaged the Soviets in talks about limiting strategic arms (SALT), and secretly Kissinger began contacts with the Chinese and with the North Vietnamese. The president declared the Nixon Doctrine, which called on U.S. allies to assume more responsibility for their own defense and signaled that the United States would try to avoid involvement in revolutionary wars. Détente also could help with Vietnam; the administration began pressuring the Russians, who were supposed to press the North Vietnamese to stop fighting and negotiate peace with the Americans.

Vietnam, of course, was the most important foreign policy issue. Nixon believed in the domino theory, once stating that "If the United States gives up on Vietnam, Asia will give up on the United States and the Pacific will become the Red Sea." Neither Nixon nor Kissinger understood Vietnamese nationalism and that although the Russians gave military supplies to the North Vietnamese, Moscow actually had little influence in Hanoi. To Nixon, victory depended on "the will to win—the courage to use our power," and he boasted to Kissinger that unlike Johnson, "I have the *will* in spades." Apparently, victory had nothing to do with the will of the enemy or the South Vietnamese. In 1969 Nixon said the same thing as LBJ in 1965: "I will not be the first President of the United States to lose a war."

Nixon announced his plan—Vietnamization. U.S. forces would train the South Vietnamese Army (ARVN) to fight and win the war against the Vietcong and North Vietnamese Army. Supposedly, that would allow the president to bring home U.S. troops so he could claim he was "winding down the war" while Kissinger negotiated peace with honor in Paris. Vietnamization, one critic noted, was "withdrawing with guns blazing."

Yet Vietnamization was flawed. It was not a new plan, for since the fifties U.S. troops had been training ARVN to confront the enemy, but with little success. Most ARVN soldiers did not have the desire to die defending the Saigon regime, the reason why LBJ had to send over a half million Americans to Vietnam in the first place. Moreover, Vietnamization raised a military question: Because U.S. troops were waging most of the war, how could Nixon win the conflict while demobilizing from it?

The president secretly answered that question just weeks after his inauguration: bombing. Nixon and his adviser wanted to impress the enemy that now America had a new tough team. "I refuse to believe," Kissinger told aides, "that a little fourth-rate power like North Vietnam doesn't have a breaking point." Nixon quietly presented himself to the enemy as a man of iron will who would do *anything* to win in Vietnam. The "madman theory," he called it: "We'll just slip the word to them that, 'for God's sakes, you know Nixon is obsessed about Communists. We can't restrain him when he's angry—and he has his hand on the nuclear button'—and Ho Chi Minh himself will be in Paris in two days begging for peace."

As the bombs dropped on Vietnam, Nixon secretly ordered the bombing of Cambodia, an act of dubious constitutionality. Bordering South Vietnam, Cambodia had declared neutrality and had attempted to stay out of the war, but that proved impossible. The North Vietnamese had violated its neutrality by establishing supply lines in Cambodia and Laos, the Ho Chi Minh Trail. Through this dense jungle they sent men and material into the South. Nixon and Kissinger aimed to destroy the supply lines and cut enemy troop infiltration, and so they enlarged bombing throughout Southeast Asia.

Nixon's bombing campaign was massive. In just the first two years of the administration, the United States dropped more bombs on Southeast Asia than the entire tonnage used on all its enemies in World War II. Throughout the Vietnam War, U.S. military forces dropped three times the bomb tonnage in Southeast Asia as it did during World War II, some 268 pounds of explosives for each person residing in Vietnam. Obviously, bombing did not win the hearts and minds of the people, or as historian Stephen Ambrose wrote, "The power to destroy is not the power to control."

The public, of course, did not know about the extent of the bombing or the madman theory, and most agreed the president deserved some time to wind down the war. Activists attempted to convince the administration to end the conflict as soon as possible, and on Easter Sunday 1969 hundreds of thousands marched in the first major antiwar demonstration during the Nixon administration. Enormous crowds appeared in New York, Philadelphia, and San Francisco; the largest parades to date were held in Chicago, Atlanta, and Austin.

The administration at first tried to placate critics. "Give us six months," Kissinger told peace activists, "and if we haven't ended the war by then, you can come back and tear down the White House fence." Nixon, who told an aide he could end the war by the 1970 elections, publicly pledged to cut draft calls and announced the first withdrawal—25,000 troops of about 540,000 in Vietnam.

Yet placating critics ran counter to Nixon's dark side. He was "appalled" by protesters, who he said were "mindless rioters and professional malcontents," and he announced that "under no circumstances" would he be influenced by the antiwar movement. To maintain law and order, supposedly, he began a domestic policy aimed at silencing his critics. "Those who are against us," presidential aide Egil Krogh said, "we will destroy." The administration enlarged investigations aimed at proving that the movement had links with Hanoi or Moscow. The CIA could not find any foreign ties, but the White House ordered the agency to break their charter and conduct domestic infiltration of antiwar organizations, code name Operation Chaos. Nixon also formed the Committee of Six. Composed of young conservatives such as Pat Buchanan and a former president of the Young Americans for Freedom, Tom Charles Huston, the committee encouraged the Internal Revenue Service to harass movement organizations. Moreover, the administration boosted the counterintelligence, or COINTELPRO, program, eventually employing 2,000 agents, that infiltrated, provoked disturbances, and began a massive program of "disinformation," a euphemism for "spreading lies."

As would be revealed later, the administration's behavior was shocking. After someone in the administration leaked the secret U.S. bombing of Cambodia to the press, the White House instructed the FBI to conduct illegal wiretaps of several government officials, journalists, and activists—from Kissinger's aide, Morton Halperin, to musician John Lennon. FBI informers provoked fights and shoot-outs between Black Power groups, and to discredit the Hispanic movement, agent Eustacio Martinez even attacked a U.S. senator, kicking him and smashing his car. State and local officials joined in; a brutal example was in Chicago, where police held a dawn attack on Black Panther local headquarters, spraying 90 bullets into the apartment, wounding four and killing two. Police tactics were so questionable that the *New York Times* wondered if authorities were engaged in "search and destroy campaigns rather than in legitimate law enforcement." Later, FBI documents confirmed that the raid was part of COINTELPRO, that the bureau was criminally complicit, and eventually the agency paid almost $2 million to the families of the deceased. During 1969 government repression devastated the Black Panthers and resulted in the imprisonment of hundreds of members and the deaths of at least 28.

Just months after his inauguration, then, the new president was breaking the law, yet to no avail, for his actions did not stifle the movement. In fact, the number of protesters soared because there were more baby boomers and because the reasons for activism had not disappeared with Nixon's election. Discrimination persisted, the war continued, and both divided the nation and created days of discord.

Third-World Revolutionaries and Militants

Discord was loudest on campuses throughout 1969, where minority empowerment was emerging. The sixties culture began striking at America's educational tradition, and a shocking case was San Francisco State University. With 18,000 students, the university only had about 700 black students, less than 4 percent in a city with a 20 percent black population. A hundred had banded together to form the Black Students Union (BSU), and they felt the rising tide of black consciousness and supported the idea of a "third-world revolution" in which all nonwhite peoples would empower themselves in their own communities. On campus that meant something startling: instead of classes taught by white males on the European experience, the BSU demanded that the university establish a black studies department and have black instructors teach the African American experience.

San Francisco State exemplified problems faced by many universities. At that time it was very difficult to find African American, or Mexican American, professors with advanced degrees from reputable institutions. Few had been encouraged to go to college and especially to graduate school, and so there was a national shortage. Eventually that could be alleviated by admitting more minority students, but because they often came from segregated neighborhood schools many had weak educations and could not gain normal admittance to the better undergraduate institutions, the door for graduate study and a professorship. It would take years to overcome that situation, but the civil rights campaign had sparked a demand for such classes—taught by black or brown faculty—now! At San Francisco State, BSU even insisted that the university admit all blacks applying without fees or tuition.

Late in 1968 the university agreed to hire one black professor, which enraged minority students. Tempers grew short, and meetings were filled with wild statements and angry denials. One black radical even declared that third-world students should "bring guns on campus to defend themselves against racist administrators." The radicals declared a strike—boycott classes—and after a few stormed offices, the university president called police to campus. That irritated many more students and some faculty members who joined the strike, while blacks taunted the cops, "Pigs off campus!" The police exploded into the students, nightclubs swinging, after which one radical declared to television cameras, "You can tell every racist pig in the world, including Richard Milhous Nixon, that we're not going to negotiate until our demands are met."

The board of trustees demanded that the university president keep the campus open for classes, "at the point of bayonet if necessary," declared Governor Ronald Reagan. Overwhelmed, the president resigned, and the board appointed a conservative professor, S. I. Hayakawa, to the job. He declared a "state of emergency," that the campus would be kept open by police, and that professors supporting student strikers would be fired, which enraged most faculty. When the president expelled some radicals, more angry students assembled, provoking police to march into the crowd. The scene turned bloody. A policeman was knocked unconscious and many students were beaten and arrested. While about 600 police occupied the campus, students and many faculty continued to boycott classes and demonstrate. Hayakawa responded by ordering mass arrests, some 450 students and professors at one rally, and declaring that any student arrested on campus since the beginning of the strike would be suspended.

After months of conflict both sides grew weary, and they held serious discussions during spring 1969. The administration agreed to a black studies department of 11, to waive admission requirements and admit numerous third-world students, even to grant many of them financial aid. Yet the price was high. Police charges against 700 arrested activists were not dropped, and a few served jail sentences. The administration also fired about two dozen faculty members. Frankly, considering the tense situation during a strike lasting 134 school days, it was amazing no one was killed.

Calm returned to San Francisco State, but the affair demonstrated how divided the sixties culture was with mainstream America. During the strike, angry Californian taxpayers sent the board of trustees 180,000 letters, most demanding law and order, "swift, sure (and if necessary violent) action against the demonstrators, including suspension, expulsion, firings, revocation of tenure, fines, arrests and/or jail terms." The California legislature proposed two dozen bills, including ones that would immediately dismiss any university employee or faculty member for striking, and another aimed at students for disrupting normal campus activities, an action that could result in a five-year prison sentence. Most students responded differently. As one noted, the university administration's uncompromising stance and use of police "played an important part in causing a large number of courageous and idealistic young Americans to come to despise the major institutions of their country."

San Francisco State also inspired more minority student militancy, and throughout 1969 they began advocating a "third-world revolution" against the white college Establishment. Asian Americans, Chicanos, and Native Americans joined African Americans and demanded classes on their history and culture. During the spring semester, students protested at over 230 colleges across the nation. At Rutgers campus in Newark, the Black Organization of Students took over the main classroom building and renamed it "Liberation Hall"; at Texas, the Afro Americans for Black Liberation insisted on converting the Lyndon B. Johnson Presidential Library to a black studies building and renaming it for Malcolm X. At the University of California at San Diego, Angela Davis, a black radical studying with Marxist philosopher Herbert Marcuse, organized a coalition of black and brown students who advocated a college named for the African and Mexican revolutionaries Patrice Lumumba and Emiliano Zapata. Similar demands at Wisconsin and Berkeley resulted in riots, forcing governors to call on the National Guard to occupy the campuses. At Cornell, 100 black students seized a building and demanded a black studies department. After the university agreed, the black militants marched out and stunned the nation—they were armed with shotguns and rifles.

The scene epitomized the word *militant* and demonstrated how far black empowerment had spread in two years. It was one thing in 1967 to see armed Black Panthers march into the California State Legislature. White suburbanites could say that the militants were simply ghetto thugs. But it was something else to see black students waving shotguns at an elite white university—confronting authorities,

Black Power reaches Cornell University;
some militant students advocated "armed self-defense."

clamoring about "armed self-defense." Black power seemed to be reaching an omi-
nous phase in the summer of 1969, and so was white militancy.

In June SDS held its ninth and last annual convention in Chicago. Because the
media had anointed SDS the most important radical student group, almost as many
journalists, undercover agents, and police officers arrived as SDS members. Actually, SDS had been losing influence for years. The nation's students came from all
walks of life and never could be organized into any group, and SDS's rhetoric had
become more revolutionary; even in 1969 most students simply wanted an education

and a job. The SDS meeting quickly deteriorated into shouting gangs of self-proclaimed revolutionaries fantasizing about "guerrillas" and "vanguards."

SDS disintegrated, but one splinter group, the Weathermen, declared they would launch an attack on "Amerika." They boasted that their "Days of Rage" would lure 20,000 angry youths to "pig city" (Chicago) in October. In a stark demonstration of how much support militants ever had, about 300 appeared—while two months earlier 400,000 went to Woodstock and a week later a few million participated in the antiwar Moratorium. Dressed in denim or leather jackets, some with football helmets or gas masks, armed with pipes and chains, the Weathermen met in Lincoln Park and chanted, "Revolution's begun! Off the pig! Pick up the gun!" Then they attacked Chicago, running down streets smashing windows, knocking people down—until they met the police. Fifty were injured, 100 arrested, and the entire affair was denounced by the Establishment, and by other activists who ridiculed them as "kamikazes."

This was not revolution, just senseless violence, which seemed to be sweeping the nation during the days of discord. In 1969 the government reported increasing crime rates in all categories, even airplane hijackings, prompting Congress to pass and Nixon to sign a bill mandating metal detectors in airports. The violence resulted from the swelling numbers of youth, but also because a few activists had become so frustrated with the war that they tried "trashing," a tactic aimed "to stop business as usual." Some radicals vandalized public offices, cut electric or telephone wires, even burned or bombed buildings, especially selective service or ROTC offices. Most of the bombs were fire or pipe devices, exploded at night to avoid casualties but disrupt businesses and public agencies. The most deadly bombing was in Greenwich Village, New York, where three members of the Weathermen were making bombs—and blew themselves up. In comparison, the most deadly bombing in American history was the federal building in Oklahoma City in 1995 that killed 168 people, but in 1969 and 1970 radicals issued bomb threats, forcing numerous evacuations from businesses, university classrooms, and government agencies. When the president was outlining plans to counter these scares at a White House meeting, he was interrupted by a bomb threat at a nearby federal building.

As usual, radical tactics backfired. Students were appalled, for numerous campus opinion polls demonstrated that they overwhelmingly disapproved of violence and supported peaceful demonstrations to bring about a campus, and a nation, that reflected their sixties values. Moreover, radical behavior only alarmed the silent majority and boosted conservatives shouting for more law and order. Deputy Attorney General Richard Kleindienst could not provide accurate facts on the number of bombings, or injuries, but nevertheless he scared the public with incredible numbers and by declaring there were "persons in our society who seek to destroy our Government by violent means." The president proposed a federal law mandating 5 years of imprisonment for making a bomb threat, 20 years for exploding a device, and the death penalty if a fatality resulted. Attorney General John Mitchell stated what many citizens wanted to hear: "The time has come for an end to patience."

Empowerment

Patience also had ended with the sixties culture, for throughout 1969 minority empowerment swept across the nation, challenging the tradition of white America, contributing to the discord. "The emergence of yellow power," wrote Amy Uyematsu. "A yellow movement has been set into motion by the black power movement." Indeed, African American activists were having an impact on other minority groups. Later that year, Native Americans landed on Alcatraz Island, and after citing an old treaty declared it "Indian property," taking down Old Glory and raising their own flag. Some 10,000 Native Americans from dozens of tribes visited the island, and *Newsweek* declared that Alcatraz had become "a symbol of the red man's liberation."

Native Americans make demands at Alcatraz Island.

All the while, the nation's second largest minority group then, Mexican Americans, were becoming involved in what *The Nation* proclaimed was "The Chicano Rebellion."

The Chicano movement had been developing for years in the Southwest, and one of the main reasons was Cesar Chavez. During his early years Chavez had been a migrant worker in California, and in the sixties he organized an agriculture workers union, the United Farm Workers. Until then, union leaders had considered it impossible to unite these workers because they usually were illiterate, indigent migrants. They had little support from local communities, virtually no political benefactors, and so migrant workers were excluded from laws that gave most laborers the right to collective bargaining and the minimum wage.

The result was a dismal existence for most of the 5 million Hispanic Americans. In California, their median annual wage was half the poverty level; in south Texas counties, almost two-thirds lived below the poverty line. Most of these citizens lived in barrios of large cities or in squalid conditions on farms. Migrant work also was hazardous, and in California the job accident rate was three times and infant mortality double the national average; life expectancy was under 50. Moreover, the usual avenue of mobility in America—education—was filled with roadblocks for Latinos. Although there were few Jim Crow laws, there was ample de facto segregation throughout the Southwest. Many public facilities and schools were segregated and at most speaking Spanish was prohibited. In California and Texas, teaching classes in Spanish was illegal. President Johnson reversed these state laws by signing the Bilingual Education Act in 1968, but local Anglos refused to abide by the law and continued the English-only tradition. Thus educational levels for most Hispanics were pathetic; about 40 percent of Mexican American adults were functional illiterates, having less than a fifth-grade education, and in Texas almost 90 percent had not graduated from high school.

A few Mexican Americans, of course, had made progress in the Southwest. Some were enrolled in college, others had become successful in business and ranching, and Texas Hispanics had elected Henry B. Gonzales to the U.S. Congress. Conservative Mexican Americans thus could point to some advancements, and they usually shunned the term *Chicano* in their attempt to assimilate into American society.

Yet for most, there was little progress. Politically, Mexican Americans were a large percentage of the population in cities such as San Antonio, Albuquerque, Phoenix, San Diego, and Los Angeles, yet election districts were so gerrymandered that few were elected to the city councils and only one had become mayor, in El Paso. California had about 2 million Latinos in 1968, but not one was elected to the state government. Legally, they were second-class citizens. The U.S. Civil Rights Commission exposed numerous cases in which white police gave brown suspects unduly harsh treatment, physical and verbal abuse, arrested them on insufficient grounds, and then dispensed penalties "disproportionately severe." Few Hispanic police officers worked in the Southwest, and only 6 of over 1,000 agents were working the area for the FBI. And Anglo police held racial stereotypes, exemplified by a Los Angeles official who stated that people of Mexican descent were "biologically crime prone."

Racism, at least publicly, had decreased toward African Americans during the sixties, but that was not the case with Mexican Americans. Anglos commonly referred to them as lazy, dirty, or sneaky, and called them "greasers," "spicks," "wetbacks," or "meskin." They could not win, for if they were too fast they were "Speedy Gonzalez" or too slow "Pancho."

Such was the typical Mexican American life, and so the reasons for the rise of Brown Power were similar to those for the black civil rights movement—discrimination based on race, which kept the doors of opportunity closed, and naturally led to poverty. For most Hispanics, America was not living up to its dream.

Chavez, of course, was well aware of such conditions, and they had prompted him to begin *La Causa*, the cause or movement. In 1965 he and 1,200 supporters announced *Huelga!*, strike, against the large fruit and grape growers in California's San Joaquin Valley, but the growers stifled the union with the support of the local police, and little was accomplished or reported in the national press about Mexican

Rise of Brown Power. Cesar Chavez leads
a United Farm Workers strike in Delano, California.

Americans until spring 1968 when Chavez went on a hunger strike that captivated the nation. After 25 days he ended the strike—and exposed the nation to the plight of Mexican Americans. Next year, *Time* put Chavez on their cover, declaring, "The Grapes of Wrath, 1969. Mexican-Americans on the March."

Hispanics organized across the Southwest, demanding more political empowerment in their communities and more opportunity in the job market. In East Los Angeles, David Sanchez and others founded the Brown Berets, a "highly disciplined paramilitary organization" to fight police brutality, and brown students joined numerous organizations such as Mexican American Youth Organization (MAYO). They began demanding Mexican American studies at universities from California State at Hayward to the University of Texas. At Berkeley 100 occupied the president's office during spring semester 1969, and another group invaded the chambers of the Los Angeles Board of Education. For six days and nights they conducted a sit-in and sleep-in, an event that one Hispanic commentator labeled "the first important public appearance of something called Brown Power."

Brown pride swelled in 1969. "Our main goal is to orient the Chicano to *think* Chicano so as to achieve equal status with other groups, not to emulate the Anglo," proclaimed an activist at San Jose City College. *Viva la revolución!* declared posters in high school lockers, or referring to the great Mexican revolutionary, *Viva Zapata!* A new, dynamic sense of community was obvious as Mexican Americans began saying "brown is beautiful," as young men grew *guerrillero* beards, as females demanded to be called *Chicana*. Brown Berets and MAYO membership soared, and cultural activists created Teatro Chicano in the barrios of Los Angeles, Fresno, and Denver. Others formed the Chicano Press Association and began publishing movement newspapers such as *El Papel* in Albuquerque and *La Raza* in Los Angeles. Large crowds attended conferences held in cities from Santa Barbara to the Chicano Youth Liberation Conference in Denver, where the term *Chicano* became vogue among the 1,500 delegates. The event was much more than a conference, said Maria Varela, it was "a fiesta: Days of celebrating what sings in the blood of a people who, taught to believe they are ugly, discover the true beauty in their souls during the years of occupation and intimidation. . . . We are beautiful."

Armed with a new pride, Chicanos declared their empowerment and shocked the Anglo Establishment. From San Diego to Houston school boards were overwhelmed with Mexican American parents insisting that board members end "Anglo education" and hire Hispanic teachers and counselors, provide bilingual education and heritage classes, and serve Mexican food for school lunch.

Another pressing issue was equal employment opportunity, which excited all minorities. As stated, President Johnson expanded affirmative action, declaring that jobs funded by the government had to be open to all taxpayers. Some civil rights activists began demanding that if there were about 20 percent minorities in a certain community, then there should be about that same percentage holding tax-supported jobs. In California, for example, Hispanics made up 10 percent of the population but only held about 3 percent of federal jobs. And there was another issue: the quality of those jobs. In San Antonio, a government official asked a haunting question. Noting that Hispanics made up about 45 percent of the local population and held about 30 percent of jobs at Kelly Air Force Base, he wondered why they had only 12 percent of the better jobs at the base. "Would you consider that a broad and glaring inequity?"

The Nixon administration answered such questions in 1969 with their own affirmative action policy—the Philadelphia Plan. Approximately 30 percent of Philadelphia's population was black, and the federal government was planning to fund a new hospital, some university buildings, and construct a new U.S. Mint, at a cost of $550 million to taxpayers. Would all taxpayers be hired? Probably not, for local unions in the sheet-metal trade had 1,400 members, elevator constructors had over 600, and stone masons had more than 400—and not one was a minority. Thus Secretary of Labor George Shultz required construction unions that accepted government contracts in that city to establish "goals and timetables" for hiring minority apprentices, a regulation the administration expanded the next year for all federal hiring and contracting throughout the nation. That regulation affected millions of employers and workers, because government contracts to private companies employed about a quarter of America's work force. Thus the Nixon administration boosted affirmative action. LBJ had banned job discrimination against individuals based on race, sex, religion, or national origin, and he encouraged government and businesses to hire and train African Americans. Shultz and Nixon extended the idea by placing more pressure on contractors to have annual "goals and timetables" to hire minorities—giving favor to minority and especially African American applicants.

Unions and other critics cried "quotas!" But to Schultz there was no realistic alternative; if the government wanted an integrated work force then it had to pressure contractors to establish goals and timetables. America's "skilled building trades unions," claimed *Newsweek,* "are nearly as lily-white as the snootiest country club," and after a Detroit union leader surveyed the pace of integration in the local building trades he declared, "At the present pace it will be somewhere around 2168 before Negroes achieve their full equality."

The Philadelphia Plan, of course, contributed to the days of discord because minority demands clashed with tradition: those jobs had been held by white males. "The niggers are all organized," declared a construction worker. "So are the Mexicans, even the Indians. But who the hell speaks for me?" The white backlash intensified. When blacks demanded jobs, white construction workers reacted with rambunctious demonstrations in many cities, including Chicago, Seattle, and Pittsburgh.

Why did Republican Nixon mandate this plan? John Ehrlichman saw cynicism and politics, later writing that Shultz had constructed a "political dilemma" for two Democratic Party supporters: white labor unions and black civil rights groups. The former resented affirmative action and the latter favored it, and the resulting tension was supposed to undercut white union allegiance to the champions of civil rights, the Democrats, and increase labor support for the Republicans instead of for Wallace.

Also, 1969 was a time of booming economic expansion, extremely low unemployment, and creeping inflation. The administration maintained that there were enough jobs for everyone and that their policy would increase black employment and capitalism. Significantly, the plan concerned only race, not gender, and so it raised new questions about employment opportunities for a majority of citizens—women.

Liberation

Tradition again clashed with the emerging sixties culture: like their mothers, baby boomer females had been raised to accept the role of girlfriend, wife, mother, homemaker. Men had been raised to think of themselves as decision makers and providers in a man's world. After courtship and matrimony, husbands expected wives to serve them, and in many states laws mandated males head of the household and primary guardian of the children. In return, they pledged to provide support for life. A woman's most important decision, therefore, was to find the right man, the best possible provider. Her man—not her*self*—was her future, for there were few other opportunities. "If anybody had asked me to marry them between April and September of 1962," Elizabeth Holtzman said of the year she graduated from Radcliffe, "I would have said yes. It appeared to solve so many problems."

That tradition rarely had been questioned, but during the first half of the sixties a number of factors merged to stimulate some women to demand change. As mentioned, Betty Friedan published *The Feminine Mystique* and it became a best-seller, and many women became involved in marches against atmospheric atomic bomb testing and for civil rights. More baby boomer females joined the work force. On the job they often found discrimination, which was not being addressed by the Equal Employment Opportunity Commission and which resulted in activists forming the National Organization of Women.

NOW advocated equal opportunities for women, ending stereotypes, and a "truly equal partnership with men." NOW's position defined moderate feminism. The activists opposed the tradition that men must carry the sole burden of supporting the family and that married women were entitled to lifelong support. They wrote a Bill of Rights for Women, which for the time was too liberal for some conservative members who formed their own organization, the Women's Equity Action League (WEAL). NOW's demands included equal access to education and jobs, enforcement of laws banning sex discrimination, maternity leave for working mothers, federally funded day care centers, and they presented two issues that would dominate politics for years—a woman's right to control her own reproductive life, including abortion, and adoption of a proposal first introduced by an older generation of feminists in 1923, the Equal Rights Amendment to the U.S. Constitution.

While older women were setting the political agenda, daughters were challenging social traditions. The "pill" became available in 1961, placing birth control in the hands of the female and giving her a powerful tool to control not only birth, but her own sexuality. Then at mid-decade medical researchers William Masters and Virginia Johnson completed their extensive experiments and published a classic work concerning the physiology of sexual intercourse, *Human Sexual Response*. Describing the four phases of intercourse—excitement, plateau, orgasm, recovery—the book became a best-seller, and more importantly it exploded numerous myths about sexuality: it was difficult for women to have orgasms; women did not enjoy intercourse as much as men; and women were "frigid" if they did not have vaginal orgasms with their husbands, thus being dependent on males for climax (when in reality they could have multiple orgasms by stimulation of the clitoris). The book demonstrated that males and especially females had the physical ability to obtain a mutually satisfying sex life.

Sexual double standards began fading while numerous young women were participating in the movement, often with ample discrimination. In 1965 civil rights activists Casey Hayden and Mary King circulated a letter to females in SDS and SNCC claiming parallels "between treatment of Negroes and treatment of women in our society as a whole. . . . It is a caste system which, at its worst, uses and exploits women." When some female activists introduced the topic at the national SDS conference, the men booed, one yelled, "She just needs a good screw," while another assessed the role of women in the organization: they "made peanut butter, waited on tables, cleaned up, got laid." A popular antiwar button concerned draft resistance: "Girls Say Yes to Men Who Say No." On campus, male activists held traditional stereotypes. During the Columbia University strike, for example, young men made the proclamations to television cameras and ordered female strikers to answer phones, type statements, and make dinner. That also occurred in the so-called liberated counterculture. Too often, as female communards complained, "The guys would gather around at about five o'clock and say, 'When's supper going to be ready?'" While hippies questioned ideas of virginity and marriage (if it feels good, do it), the result often was that females were expected to have many sex partners, "free love," leading to feelings of exploitation. Hippie button: "Peace, Pussy, Pot." And exploitation in the music scene was demonstrated by Bill Wyman of the Rolling Stones, who coined the word *groupie* for female admirers of the band; he added up the number of women the band had slept with in two years: 444.

Sexism was pervasive in America. Men told "women driver" jokes, and popular magazines belittled females with a continual barrage of caricatures. Officials of famous races like the Boston Marathon refused female entrants, declaring, "It is unhealthy for women to run long distances." Women were excluded from men's clubs and bars, even in hotels that catered to the public, a violation of the Civil Rights Act. And the myths: it was *natural* that women were weak, passive, emotional, and a legion of experts from Sigmund Freud to Erik Erikson told them they could avoid suffering from "penis envy" if they realized they were different and if they did not attempt to do things beyond their "female dispositions." Moreover, men commonly used scores of slurs to describe women—bitches, whores, sluts, tramps, broads, pussies—and even so-called compliments grated the "girls," "dolls," "foxes," or "chicks."

Yet with the issues of war and race, few citizens thought about the status of women until September 1968 when two dozen feminists demonstrated at the Miss America Pageant. The protest stunned the nation, and during 1969 *women's liberation* became household words and flourished, partly because female baby boomers flooded the ranks of the movement and also because the press began publishing hundreds of articles while television networks ran special programs.

What did this barrage of media coverage reveal? The reasons for the women's liberation movement: not only did stereotypes and sexism enrage some females, but more importantly, legal, educational, and economic discrimination affected almost all of them, and resulted in second-class citizenship—or what Mary King labeled the "caste system for women."

The caste system was apparent throughout American society during the late sixties. On campus, females usually found doors closed; regardless of their interests, advisers steered them away from "male professions" like business, science, engineering, and toward "female occupations" like nursing, teaching, and home economics. Deans had *quotas* to maintain male dominance in professional and graduate schools, and so only 2 percent of dentists were female, 3 percent of lawyers, and 7 percent of physicians. There were very few female professors, journalists, and executives. Nevertheless, by the end of the decade millions of females stood in line for interviews. Armed with diplomas, they sought an opportunity, perhaps a career at a time when the economy was booming. What did they find? Tradition: They were denied interviews, or if lucky, then male interviewers asked, "Are you engaged?" and if not then, "Can you type?"

Most women with college degrees had three opportunities—teach, type, and take temperatures—all meaning lower pay and little chance for advancement. One survey of 1,000 male executives found that 80 percent of them felt women made valuable contributions to management, but only a third favored giving them such opportunities. That also was the case for female law school graduates, for they cited almost 2,000 cases in which they had been told by law firms, banks, corporations, unions, and agencies "we do not hire women." Ruth Bader Ginsburg, who graduated first in her class at Columbia Law, could not get a job offer or a judicial clerkship. "Does she wear skirts?" inquired Supreme Court Justice Felix Frankfurter when he was asked to consider Ginsburg. He refused, saying, "I can't stand girls in pants!"

Job discrimination was pervasive. In higher education universities advertised for male professors only; thus, although female tuition payers made up over 40 percent of students at the top 100 universities, they were only 10 percent of faculty. Female taxpayers also funded the U.S. military academies, but no women were allowed to enroll. Discrimination even existed in the so-called traditional female occupations.

Women made up about 80 percent of teachers, yet about 10 percent of school principals and 3 percent of superintendents. Airline stewardesses were fired when they married or reached age 32, but not male stewards, prompting Congresswoman Martha Griffiths to write the personnel director of United Air Lines, "You are asking . . . that a stewardess be young, attractive and single. What are you running, an airline or a whorehouse?"

On payday many women felt their work was little more than prostitution. A survey found that only half of men favored equal pay for equal work, and that was the case. The average salesman earned $8,500 a year and a saleswoman made $3,500. Wage discrimination was traditional, and it even was practiced by the federal government, which by law was an equal opportunity and pay employer.

Legal discrimination also was rampant. Eighteen states exempted only women from serving on juries, increasing the probability that a female suspect would face a male jury. Factory health and safety "protective laws" in some states applied only to women, rewarding businessmen who avoided such regulations and hired only men. In 17 states women could not work in mines, in 10 they could not tend bar. Other states "protected ladies" from lifting more than 15 pounds (the weight of a 1-year-old child) and from working nights, except if they were nurses or telephone operators. In a half dozen states women were considered incapable of handling their finances. Without a male cosigner they could not establish a business, buy stocks or bonds, or get a loan, meaning it was difficult for a single female to purchase a car or home. In four states the married couples' earnings were joint property, and all the earnings were controlled by him.

The double standard was even legally institutionalized in some states. Only a woman in Arizona using obscene language was committing a crime, and only a female juvenile in New York could be put in jail for promiscuous behavior. Schools expelled pregnant girls, not their boyfriends, and rape laws usually stated the woman must physically resist; if she was not a virgin, attorneys were allowed to present evidence of her previous sexual behavior to discredit her testimony. In state law it was inconceivable a husband could rape his wife. Some states prohibited single women from obtaining contraception, and all forbade her from making the choice herself and then obtaining an abortion. The result, according to the President's Crime Commission Report in 1968, was that nationally there were 1 million illegal abortions a year and at least 1,000 women died annually from botched attempts.

By the end of the decade *Time* noted that the "status of American women is, in many ways, deteriorating." Female workers in the fifties earned about 64 cents for every dollar by a male, and during the sixties that figure *declined* to about 58 cents. Politically, women lost 50 seats in state legislatures and the number of congresswomen decreased from 17 to 10. In education, they held fewer faculty positions at the end of the decade, received a lower percentage of doctorates, and were a smaller percentage of elementary school principals.

Conditions were worse for minority women. Elvira Saragoza declared that Chicanas were tired of being treated like "inferior beings," and as for black women, Pauli Murray stated they were "doubly victimized by the twin immoralities of Jim Crow and Jane Crow." In fact, minority females were the least educated and the poorest in the nation; for every dollar earned by a white male, a black female made about 45 cents.

"What is women's liberation?" Activist Marilyn Salzman Webb declared, "It is simply organized rage against real oppression." Women began to realize, and then proclaim, that opportunities and thus destiny in America were shaped not only by race and class, but also by gender. The publicized facts struck home: Awakening. A Gallup poll early in the sixties revealed that less than a third of females felt discriminated against, but by 1970 that percentage was over half, and it climbed to two-thirds during the Nixon years.

Oppression, a term almost never heard in the land of the free, became common parlance in 1969, and it even appeared in the most unusual places—such as gay bars.

"Hundreds of young men went on a rampage in Greenwich Village," reported the *New York Times* in June 1969, "after a force of plain clothes men raided a bar that the police said was well known for its homosexual clientele." The Stonewall Inn was a famous gay bar. Police often raided such businesses and harassed patrons, but this time, and for the first time in memory, gay men stood and fought back.

Like all minorities and women, gays faced ample stereotyping and discrimination. Although the Kinsey survey 20 years earlier reported that about 4 percent of males were exclusively homosexual, and about 2 percent of females, they were ridiculed as "fags" or "queers," their sexual behavior *illegal* in every state. Public pressure was severe, and if discovered, gays were dishonorably discharged from the military and usually fired from the federal government. To avoid such sanctions many would suffer unhappy marriages, such as actor Rock Hudson. As Jonathan Katz lamented, "We have been the silent minority, the silenced minority—invisible women, invisible men."

To be sure, gay liberation had been developing quietly during the decade, with homosexuals such as Allen Ginsberg and Bayard Rustin participating in the various movements, and with a few gay advocates emerging, such as Frank Kameny. But gay liberation exploded in the late sixties, because as Charles Kaiser wrote, "everything was being questioned," and "for a moment anything could be imagined—even a world in which homosexuals would finally win a measure of equality." After Stonewall the movement spread with lightning speed, and within a year gays had organized 50 groups, one of the most outspoken being the Gay Liberation Front. They began picketing companies that discriminated against them, publishing underground papers, and marching in Gay Day or Gay Pride parades. On the first anniversary of Stonewall, 10,000 paraded down Sixth Avenue in New York. Some chanted, "Two, four, six, eight! Gay is just as good as straight!" Others held signs: "Hi Mom! Me Too!"

The first Gay Day, or Gay Pride Parade. New York City, 1970.

"'Enough!' to War"

The days of discord witnessed a legion of protesters who challenged traditions and the Establishment, and for the first time that included combat troops in Vietnam. In May 1969 an American colonel ordered his troops to attack Hill 937. The heavily fortified hill was defended by the North Vietnamese Army. Deeply entrenched in bunkers, the enemy continually repelled the onslaught. Officers called in an artillery attack that lasted 36 hours and then ordered another attack. It too was repulsed, again with heavy casualties. After ten days the men grew tense and irritable, but the colonel obtained reinforcements and ordered another attack. Soldiers grumbled, but complied, and four battalions finally drove the enemy off the position, an area where troops had been so bloodied, so ground up, that they called it "Hamburger Hill." After controlling the position for a few days, the colonel ordered a withdrawal, commenting to the press that the "only significance of Hill 937 was the fact that there were North Vietnamese on it." After all, it was a war for hearts and minds, not for real estate. Shortly thereafter the enemy reoccupied Hamburger Hill.

The sacrifice, and the withdrawal, led to a political debate in America, enraged many troops, and boosted the antiwar movement. The underground newspaper, *GI Press Service*, proclaimed "Hamburger Hill is Nixon's 'secret plan' for ending the war," and another underground advised soldiers, "Don't desert. Go to Vietnam and kill your commanding officer." Soldiers advertised a $10,000 bounty for anyone who killed the colonel who ordered the attack, and the army shipped him back to the United States. It was a lesson learned, for as one combat officer stated, "Another Hamburger Hill is definitely out."

Indeed, later that year an entire unit flatly refused orders to advance on the enemy, an act filmed and aired on CBS-TV. While a few individual soldiers had refused to engage in combat, in 1969 entire units began to do so. In 1970 about 30 units rejected orders, a year with so many cases of troop disobedience that the army developed an official euphemism: "combat refusal."

There were many reasons for combat refusal and for the decline in U.S. troop morale in Vietnam. By 1969 the war had dragged on for four years, soon would become America's longest war, and there was no end in sight. By then, many troops had been influenced by the antiwar movement and the counterculture, and before they were drafted many had been questioning the war. The soldiers in Vietnam were young; the average age of an enlisted man was 19 (versus 26 in World War II), and these teenagers were frustrated living in and fighting an alien culture, especially one in which the enemy often did not wear uniforms and friends and foes looked alike. "The hard part, the really hard part," Marine George Kulas wrote to his parents, "is trying to decide which ones are the bad guys and which ones are the good guys." Moreover, the army's policy of a one-year tour of duty meant that few soldiers wanted to risk their lives in their final months before going home, or as one said, "I don't want to die on my last day of the war."

Vietnamization, then, killed what remained of American troop morale in Vietnam, and actually, it was not a military policy for South Vietnam, but a political one for the Nixon administration. The slow U.S. withdrawal meant that eventually ARVN would have to defend the Saigon government, which was very unlikely, so the enemy probably would win. For American troops, then, the objective shifted from search and destroy to staying alive. "We did a very good job of avoiding the bad guys," said Army Captain Pete Zastrow, "search and avoid."

"By 1969 the war was finished," recalled America's most decorated Vietnam veteran, Colonel David Hackworth. "Service there was no longer regarded as a patriotic duty—not even by those who served." During and after that year many army units stopped fighting—and began surviving—in Vietnam. The army itself documented that fact, citing dozens of cases of combat refusal. Whereas in previous wars refusing orders was one of the most serious offenses, punishable by death, that was not the case during Vietnamization. Faced with demoralized troops who wanted to go home, generals did not even give reprimands to most soldiers refusing orders. Vietnamization had changed the mission. As James Reston noted, Nixon was asking soldiers "to fight for time to negotiate a settlement with Hanoi that will save his face but may very well lose their lives. . . . He wants out on the installment plan, but the weekly installments are the lives of one or two hundred American soldiers, and he cannot get away from the insistent question: Why?"

Many more Americans were asking that question in 1969, and to counter Nixon's slow withdrawal, activists declared a one-day pause in their usual business, a peaceful "Moratorium" on October 15 for the purpose of generating popular support for either immediate withdrawal or a fixed date to evacuate all U.S. troops.

"Bells Toll and Crosses Are Planted Around U.S. as Students Say 'Enough!' to War," reported the *New York Times*. The Moratorium was the largest antiwar protest of the era, and according to historian Mel Small, "the single most important one-day

The Moratorium on the Washington Mall, which was
the largest one-day antiwar demonstration of the sixties.

demonstration of the entire war." Millions participated, some attending church services or joining processions through their cities, others simply wearing black armbands symbolizing peace or boycotting classes. An airplane sky-wrote a peace symbol over Boston. Actors held a moment of silence during plays in New York; judges recessed trials. Students at Bethel College in Kansas struck a bell every four seconds for each death in Vietnam, and 200 Vassar women walked through the gates of the military academy at West Point, handed flowers to cadets, and sang "America the Beautiful." In Vietnam, some troops went on patrol wearing black armbands, and at home thousands conducted quiet candlelight processions, one of the largest from the Washington Monument to the White House. A "Political Woodstock" declared the Boston *Globe*, for more than ever before the massive, peaceful Moratorium revealed a yearning in America, as many marched and sang, "All we are saying, is give peace a chance."

Nixon was enraged. After telling colleagues that he was "not going to be pushed around by the demonstrators and the rabble in the streets," he unleashed his vice president. Agnew attacked the "mob," the "strident minority" who did not support the president. Student protesters, he declared, had "never done a productive thing in their lives. They take their tactics from Fidel Castro and their money from Daddy." He also assailed the press, charging that "a small and unelected elite" distorted the news, and raised doubts about the president's policies; these "nattering nabobs of negativism" promoted dissent. Then on November 3 the president launched his own attack, his *silent majority* speech to a television audience of 50 million. Although the term had been used before, that evening it became part of the sixties lexicon. Nixon asked for time to "wind down the war" and then turned up the heat on antiwar critics who threatened America's "future as a free society." The enemy, apparently, really was at home: "North Vietnam cannot defeat or humiliate the United States. Only Americans can do that." And "to you, the great silent majority of my fellow Americans, I ask for your support."

A "remarkable speech," declared columnist Joseph Alsop, and Nixon's approval rating soared to 67 percent as 80,000 letters and telegrams flooded into the White House. As usual, Americans would support their president in a time of crisis. The administration's attack on the press also had an impact; when 250,000 demonstrated against the war in Washington, D.C., on November 15, there was no live coverage on TV.

Yet opinion polls after Nixon's speech also revealed confusion. As much as 70 percent of the nation identified with the silent majority, demonstrating that the emerging sixties culture always was a minority, but most people remained bewildered about Vietnam. Half of citizens now felt the war was "morally indefensible," 60 percent said it was a "mistake," and 80 percent were "fed up and tired" of the conflict. Other polls showed more contradictions. Three-fourths of Americans would give the president time to wind down the war as long as he continued to negotiate with the enemy, decrease draft calls, and withdraw U.S. troops. Eighty percent felt activists raised important issues that should be discussed, but over 60 percent agreed with Nixon that demonstrations harmed the prospects for peace. By the end of 1969, then, Americans were frustrated, angry, and confused; they simply wanted peace in Vietnam, preferably with honor.

Many also wanted peace at home, but as the year and decade ended, that too was not to be; discord over empowerment and liberation continued in 1970, and during that spring the evening news became a pageant of demonstrators—antiwar activists, blacks, browns, women, gays, Native Americans—and others who boosted a new cause: ecology.

Green Power

The environment, of course, had interested citizens throughout most of the decade, and the Johnson administration responded by passing air- and water-quality acts, which slowly were attacking pollution. But in 1969 and 1970 industrial accidents and corporate behavior provoked activists. Off the coast of Santa Barbara, California, an oil rig ruptured, creating an enormous slick that fouled 200 miles of valuable coastline. Wells off Louisiana caught fire, creating the largest spill yet in American history, and a tanker off Florida punctured, making an oil slick of Tampa Bay. "The Ravaged Environment," *Newsweek* proclaimed in a 1970 cover story: the "Dawn for the Age of Ecology."

Ecology quickly became another form of empowerment: Green Power. Activists began confronting local companies that polluted the air, such as Commonwealth Edison power company in Chicago. Demanding that the company cut sulfur emissions and electricity rates, some 800 invaded the annual meeting of the board of directors and chanted "Let us breathe!" In a few months they won their demands as the movement spread to campuses. At Berkeley students formed Ecology Action and membership soared nationwide. Northwestern students staged an environmental "teach-out" that attracted 10,000, and those at MIT, Harvard, and Brandeis demanded stricter water controls and marched on the statehouse. Berkeley and Stanford students ignited the "Save the Bay" campaign, and those at Texas filed almost 60 complaints against their university for polluting a campus creek.

During spring 1970 polls showed that Americans were more concerned about the environment than any other domestic issue, and that became apparent as they participated in the largest one-day demonstration of the sixties era—Earth Day. Senator Gaylord Nelson of Wisconsin and Representative Pete McCloskey of California had proposed that citizens conduct a "moratorium" to discuss the environment, and thousands of students heeded the call, working on their campuses to devise programs aimed at ecological awareness. On April 22 students and hippies, workers and professionals, urbanites and suburbanites, mingled at hundreds of parks, 2,000 colleges, and 10,000 high schools. Indiana University females handed out birth control pills to illustrate overpopulation; Cal Tech held an Ecological Fair, and Minnesota had a

Festival of Life Week. At Michigan, some protested auto emissions by smashing a Ford; at Wisconsin, students handed out flyers advocating the use of returnable bottles, biodegradable detergent, and a new idea—recycling.

"It was Earth Day," reported the *New York Times,* "and like Mother's Day, no man in public office could be against it." Indeed, during the months before and after Earth Day, Congress passed and Nixon signed amendments to the Clean Air Act, which tightened pollution standards, and the National Environmental Policy Act, establishing the EPA, which had the power to require businesses and contractors to file acceptable environmental impact statements before beginning construction. States followed as many governors signed legislation creating state agencies. Companies pledged buying pollution control equipment for plants and establishing environmental departments, and many activists wore a new button: a green peace symbol.

By the end of the week about 20 million had participated, and it appeared that this celebration indicated the emergence of the sixties culture, perhaps the greening of America. E-Day created a mellow, gentle glow, which rekindled hope. "Should the campaign to clean up our air, water, and soil fizzle—for whatever reason—and destroy the faith or idealism of the young people again," said newsman Murray Fromson, "I would not like to imagine the scope of disenchantment and cynicism that will emerge on our campuses."

Civil War

A week later President Nixon suddenly extinguished the glow of E-Day with his D-Day. On April 30, 1970, he announced ARVN and U.S. troops were crossing the border into Cambodia. Since the Geneva Agreement, Nixon lied, American policy "has been to scrupulously respect the neutrality of the Cambodian people. . . . This is not an invasion of Cambodia." His "incursion" was not expanding the war, but aimed to destroy enemy bases and supplies and thus speed the pace of American withdrawal and Vietnamization. Nixon proclaimed he would rather be a one-term president than see "America become a second-rate power." The war was a test of the nation's "will and character. . . . We will not be humbled. We will not be defeated."

Nixon's invasion reignited the antiwar movement that had been smoldering that spring. Many activists had become more interested in minority empowerment, women's liberation, the environment, or the flourishing counterculture. Moreover, the president had defused antiwar critics by continuing negotiations with the North Vietnamese, cutting draft calls, establishing the lottery, and announcing the withdrawal of another 150,000 troops. But then Cambodia. More than any other event of the era, the invasion pushed the sixties culture into the streets. Most felt betrayed: Nixon had promised he was winding down the war, only to expand it into Cambodia.

Minutes after the president's address, activists rallied in Philadelphia and New York, and the next day students began protests on campuses from Maryland to UCLA. The president referred to demonstrators as "bums blowing up the campuses," prompting more students and faculty to participate, some calling for a national strike and others advocating a massive demonstration in Washington, D.C. Strikes spread to 60 colleges across the nation, and then into the cities. Activists rallied at federal buildings in Nashville, Chicago, and 1,000 students blocked traffic in downtown Cincinnati.

Most rallies were peaceful—until Kent State. On May 4 nervous Ohio national guardsmen fired over 60 times into a crowd of about 200 students, wounding 9 and killing 4. "My God, they're killing us!" cried one female, as blood ran from the wounded. In ten terrifying seconds, *Time* reported, the usually placid campus was converted "into a bloodstained symbol of the rising student rebellion against the Nixon Administration and the war in Southeast Asia."

The sixties culture, liberal politicians, and a surprising number of college officials were outraged. Thirty-five university presidents called for withdrawal from Cambodia, and 225 student body presidents called for the impeachment of President Nixon. In the week after Kent State, students at 350 universities went on strike, and protesting resulted in closing about 500 campuses, 50 of them for the remainder of the semester.

Frustration boiled over and erupted into violence. Students and police clashed at two dozen institutions, even at tranquil campuses such as New Mexico and Eastern Michigan. Students attacked and damaged ROTC buildings at over 30 universities, including Nebraska, Virginia, and Case Western Reserve. At Temple University, students broke windows of military trucks; in Buffalo, 2,000 blocked traffic and smashed windows of local banks; in Madison and Iowa City, they shattered storefront windows. The governors of Ohio, Michigan, Kentucky, and South Carolina declared their universities in a state of emergency, and governors of 16 states activated the National Guard to curb rioting at 20 universities. In other words—the government was forced to employ its military to occupy the nation's campuses to quell the insurrection of its own youth.

Then, Jackson State. Just as the fires in the streets began to smolder, white state troopers in Mississippi opened fire on black students, shooting 300 bullets into a dormitory, wounding 12 and killing 2 females who were watching events from their window. Amid cries of racism, students again rebelled, demonstrating at 50 campuses.

Tired, exhausted, students limped home, only to find most citizens staunchly opposed—not to the invasion of Cambodia or the Kent State killings—but to them, those who demonstrated against America and its president. Opinion polls showed that a majority supported the invasion and now felt campus demonstrations were the nation's primary domestic problem. Three-fourths opposed protests against the government and even would support restricting basic freedoms guaranteed by the Bill of Rights. The mother of one Kent State student declared, "It would have been a good thing if all those students had been shot." Alarmed, her son responded, "Hey Mom! That's me you're talking about," and she replied, "It would have been better for the country if you had all been mowed down."

College student mood after Kent State.
Graduation at the University of Massachusetts, May 1970.

Few could be neutral any longer, and few could remember Nixon's campaign slogan, "Bring Us Together." The presidential commission investigating the upheaval wrote about a "division of American society as deep as any since the Civil War. . . . If this trend continues, if this crisis of understanding endures, the very survival of the nation will be threatened."

Conservatives lined up behind their president and his calls for law and order. Staunch Republicans proclaimed the "raw personal courage" of the commander in chief, and flag-waving construction workers in New York City attacked antiwar students, injuring 70, prompting an observer to note, "They went through those demonstrators like Sherman went through Atlanta." Impressed, Nixon invited union leaders to the White House and posed for pictures in a hard hat.

Liberals condemned the events, from politicians to ministers to university presidents, even government employees. Over 200 State Department officers and workers resigned in protest, as did some of Kissinger's staff. The Democratic Senate overwhelmingly repealed the Gulf of Tonkin Resolution and began talking about cutting off funds for the war.

On campus, Cambodia and Kent State resulted in a major shift in opinion. The percentage of students calling themselves conservatives dropped in half to 15 while liberals doubled to over 40 and radicals reached the highest percentage of the era at 11. Eighty percent of students felt that new laws were needed to restrict the president's power to make war, and 60 percent felt the nation had become a "highly repressive society, intolerant of dissent."

Radicals intensified their attempts to "stop business as usual," issuing a record number of bomb threats during fall semester, forcing faculty and students at Boston University to vacate classes and dormitories 80 times, some 175 times at Rutgers. And there were bombings. Radicals firebombed many federal buildings, and over 20 branches of the Bank of America, but the most destructive bombing of the era was at the University of Wisconsin. On an early August morning three radicals blew up a building that housed the Army Mathematics Research Center, killing one innocent researcher.

The Campus Commission on Student Unrest, led by Republican Governor William Scranton, surveyed universities and reported the main reason for campus demonstrations: Nixon's policies in Vietnam. The Bank of America stated they were a target because of their name and the "national uprising of young people against the war in Indochina." The president immediately rejected such views and blamed the riots on "the rock throwers and the obscenity shouters" who wanted to "tear America down."

"There was this civil war," recalled White House operative G. Gordon Liddy, "and we were determined that we were going to win." Thus the president expanded illegal activities. The administration enlarged Operation Chaos and COINTELPRO, directing the U.S. armed forces, National Security Agency, and Internal Revenue Service to conduct additional wiretaps, surveillance, disinformation, even "surreptitious entry," a euphemism for burglary. "Kent State," recalled presidential aide H. R. Haldeman, "marked a turning point for Nixon, a beginning of his downhill slide toward Watergate."

These were the days of discord. A *Newsweek* survey in 1969 concluded the "average American is more deeply troubled about his country's future than at any time since the Great Depression," and another poll in summer 1970 found that conservatives and liberals, whites and blacks, suburbanites and hippies, could agreed on one thing: "Something is wrong with America."

Americans were fighting for the soul of their nation. The silent majority defended the traditions: the sixties culture challenged, demanding empowerment and liberation. The battle would continue for the next two years as the sixties reached its climax.

Chapter 7

The Climax and Demise of the Sixties, 1970–1973

T he "significant movements of a decade rarely begin with the opening year and then stop neatly on calendar cue ten years later," wrote *Life* in December 1969. "These explosive years will carry over into the '70s, and it is impossible to predict when they will end."

That was the case. The sixties had set the social, cultural, and political forces in motion, and the era not only carried over into the seventies, but reached its climax, creating a nation in 1972 that was vastly different from 1960, 1965, even 1968. A legion of activists demanded liberation and empowerment, confronting the establishment on almost every level and at almost every institution.

Sixties Culture

During the early seventies the sixties culture flourished, one that included hippies, women demanding liberation, many young minorities, college students and ecologists, even a surprising number of older folks. Youth called it the Woodstock Nation, Aquarian Age, or New America, and one wrote in an underground paper that the "Sixties have seen the dawn of a new culture. The Seventies will see its flowering." Most older observers agreed. Editors at *Saturday Review* declared in 1971, "The new American revolution has begun." Feeling the prevailing winds that year, even President Nixon changed the name of his domestic policy from the New Federalism to the New American Revolution and pledged to return "power to the people."

The sixties culture appeared all over the nation. College polls showed that half of students favored legalization of marijuana, that 80 percent felt their most important objective was to "develop a meaningful philosophy of life" and less than half that favored making a lot of money. The president of Columbia University estimated that half of all collegians belonged to "an alienated culture . . . which is growing at a very rapid pace." Thousands of young professionals established "counter-institutions" such as law collectives, day care cooperatives, free schools and health clinics, or alternative FM radio stations. Activists developed food co-ops near most universities; others attended workshops and conferences aimed at creating their own communities. Simon and Schuster published *The Underground Dictionary,* which included over 200 pages of hip lingo, and the government reported in 1970 that marijuana use was soaring; border agents were seizing massive quantities and some 10 million were smoking the weed, a record at that time. Rock festivals proliferated, from Atlanta to Portland, and overseas—Australia, England, France, Germany, Japan, Sweden, even in South Vietnam. Meanwhile, 2 million youth hitchhiked from California to Maine, from Allahabad to Zagreb. Back home, communes flourished. *Time* estimated 2,000 communes nationwide in 1970, and the Associated Press declared that the "movement reached massive proportions in 1971," with 3,000 communes and perhaps 3 million communards. "We are trying to create a whole new culture," said a hippie, "with its own economics and values."

The sixties culture was having an impact, for by the early seventies America had a new appearance. Throughout the postwar era the nation had a white male face, a crew cut, dark suit, white shirt, and tie. But the sixties culture created a multicultural renaissance. Street art flourished; color flooded the nation. Black men wore jumbo Afro hairstyles and the women sported vivid African dress, many discussing "soul" while transforming themselves from "Negroes" to "blacks." Native Americans took off "white man's clothing" and donned traditional dress; Chicanos painted "walls of fire" on buildings and declared *La Raza,* a race of "bronze people with a bronze culture." Young women "liberated" themselves from bras, wore hip-huggers and tank tops, or donned floral granny dresses. Hippies wearing bandannas and bell-bottoms invaded the streets, setting up shop and selling jewelry, bells, leather; sunlight streamed through cut glass. Farmers' markets proliferated as communards hawked whole wheat bread or organically grown vegetables. White T-shirts became passé as the new culture wore slogans across their chests, buttons, green peace symbols.

Strike for Equality

Long hair flying, the sixties culture marched across America, and a significant example was in August 1970 when women nationwide participated in the first major feminist demonstration in a half century—the Women's Strike for Equality. With the slogan "Don't Iron While the Strike Is Hot," they boycotted work and paraded on

Women's Strike for Equality in Washington, D.C.

main streets of many cities. The largest demonstration was in New York City, where thousands joined Betty Friedan, who marched down Fifth Avenue between a young radical in blue jeans and Dorothy Kenyon, age 82, who had demonstrated for her vote on the same route 50 years earlier. Grandmothers, mothers, daughters held hands. Husbands carried kids on their shoulders. Female employees waved from office windows. "It made all women feel beautiful," wrote a participant. "It made me feel ten feet tall." The message was clear, as Kate Millett declared to a crowd of almost 40,000: "Today is the beginning of a new movement."

It was, for the Strike had an immediate impact. The *New York Times* declared liberation a "serious revolution," that the Equal Rights Amendment was an "idea whose time has come." The *Los Angeles Times* said equality was long overdue, and suddenly, so did Congress. The House of Representatives, which had not held a hearing on the amendment for 20 years, began debating it. The Strike also boosted NOW as the leading feminist organization, and its membership expanded rapidly among working women and on campus.

The Strike also had an impact on those who supported traditions. "Women's lib," declared conservative Phyllis Schlafly, "is a total assault on the role of the American woman as wife and mother and the family as the basic unit of society." An elderly male representative in the House attempted to block debate of the "blunderbuss amendment," and the director of the National Council of Women contended the feminists did not have a legitimate purpose because there was "no discrimination against women. . . . And so many of them are just so unattractive." Other women were not repulsed by male behavior, but enjoyed it: "I don't know what those women are thinking," declared Posey Carpenter. "I love the idea of looking delectable and having men whistle at me." Thousands joined HOW, Happiness of Womanhood, or FAF, Feminine Anti-Feminists, but Phyllis Schlafly had a larger aim in mind: organizing Stop-ERA.

Nixon

The sixties culture again clashed with tradition, and while President Nixon cautiously supported traditional values during autumn 1970, he vehemently attacked those who did not support his Vietnam policy. The November congressional elections became one of the more ugly political campaigns in American history. Activists met Nixon and Agnew at every stop, taunting and heckling, shouting obscenities. In Burlington, Vermont, demonstrators threw trash at the vice president, and in San Jose, California, 1,000 chanting youths tossed stones, bottles, and eggs at the president's limousine, almost hitting him with a rock. Such behavior played into the administration's plans as spokesmen deflected criticism away from their policies and on to college students and administrators. The president called the San Jose incident "the action of an unruly mob that represents the worst in America." Agnew blamed "radical liberals" for national problems: the Republicans equal law and order, he said, the Democrats equal permissiveness and violence. As Democrats complained that the campaign was not addressing the real issues, Nixon declared it was "time to draw the line." Agnew put it bluntly, urging blue-collar Democrats to prove their patriotism by voting Republican. As for protesters, he said, it was "time to sweep that kind of garbage out of our society."

The administration's politics of discord failed. Although citizens were concerned about campus unrest and frustrated with demonstrations during the November elections, opinion polls found that besides local items important in all congressional elections, the war remained the most significant issue that fall, followed by new concerns about declining economic growth and rising inflation. On the state level, Republicans were battered, losing 11 governorships, and conservative Georgia elected a moderate Democrat who promised equal rights, Jimmy Carter. Nationally, the Republicans could not beat seven of eight Democratic senators whom they had labeled "extremists," peace candidates, and the conservatives won only two seats in the Senate while antiwar liberals were easily reelected. In the House, 24 peace candidates won and 5 lost. Democrats picked up nine seats, including one by feminist

Bella Abzug of New York City, a founder of Women Strike for Peace, and another by black militant Ronald Dellums of Berkeley, resulting in a more liberal and antiwar House. Although election results were cloudy, it seemed citizens were tired of the war and wanted their government to address domestic problems.

Nixon attempted to address those problems in 1971, but with little success. He announced his New American Revolution, claiming he would return power to the people by establishing revenue sharing with states, reorganizing the federal government, and, again, reforming welfare. Those bills stalled for months in the Democratic Congress as a more pressing problem appeared—a sluggish economy with both 6 percent unemployment and inflation, a result of increased federal spending and the demobilization from Vietnam. The president again stunned conservatives. He increased taxes by imposing a 10 percent surcharge on imports, and he took the nation off the gold standard, allowing the value of the dollar to float on world markets. He also announced wage and price controls for 90 days, which only slowed inflation momentarily.

The president was more successful with his two new nominees to the Supreme Court, Lewis Powell of Virginia and William Rehnquist of Arizona. Although Powell was from the South, he had a strong legal reputation and easily won Senate confirmation. Rehnquist had a more difficult time because he had not been a supporter of desegregation or privacy rights, but he was approved after debate. Nixon's four appointments began the shift toward a more conservative Court.

Meanwhile, the administration amplified the attack on its critics, and that became public in January when the *New York Times* reported 1,000 U.S. Army agents were using computers to collect the names of civilians: operation Continental US Intelligence, or Conus Intel. LBJ began the operation, the newspaper noted, but it had been greatly expanded by Nixon. Congress began investigations, and during hearings Pentagon officials admitted the military had compiled dossiers on 25 million Americans! FBI documents surfaced which revealed that director Hoover had ordered surveillance of student and peace groups and had gathered files on citizens, some with no criminal records. In addition, the agency had bugged the phones of some movement organizations; without a court order, those wiretaps were illegal.

The surveillance was far more extensive than generally known, and it concerned many in Congress who demanded an explanation. Attorney General Mitchell claimed the government had "inherent power" to wiretap dissident groups without court orders, but federal courts and many senators disagreed, calling for new legislation to prevent the abuse of power. House of Representatives majority leader Hale Boggs demanded the resignation of FBI director Hoover, age 76, accusing him of tapping phones of congressional members and of using "tactics of the Soviet Union and Hitler's Gestapo."

The congressional challenge placed the administration on the defensive during spring 1971 while at the same time it scrambled to end the unpopular war. Opinion polls now demonstrated that over 60 percent favored a withdrawal, even if that meant the collapse of South Vietnam. Nixon responded by announcing more troop withdrawals while again quietly escalating the bombing campaign as Kissinger tried to convince the Soviets to pressure the North Vietnamese. In February, the administration again stunned the nation, declaring the South Vietnamese Army was invading Laos: Operation Lam Son. The aim was to stop supplies flowing down the Ho Chi Minh Trail and to prove that Vietnamization was working—that ARVN could stand alone and beat the North Vietnamese Army.

Lam Son was a disaster. Spies in Saigon had given ARVN military plans to the enemy, and the North Vietnamese Army was waiting to attack. To prevent ARVN from suffering a total slaughter, the United States called in massive air strikes—some 277 in just one day. Meanwhile, American helicopters evacuated the remnants of ARVN, losing 140 helos and crews. Clearly, the invasion demonstrated that Nixon's policy of Vietnamization was a failure. Nixon's strategy was no closer to winning the war in 1971 than when he took office in 1969 or, for that matter, when LBJ escalated the conflict in 1965. It might be many years, if ever, before South Vietnam would be able to defend itself.

Vietnam: Fatal Wounds

The invasion prompted protests, of course, but more important in boosting antiwar feelings were shocking revelations about U.S. troop conduct in Vietnam. During December 1970 and early 1971 the nation watched the trial of Lieutenant William Calley Jr., charged for murder in the Vietnam village of Mylai. Two years earlier he and his soldiers had taken fire in the area, lost companions, and became frustrated. They attacked Mylai, went berserk, shooting about 300 unarmed civilians, mostly women and children. Eventually, a few of those soldiers, discharged from the army, began having psychological problems, and they revealed the incident, prompting an investigation.

The Calley trial divided the nation. War supporters claimed the deaths were an isolated incident and the inevitable consequence of war; opponents wondered how killing civilians would win the hearts and minds of the South Vietnamese. A jury of combat veterans ruled that Calley was guilty of murder of at least 22 villagers, and then the commander in chief stepped in, placing the soldier under house arrest instead of stockade confinement. Eventually, Calley served almost no jail time, was paroled, and dishonorably discharged.

In February 1971 more veterans came forward, and the Vietnam Veterans Against the War (VVAW) conducted its own "Winter Soldier Investigation." More than 130 vets testified, many on television with horrifying tales. Beating enemy prisoners: "I personally used clubs, rifle butts, pistols, knives." Body counts: "If it was dead and Vietnamese, it was a VC." Rape: "He ripped off her clothes, they stabbed

As support for the Vietnam conflict declined, American magazines published pictures depicting the horrors of war. This young girl was severely burned during a napalm attack on her village. Nguyen Kong's picture won the Pulitzer Prize.

her in both breasts, they spread-eagled her and shoved an E tool up her vagina." Murder: "When you shot someone you didn't think you were shooting at a human. They were a gook or a commie and it was okay."

Shocking stories—beatings, maiming, rapes, strafing, defoliating, napalming, body counts, free-fire zones, tossing enemy prisoners out of helicopters: "Don't count prisoners when loading, only upon landing."

The statements repulsed the American public, and so did other revelations. *Life* published pictures proving the Thieu regime in Saigon was holding thousands of its own citizens as political prisoners in tiny bamboo pens or "tiger cages." *Time* reported a $40 million corruption scheme in the U.S. military in Vietnam, and *U.S. News* described drug abuse, including that half the soldiers were smoking marijuana. The Pentagon confirmed such findings, even admitted *fragging* in the war zone, a term taken from the fragmentation grenade, meaning assassination attempts against superiors. Eventually the army reported that fragging had resulted in at least 600 and perhaps as many as 1,000 murders, mostly gung ho junior officers, and they could not account for the deaths of another 1,500—the army was at war with itself over the war in Vietnam.

During 1971 the U.S. armed forces almost collapsed. Desertions increased to a stunning rate: for every 100 soldiers that year, 17 went AWOL and 7 deserted, the highest numbers in army history. In fact, over a half million soldiers deserted during the war—again, record numbers. That year some 25,000 personnel took undesirable discharges. Although a less-than-honorable discharge in previous wars would have doomed the person's future, that was no longer the case because so many citizens opposed the war, and many employers would no longer ask to see the applicant's discharge. For those who remained, discipline plummeted. An army survey found that over *half* of troops had participated in either drug offenses or acts of dissidence or disobedience. Many commanders felt their own troops could not be trusted and they began restricting access to explosives and rifles. As the commander in chief shifted more of the war burden from land to air and sea, some sailors rioted on ships and a few pilots refused to fly missions. The navy reported almost 500 cases of arson, sabotage, or wrongful destruction on its ships; 1,000 sailors on the USS *Coral Sea* appealed to Congress to stop its cruise to Vietnam. In Vietnam, troops signed petitions, joined VVAW, and even marched against the war in 1971. On July 4, over 1,000 GIs at Chu Lai held a peace rally, which they reported as the "largest pot party in the history of the army." The troops hated the war, and as one veteran predicted, "If Nixon doesn't hurry up and bring the GIs home, they are going to come home by themselves."

The generals knew it. General Matthew Ridgway lamented, "Not before in my lifetime—and I was born into the army in the nineteenth century—has the Army's public image suffered so many grievous blows and fallen to such low esteem in such wide areas of our society." Former Colonel Robert Heinl agreed; after he returned from the war zone he reported "drugged soldiers near mutiny," and summarized, "By every conceivable indicator our army that now remains in Vietnam is in a state approaching collapse." Vietnam and Vietnamization were killing the U.S. armed forces.

Back home, most American men would no longer serve in the military. Reenlistments fell to the lowest on record, and ROTC enrollment plummeted as the number of men filing for conscientious objector status soared to record levels, over 60,000 in 1971. That year the government reported that 15,000 men refused induction, 100,000 did not appear for their physicals, and there were 190 attacks on local selective service offices. Men—of all political persuasions—attempted to avoid service in Vietnam. College graduates studied or traveled overseas, and as many as 100,000 young Americans moved to Canada, including as many as 10,000 deserters from the U.S. armed forces. Other youths flocked to National Guard and armed forces reserve units, where they would have to spend only six months on active duty and could remain in the United States. The Dallas Cowboys had ten players assigned to the same Guard division while promoting themselves as "America's team," and two scholars later noted that mobilizing the Guard would have canceled the NFL football season.

Vietnam Veterans protest the war in Washington, D.C., April 1971.

In 1971 it was difficult to find anyone who wanted to volunteer for Vietnam. Americans demanded peace, from businesspeople to union members, from clergy to veterans, from Democrats to Republicans. On April 24 a half million people demonstrated in Washington, and about 125,000 in San Francisco, marking the second largest gathering in the nation's capital and the largest on the West Coast. The demonstrators urged Nixon to "set a date" for the end of American participation in the war; some wanted the Fourth of July and others advocated December 31.

The demonstration was very peaceful, gentle, and most activists returned home; yet about 30,000 stayed in the capital and camped in Potomac Park. The May Day Tribe, they called themselves, and organizer Rennie Davis declared that on Monday, May 3, they would force the administration to sign the "People's Peace Treaty" by using a new type of nonviolent direct action: "Unless the Government of the United States stops the war in Vietnam, we will stop the Government of the United States."

Nixon struck first. At dawn on Sunday, federal officials appeared at the encampment and made a few hundred arrests. The May Day Tribe regrouped, and on Monday it converged downtown, putting up barricades, letting air out of tires, momentarily impeding traffic. The administration then struck again, harder. City police and 10,000 soldiers quickly swept the downtown and occupied federal buildings. In battle dress, many armed with machine guns, soldiers patrolled the streets, helicopters overhead, while police shot tear gas and chased virtually everyone who looked like a protester. A few scattered skirmishes erupted, resulting in 150 injured activists. But mostly officials conducted mass arrests, some 7,000—the most in one day in the nation's history. On Tuesday, May Day, forces tried to protest the severe treatment by marching on the Justice Building, again resulting in mass arrests, including unlucky shoppers, jaywalkers, and even federal employees. By that evening 12,000 people were incarcerated in the Washington Coliseum or at a practice field near RFK Stadium. Attorney General Mitchell called demonstrators "Hitler's Brown Shirts," later commenting that some of them had "Communist-oriented or related backgrounds." The president would not tolerate critics, proclaiming to aides, "We'll get them on the ground where we want them. And we'll stick our heels in, step on them hard and twist . . . crush them, show them no mercy."

The May Day incident was significant. A few antiwar activists had become so frustrated, so radicalized, that they aimed to shut down the U.S. government for peace in Vietnam. In response, the Nixon administration called on the nation's military to arrest some 12,000 Americans, of which only 63 were found guilty of breaking any law. Vietnam was prompting more and more citizens, in and outside of the administration, to use radical tactics.

May Day, of course, failed to stop the war, but the war effort was fatally wounded in June when the *New York Times* and *Washington Post* began publishing the secret history of the war, The Pentagon Papers. In 1967 Secretary of Defense McNamara had put together a team of 40 researchers to examine how the United States had become involved in the war in the first place; that in itself was an incredible admission while soldiers were giving their lives for their country. One of the researchers, Daniel Ellsberg, copied the documents and delivered them to the newspapers, which began publishing them. Alarmed, Nixon's Justice Department issued a restraining order to block publication, citing "national interest." The *Times* took the issue to the Supreme Court, arguing the government had failed to prove its case. The court agreed, six to three, and allowed publication.

The secret history was "deeply disturbing" said *Newsweek*, for it exposed the delusions and deceptions of previous leaders, especially in the Kennedy and Johnson administrations. The documents revealed a war kept secret from Americans—covert military operations against North Vietnam, bombing missions in Laos, while such actions were being denied by the United States. Memoranda contradicted official statements: JFK knew of and approved the plot that led to the coup d'état against Diem in 1963; the next year the CIA reported it did not believe the domino theory was relevant to Asia; intelligence experts in Vietnam had informed LBJ then that the insurgency against the Saigon regime was primarily indigenous instead of being directed from Hanoi; the administration knew that air strikes did not soften—but had hardened—the attitude of the enemy; the various Saigon regimes were not free and democratic but corrupt and controlled by Washington. The Papers exposed how

Johnson did not tell legislators or the people the full details of the attack in the Gulf of Tonkin, how in 1965 he wanted to avoid publicity about his expansion of American involvement. It was clear—as activists had said all along—elected officials had lied about the war.

In the hearts and minds of most Americans, the Vietnam war ended during the first half of 1971. The deception and lies disclosed in The Pentagon Papers, the revelations about the U.S. military, ARVN's failure in Laos, the nature of the Thieu government in Saigon—all revealed the dark underside of the war and ended lingering doubts: the effort was no longer worth the price. Opinion polls between March and June revealed that only 15 percent wanted to continue the war, almost 60 percent thought U.S. involvement was "immoral," and over 70 percent thought the war was a "mistake" and favored withdrawal. Opposition reached the highest levels yet while popular confidence in political leaders plummeted and the president's approval ratings fell to the lowest of his first term; his "credibility" problem was becoming ominously close to that of LBJ in 1968. Even the few conservatives who still supported the effort phrased their position as supporting their president's policy, not the war; other former proponents simply abandoned the crusade. "Everybody's just sick and tired of the war," said a conservative, and a Republican senator told the secretary of defense, "The hawks are all ex-hawks. There's a feeling that the Senate ought to tell the President that we should get the hell out of the war." Business complained that the war was hurting profits and creating labor unrest. Unions said it was fueling inflation and hurting workers. The foreign policy establishment preached it was no longer strengthening but weakening U.S. credibility and alliances. As for the average citizen, most could sympathize with columnist Arthur Hoppe, who admitted his reaction when he heard about ARVN's failure in Laos. "Good. And having said it, I realized the bitter truth: Now I root against my own country. . . . I don't root for the enemy. I doubt they are any better than we. I don't give a damn any more who wins the war. But because I hate what my country is doing in Vietnam, I emotionally and often irrationally hope that it fails."

It was failing, but Nixon could not admit it, and his dark side appeared as he blamed and intensified the attack on his critics. After Daniel Ellsberg disclosed the Pentagon Papers, the president established the "Plumbers," who supposedly would stop government "leaks." Composed of operatives such as G. Gordon Liddy and E. Howard Hunt, the Plumbers conducted more illegal wiretaps, hired thugs to attack antiwar demonstrators, and in an attempt to obtain damaging material on Ellsberg, they burglarized the office of his psychiatrist. The president established an "enemies list," and to put more pressure on them he told an aide he wanted a new director of the IRS: "I want to be sure he is a ruthless son of a bitch, that he will do what he's told . . . that he will go after our enemies and not our friends."

Yet the president's enemies were not the reason why his policies were failing in Vietnam. Nixon was in a hopeless situation. To get elected he had promised peace with honor, but that was impossible—for him or for any previous president because the phrase meant different things to the three sides. To the North Vietnamese it meant the eventual unification of Vietnam, which in turn meant the end of South Vietnam. The Thieu government could not agree to self-destruction, they wanted to survive, and although most Americans felt a commitment to South Vietnam was honorable, they no longer supported the only possible way to keep an independent South—a war conducted by U.S. troops.

Nixon had no recourse. He had to disengage from the war, regardless of the outcome. He announced he would try to end the lottery and institute the first "all-volunteer armed forces" since before World War II, and he pledged withdrawing another 100,000 troops by the end of the year, which would leave about 150,000 in South Vietnam. He also had to negotiate some sort of settlement, which Kissinger continued to do in Paris, and the administration played the trump card—fear. If the United States pulled out entirely, officials stated, the enemy would win and would conduct a bloodbath against the South Vietnamese. More persuasively, officials declared the United States could not entirely withdraw until the enemy returned all American prisoners of war. Meanwhile, Nixon privately promised Thieu the United States would "never abandon" their ally, and he made secret contacts with the Soviet Union and his old adversary, the People's Republic of China. He hoped they would pressure North Vietnam to curtail their attacks in the South.

As the administration scrambled for a way out of an unpopular war, the antiwar movement naturally faded. April 24 was the last major *national* peace demonstration. The administration's attacks on the "liberal media" had taken a toll; news executives told their journalists to cut reporting antiwar activities, and televised coverage of demonstrations significantly decreased. Antiwar protests no longer were "news." Moreover, fewer college students participated. A journalist surveyed 40 universities and found that "while student opposition to the war and the Nixon Administration is as monolithic as it ever was," activists were no longer enthusiastic for mass demonstrations, especially at colleges that had witnessed years of upheaval. Many students realized troops were coming home, draft calls and casualties were declining, and they supported a voluntary armed forces—in which they would not have to serve. Others felt powerless. "The problem," one organizer said, "is that students feel totally alienated from the administration, that it has never listened and that it will not now."

Think Global: Act Local

That being the case, many activists turned away from national issues and toward local affairs—Think Global: Act Local—and that interested and involved citizens of all ages as the sixties reached its climax. "We saw what the kids were doing," declared a middle-aged man, "and we decided to protest too."

Citizens began appearing at local businesses, pickets in hand, demanding "corporate responsibility" in the neighborhood, and asking questions: What is more important, private, community, or corporate rights? What is legitimate business behavior? Neighbors demonstrated against polluters, such as coal-firing power plants or oil companies, and against banks that "red-lined," or refused loans in low-income neighborhoods, which only continued area poverty. Consumers demanded that local businesses justify increases in food, clothing, and utility prices. In Chicago, housewives conducted a "food-in" at a Jewel Food Store, packing shopping carts with meat and refusing to pay until the president of the chain rolled back price hikes. In Philadelphia, 15,000 signed cards pledging to withhold utility payments until the electric company reduced prices, and in New York, when the Consolidated Edison board met, they were confronted with a huge picket line and a banner: "Con Ed Is Robbing Us—We're Fighting Mad." Opinion polls demonstrated a 50 percent drop in public confidence in business between 1969 and 1971, and that latter year David Rockefeller of Chase Manhattan Bank declared, "Right now American business is facing its most severe public disfavor since the 1930s. We are assailed for demeaning the worker, deceiving the consumer, destroying the environment and disillusioning the younger generation."

"You can fight city hall," declared activists, and they did when it came to urban zoning and freeways. In Los Angeles, a retiree organized a group called the Freeway Fighters and they filed a suit against the state highway department, maintaining their neighborhood by delaying construction of the Century Freeway. The "freeway revolt" also quashed planned construction on the Beverly Hills and Malibu freeways and other roadways in Boston, New York, Memphis, New Orleans, and San Francisco. In St. Louis, activists fought off developers who aimed to destroy the Italian district known as The Hill.

The activism became known as the "backyard or neighborhood rebellion," and it encouraged older citizens. *Newsweek* noted in 1971 that "an increasing number of senior groups are gradually joining the growing ranks of the country's demonstrators in an effort to publicize their demands," a movement the press labeled "Gray Power." Although the elderly had Social Security and Medicare, a fourth of those over 65, half of minority seniors, lived in poverty, and unlike all other age groups then, the percentage was increasing. Furthermore, too many citizens held the opinion that anyone retired was "used up," useless. "The old and young have three common traits," stated an official for the American Association of Retired Persons: "both have no money, no power and no identity." Like many blacks, browns, reds, and women, some gray Americans felt injustices and began to challenge the white middle-aged establishment. "We want to give old folks a new sense of power and worth," declared Maggie Kuhn, who was forced into retirement and who with other retirees formed an organization that the media dubbed the Gray Panthers. In Philadelphia, 600 Gray Panthers staged demonstrations for lower mass transit fares, better routes, and easier access to buses. In San Francisco, activists picketed cafeterias that raised prices on their so-called senior lunch special. In Miami, they demonstrated at over-priced grocery stores and held sit-ins at expensive medical offices. In Chicago, seniors began a crusade for tax relief, and in New York, they pressured state legislators to abolish mandatory retirement laws. In Washington, D.C., gray activists demanded that the government inspect nursing homes and fraudulent retirement land sales, improve health care, and reconsider retirement laws.

These demands were not lost on local politicians, or on the Nixon administration, yet as the nation withdrew from Vietnam the two most significant, and successful, movements were ecology and women's liberation. "The drive against pollution catches on at the local level," reported *Life* in 1971, as "concerned citizens all over the country are waging individual and community battles to control the nation's growing mountain of waste." Armed with the 1970 amendments to the Clean Air Act, which allowed communities to issue more restrictive environmental standards, ecologists confronted city halls and applied pressure on developers, winning significant victories. In San Francisco, activists rallied and the board of supervisors killed plans for a massive U.S. Steel office and hotel building. In New Jersey, ecologists saved wetlands from development; in Florida, they blocked construction of the Everglades jetport; and in Idaho, they halted dam construction on the scenic Snake River. The governor of West Virginia canceled permits for strip mines, and his counterpart in Delaware signed a law restricting potentially polluting industries from its coast. In Montana and Arizona, activists restricted open-pit mining, and in Texas and Washington, they forced smelters to cut pollution. Citizens of a desert town, Barstow, California, even blocked construction of a coal power plant, one official commenting, "We're not against industry. We just don't want that coal fouling our air." The ecology movement challenged business so often in 1971 that *Forbes* concluded, "Today it is nearly impossible to build an electric-power plant, a jet airport, an open-pit mine or a resort community without strong protests. . . . The intent is clear: A pleasant environment is at least as important as industrial expansion. Maybe more so."

"Women in Revolt"

To many women the most important issue was discrimination. More than any other group, feminists merged the themes of liberation and empowerment.

Throughout the early seventies feminists demanded empowerment but disagreed on ideology and tactics. Moderates such as Betty Friedan advocated reforming the system, obtaining equal opportunity, and integrating women into the positions of power in the male establishment. NOW and WEAL organized chapters, campaigned for liberal politicians, and employed a very American tool—the lawsuit—to force corporations, government agencies, and universities to abide by federal laws and end discriminatory practices. Radical feminists such as Ti-Grace Atkinson declared they should "destroy the positions of power," that women would not be liberated without a social and economic revolution, even Marxism. Others disagreed, stating the real oppressors were not capitalists, but men, and feminists should practice separatism, even withdrawing from sex with men.

While moderates marched and headed for courts, a small number of radicals took action, much of it sensational, resulting in media attention. They formed groups with outlandish names, such as WITCH (Women's International Terrorist Conspiracy from Hell) and SCUM (Society for Cutting Up Men). WITCH mocked male-dominated corporations by holding a Halloween witches' dance on Wall Street (causing a slight drop in the market) and by barging into company headquarters and putting hexes on bosses. Other radicals disrupted legislative hearings on abortion by shouting down stunned legislators; they held "nude-ins" before *Playboy* representatives, demanding the end of commercializing the female body; they held noisy sit-ins to "liberate" male-only clubs and bars. More mainstream, female employees occupied the offices of *Ladies' Home Journal, Time,* and *Newsweek,* demanding an end to "exploitative" advertisements and employment discrimination. *Newsweek* declared in a cover story, "Women in Revolt."

Many were, for between 1970 and 1972 no issue received as much national attention as women's liberation. Suddenly, topics that had not been discussed openly in the media appeared in newspapers and on television—bisexuality, lesbianism, pornography, rape—and there was more coverage than ever before about discrimination, opportunity, sexism, and abortion. The discussion created a Feminist Renaissance, which enlarged the sixties culture. The first television sitcom that concerned a professional woman, *The Mary Tyler Moore Show,* appeared in 1970, and within two years Moore was followed by other unique females, *Maude* and *Rhoda.* The message also was on the airwaves. Helen Reddy's "I Am Woman" was the number-one hit of 1972, and Carole King's *Tapestry* became the best-selling album of the decade. Feminists published provocative best-sellers: Ingrid Bengis, *Combat in the Erogenous Zone;* Kate Millett, *Sexual Politics;* Shulamith Firestone, *The Dialectic of Sex;* Germaine Greer, *The Female Eunuch;* and popular novels such as Rita Mae Brown's *Rubyfruit Jungle,* Erica Jong's *Fear of Flying,* and Sylvia Plath's *The Bell Jar.* A new breed of female scholars produced exciting books on topics ranging from *The Southern Lady: From Pedestal to Politics* to *The Rebirth of Feminism*; others were printing hundreds of new publications, from *Women: A Journal of Liberation* to *Ms.,* a magazine "owned by and honest about women," which soon had a circulation of 200,000. The Boston Women's Health Book Collective challenged the male medical establishment by publishing *Our Bodies, Ourselves,* which became a best-seller and eventually was translated into 11 languages.

All the while female activists challenged their sisters—and traditions. Many joined "consciousness-raising" groups where they explored feelings, ideas, and asked questions that were startling for the times: Should we wear makeup or bras? How aggressive should females be with men? Should I live with my man, or marry him, and if the latter, then should I keep my name or take his? Should I use Mrs., which connotes marital status like Miss, or Ms.? What are the father's responsibilities with the children or doing housework? Does your man satisfy you sexually, or do you "fake orgasm" to make him feel adequate? Can my marriage be saved, or should it be saved? Can women love other women?

Such questions also challenged men. Some feminists called men "sexists" or "chauvinist pigs," first provoking anger, but eventually prompting males to wonder about liberating themselves from traditional roles. Questions abounded, from "What is the meaning of masculinity?" to "Do I have to be the provider?" to the mundane: countless college men stood in front of doors wondering, "Should I open the door for my date, or will she be offended and think I'm patronizing?"

While the nation was buzzing about "women's lib," feminists continued their assault on other male bastions, especially education and the workplace. They filed lawsuits against institutions that received tax funds from all citizens yet continued to hire only men or had quotas that discriminated against qualified female applicants. WEAL lawyers sued 350 universities, including the entire state college systems of California, Florida, New Jersey, and New York—and all of the nation's medical and law schools, forcing them to end the quota system and open the door of opportunity for female applicants and faculty members. NOW filed a class action suit against all public schools on the grounds that they discriminated in salaries, promotion, and maternity benefits. Feminists filed complaints against 1,300 major corporations that received federal contracts, demanding affirmative action goals and timetables for equal employment, and they sued numerous companies— Southern Pacific, General Motors, Colgate-Palmolive, Martin-Marietta, Libby-Owens, American and Northwest Airlines. Female activists struck against American Telegraph & Telephone's Bell System, calling for equal pay and management jobs, declaring, "Ma Bell is a Cheap Mother!"

Women's liberation expanded rapidly, more became involved, and they broadened the attack. Servicewomen formed support groups and demanded better treatment in the armed forces. Working women attacked labor unions, demanding equal opportunity for skilled jobs in the AFL-CIO. Nuns organized, and along with Protestant women began challenging the idea that sin is based on Eve. When priests said, "God bless you," some sisters responded, "Thank you, She will."

Other females challenged state laws, especially concerning abortion and rape. They formed the National Abortion Rights Action League (NARAL) and pressured legislatures to begin reviewing abortion laws. "When we talk about women's rights," declared an activist, "we can get all the rights in the world . . . and none of them means a doggone thing if we don't own the flesh we stand in, if we can't control what happens to us, if the whole course of our lives can be changed by somebody else that can get us pregnant by accident, or by deceit, or by force." For raped and battered women, activists began establishing women's crisis centers.

Clearly, during the early seventies, feminists challenged male America. Throughout the history of the Republic men had defined gender roles. But no longer, as Vivian Gornick declared in a shocking statement of the times: "The whole *point* of the feminist movement is that each and every woman shall recognize that the burden and the glory of her feminism lie with defining herself honestly *in any terms she shall choose.*"

Climax

The sixties culture challenged the Establishment, and Congress and the Nixon administration responded during the election year of 1972. As the president ended the draft and created the all-volunteer armed forces (established the next year), Congress passed the Basic Educational Opportunity Grant program. Sponsored by Senator Claiborne Pell, these Pell grants expanded LBJ's loan program to students from upper-middle-class families, and by the end of the decade one student in three was attending college with some sort of federal loan or grant.

Concerning the environment, Congress passed the Federal Water Pollution Control Act, which increased funds for clean water, banned a pesticide that Rachel Carson had warned against, DDT, and enacted a much stronger Endangered Species Act, all of which became law. The president proposed a noise control bill, ordered the federal government to begin recycling, and supported the establishment of Big Cypress National Preserve, which protected more of the Everglades in Florida. "The astonishing thing, two years into the Age of Ecology," *Newsweek* noted, "is how much is being done."

Feminists, too, obtained stunning victories in 1972. In March, the Senate passed the Equal Rights Amendment 84 to 8, Nixon supported it, and the ERA was sent out to the states for ratification. By the end of the year 22 states had ratified it, and most pundits predicted victory, as about 35 states also were adopting their own ERAs. The federal government passed Title IX of the Higher Education Act, which forbids discrimination in any public university program or activity, opening the door to women in all programs—including athletics—and another law made it illegal for administrators to expel pregnant girls from public high schools. The Equal Employment Opportunity Act strengthened the enforcement powers of the EEOC, and amendments to the 1963 Equal Pay Act prohibited sexual discrimination in federally supported programs and expanded the jurisdiction of the EEOC to include local government agencies and educational institutions. Representative Bella Abzug called 1972 a "watershed year" and Jo Freeman proclaimed a "bumper crop" of legislation, "considerably more than the sum total of all relevant legislation previously passed in the history of this country."

Feminists also won notable cases at the Supreme Court. Beginning in 1971 the Court began striking down numerous laws that discriminated against women in unemployment insurance, maternity leave, Social Security benefits, and dependency benefits for military personnel. The Court also found state laws that prohibited single women from obtaining birth control pills or devices unconstitutional, and then in January 1973, the Court stunned the nation with the *Roe v. Wade* decision, ruling a Texas law unconstitutional that made abortion a crime except to save a pregnant woman's life. The Court's majority concluded, "The right of personal privacy includes the abortion decision, but that this right is not unqualified," meaning states could regulate abortion, which they eventually did after the first three months of pregnancy. Soon afterward, the Court struck down restrictions on places that could be used to perform abortions, giving rise to abortion clinics.

As the seventies became the decade of women's liberation, other activists pushing for empowerment were winning significant victories. The federal government began enforcing the law and opening opportunities for Mexican Americans in the Southwest, resulting in bilingual education and many elected Hispanic officials. Congress restored lands to Indian tribes, including the Alaska Native Land Claims Act, which returned 40 million acres to the Eskimos and Aleuts. Ten cities passed ordinances banning discrimination against gays, and 50 cities and half the states established consumer protection offices. The president established an Office of Consumer Affairs and Congress passed the Home Mortgage Disclosure Act, which monitored banks and discouraged "red-lining," prompting banks to become "equal opportunity lenders."

Gray Power was even more successful, especially because all politicians realized the high levels of voter participation for seniors, and because of rising inflation. To protect the value of Social Security payments, Congress passed and the president signed the Cost of Living Allowances (COLA), and payments since have been automatically adjusted for inflation. Nixon held a White House Conference on Aging, and he called on local governments to reduce taxes for the elderly. Many states did, and they also mandated generic drugs; communities established senior day care centers and special transportation services, including "meals-on-wheels." Congress passed laws protecting private pension plans and prohibited mandatory retirement before the age of 70, up from 65. The *New York Times* later noted that the "elderly have a better legislative record than almost any other group."

This was the climax of the sixties. Widespread activism demonstrated how much the nation had changed in just 12 years. At the beginning of 1960, advocating a position, demonstrating for it, challenging the Establishment, would have been rare, even suspect: when African Americans peacefully demonstrated for their constitutional rights, when students demanded more freedom on campus, when youth questioned their nation's foreign policy, many citizens labeled them communists. But by 1972 the movement had made social activism legitimate. People of all ages, races, and sexual orientations were marching for what they considered their rights, and ever since that type of democratic participation has been considered "normal behavior." So normal, in fact, that conservative citizens who usually avoided such behavior began protesting, especially in their neighborhoods over issues that concerned them, such as busing, public housing, and schools. George Wallace had touched this chord throughout the sixties and the conservative backlash expanded, strengthening the Republican Party. In an ironic twist, then, the movement inspired popular participation that contributed to the later rise of the New Right, which became the political foundation that elected President Ronald Reagan.

New Democrats versus Nixon

The conservative emergence was becoming obvious during the 1972 election, which also marked the beginning of the demise of the sixties. For many activists that election began a day after the Chicago convention in 1968. After that debacle, party reformers or "New Democrats," many of whom had participated in the campaigns of Eugene McCarthy and Bobby Kennedy, demanded changes in delegate selection for the next convention with the aim of enlarging youth, minority, and women representation. Many party rules had not been revised since the last century, meaning that in some states Democrats did not hold primary elections, in two southern states the governor picked all delegates, and there were no written rules in ten states. For the most part, then, Democratic (and Republican) delegates consisted of a white male club.

New Democrats and party regulars formed a commission and wrote a report, which was adopted, and resulted in the most significant change in delegate selection in American history: the power to nominate the party's standard-bearer and platform was transferred from the bosses to the people who voted in the primaries.

George McGovern announced his candidacy for the Democratic nomination, and eventually the liberal senator from South Dakota had rivals. New York congresswoman Shirley Chisholm appealed to many feminists because she was an outspoken African American, but she was too blunt for a national following, telling male congressmen in the Black Caucus, "I'm the only one among you who has the balls to run for President." Governor George Wallace declared this time he would run as a Democrat, and he began his attempt to capture the conservative wing of the party. Senator Hubert Humphrey had support from mainstream Democrats and he eventually announced his intentions by declaring, "Had I been elected in 1968, we would now be out of that war." But the most important contender was Senator Edmund Muskie of Maine, who had been the vice presidential candidate in 1968. Muskie was eager to end the war and was known as an honest moderate with a strong environmental record. By early 1972 Muskie had lined up a remarkable number of endorsements, and an opinion poll found he was running even against President Nixon. McGovern ranked last in the possible pack of contenders. Muskie's campaign was based on trust. "Trusty Muskie" was his campaign slogan, and he would slay "Tricky Dick," but during the next months there was little mention of specific proposals, leaving voters to say, "I trust Muskie, but to do what?"

Citizens knew where McGovern stood on the issues. He gave more speeches at universities than any other candidate, drawing large crowds, seeking the youth vote that had been enlarged because of the new voting age of 18. He supported busing to bring about school integration as "a way to reverse a hundred years of segregation." Concerning employment opportunity, he told minorities he would set up guidelines to hire them to governmental posts in reasonable relationship to their presence in the population. He was generally liberal on abortion, and, of course, he was an outspoken critic of the war. This World War II bomber pilot was blunt, calling Vietnam "a moral and political disaster—a terrible cancer eating away the soul of the nation," and he declared that after his election he would bring the soldiers home and end the war "in ninety days or less."

Such proclamations made McGovern popular with the sixties culture, and although alienation was running at record levels by 1972, many activists volunteered and got out the vote for the New Hampshire primary. Pollsters had predicted that Muskie would easily win in his neighboring state, but when he did not obtain a majority and beat the South Dakotan by only eight points, pundits declared a psychological victory for McGovern. On to Wisconsin, where McGovern won easily, and the same in Massachusetts, tossing Muskie out of the race. Senator Humphrey won in Ohio and gained momentum for the big prize, California, where 10,000 McGovern volunteers walked precincts and rang doorbells. McGovern barely won, and then he was victorious in New York and New Jersey, making him the man to beat at the Democratic Convention.

While the Democrats were politicking, Nixon played the role of statesman. Although Kissinger secretly had been talking to the Chinese for months, the president stunned the world in February 1972 when he and his national security adviser flew to Beijing. A man who had made his career lashing out against communism and "Red China," Nixon now grinned and gingerly shook the hand of Chairman Mao Zedong. The meeting itself was significant: the United States had diplomatic relations with the Nationalist government on Taiwan, not the Communist People's Republic on the mainland, and thus Nixon and Kissinger opened the door for eventual recognition. The Chinese and Americans agreed to relax tensions in Asia, increase exchanges, but basically ignored the issue of Vietnam. "We have been here a week," the president proclaimed upon departure. "This was the week that changed the world."

Not to the North Vietnamese. That nation was not a puppet of either the Soviet Union or China, and it launched a conventional attack, its first major assault since Tet 1968. During the Easter Offensive they stormed into South Vietnam in another test of Vietnamization. Only 60,000 U.S. troops remained in that country, and they reported a rout, ARVN in disarray. Within a few weeks the enemy threatened the survival of the Saigon regime. Nixon responded by ordering another massive escalation in the air war, and B-52s pulverized enemy positions and North Vietnam. The president ordered Kissinger, "You tell those sons of bitches that the president is a madman and you don't know how to deal with him. Once reelected I'll be a mad bomber." Nixon raised the stakes. He commanded the armed forces to mine Haiphong harbor and bomb rail lines from China, thereby blocking trade into Hanoi. "It was one of the finest hours in the Nixon presidency," wrote Kissinger, and the president told his daughter that if his plan did not work "the United States would cease to be a respected great power."

Activists commenced scattered campus protests, resulting in over 2,000 arrests, this time not only students but some university presidents. Large crowds also demonstrated in the streets of San Francisco, Los Angeles, Madison, Washington, D.C., and the largest in two years appeared in New York City. But by spring 1972 the peace movement had become so mainstream that the Democratic politicians fired the main shots. "The president is an international lawbreaker," declared New York Congressman Ed Koch, and Senator McGovern called the escalation "reckless, unnecessary, and unworkable, a flirtation with World War III." During the year the Senate voted six times, the House three, to end the war, and although the former approved a measure that would have forced Nixon to withdraw all remaining troops, the House could not muster a majority so it did not become law.

While the Congress debated, Nixon again surprised the nation by traveling to Moscow in May, making him the first president to arrive in the Soviet capital. With Kissinger at his side, Nixon and the Soviet Communist Party Secretary, Leonid Brezhnev, signed a strategic arms treaty, which limited the number of atomic missiles that both nations could deploy. The Americans also continued their attempts to urge the Soviets to pressure North Vietnam to stop fighting in the South.

Back home, a deranged assassin helped Nixon's reelection hopes by critically wounding George Wallace, gunning down him along with his campaign. Wallace's misfortune was Nixon's fortune: now there would be no battle for the South and for the hearts and minds of conservatives.

The Democrats assembled for their convention in Miami in July. "There won't be any riots in Miami," stated observer Ben Wattenberg, "because the people who rioted in Chicago are on the Platform Committee." State parties had adopted the new rules and had elected delegates, and who attended the convention were not the usual white males from unions, universities, and city machines. What appeared were the New Democrats. Professionals, teachers, and housewives made up half of the delegation; 80 percent had never attended a convention. African American Fannie Lou Hamer, who because of her color had been kept off the official delegation of Mississippi in 1964, now represented that state. Instead of Chicago Mayor Richard Daley, activist Jesse Jackson represented Illinois, and the New York delegation included Congresswoman Bella Abzug, *Ms.* editor Gloria Steinem, NOW leader Betty Friedan, and members of the Gay Liberation Front. Compared to 1968, the ratio of female delegates at the 1972 convention tripled to almost 40 percent, blacks tripled to 15, and those under the age of 30 soared from 2 to over 20 percent. "Where was the bourbon and broads of yesteryear?" asked Norman Mailer. "Yes, every sense of power in the Democratic party had shifted."

McGovern won the nomination: the movement that had begun at Greensboro in 1960 and had expanded to numerous causes throughout the sixties finally captured the Democratic Party in 1972. Union leaders, urban bosses, white ethnics, and some older blacks resented the new party. AFL-CIO boss George Meany labeled the delegates "hippies, women liberationists, gays, kooks, and draft dodgers," and soon opinion polls noted an unprecedented defection of mainline Democrats to Richard Nixon.

The president and his Republicans also convened in Miami, but their delegation was in stark contrast to the Democrats. The civil rights movement here was represented by actor Sammy Davis Jr., who hugged the president after singing "Dixie." The delegates were professional politicians—congressmen, senators, governors, over 80 percent had been officeholders. Journalist Theodore White reported just three beards in the entire group, no longhairs, and as for the California delegation, they "came from paintings by Norman Rockwell—stately, big-bosomed clubwomen; silver-haired men with pince-nez eyeglasses . . . and the young men all looking as if they had showered and come in fresh, with neckties, from a workout with the track team." There was little to discuss at the convention because no one seriously ran against the president. Nixon stood on stage with his arms making a V for victory while hundreds of Young Voters for the President screamed on cue, "Four more years! Four more years!"

Outside the convention hall some 3,000 activists appeared to protest four more years. A few demonstrators attempted to disrupt the convention and delay the president's acceptance speech, but police had learned from the 1968 Democratic Convention. Officials surrounded the convention hall with a barricade of buses, bumper to bumper, and when small outbursts of violence erupted they effectively used massive quantities of pepper gas to disperse protesters. Furthermore, the Nixon administration had attempted to immobilize the only group that might receive press attention and public support, the Vietnam Veterans Against the War. Before the convention the Justice Department subpoenaed two dozen VVAW coordinators, charging "conspiracy to cause disorder," keeping them occupied in front of a grand jury 500 miles away. And in Miami, the administration arrested eight VVAW members, charging that the men planned to attack authorities "with slingshots," which later prompted the following response: "Do you think these combat vets just back from Vietnam were stupid enough to think they could attack riot police with slingshots?"

Regardless of the administration's tactics, the VVAW staged an impressive demonstration at the convention. Twelve hundred of them slowly marched toward the delegate's hotel, in silence, using hand signals, some in wheelchairs or on crutches, most dressed in battle fatigues, helmets, boots, some carrying plastic rifles, many wearing peace symbols. They arrived at the hotel, came to parade rest, maintained silence, and faced 500 armed police officers. Nobody moved. Eventually, a platoon leader said, "We want to come inside," prompting Republican antiwar Congressman Pete McCloskey to rush to the vets and arrange for three of them to attend Nixon's acceptance speech. That evening Robert Muller, Bill Wieman, and Ron Kovic (who later wrote *Born on the Fourth of July*) were sitting in their wheelchairs, far back from the podium. Nixon appeared to roars of "Four more years," and the vets screamed as loud as they could, "Stop the bombing, stop the war!" Guards quickly grabbed their chairs, pulled them toward the door. A man rushed up to Kovic, spit in his face, and screamed, "Traitor!"

Traitor or patriot? Those terms had been defined so easily years before, but in 1972 many wondered, What was more patriotic, to be for or against the war? America was so divided, so confusing.

But there was little confusion concerning the election; it never was in doubt. Opinion polls demonstrated that voters usually supported Nixon two to one over McGovern. The only hope for the Democrat was to convince citizens that Nixon could not be trusted, and McGovern's slim chance appeared after a curious event: the break-in of the Democratic National Headquarters at the Watergate Hotel. In June police arrested five men burglarizing the files and planting microphones in the Democrats' Watergate offices. Evidence at the scene quickly connected them to E. Howard Hunt and G. Gordon Liddy, who worked for the Committee to Re-Elect the President (CREEP), headed by John Mitchell. The FBI began an investigation while Nixon denied knowledge. "I can state categorically that no one in the White House staff, no one in this administration, presently employed, was involved in this very bizarre incident." Yet in the Oval Office Nixon's dark side reappeared. He met with his aide H. R. Haldeman and the two men devised a plan to use the CIA to block the FBI's investigation, which was a felony—obstruction of justice. Thus Nixon took another step that would lead to his resignation.

The public, of course, had no knowledge about the emerging scandal, and most citizens felt Nixon's denial was plausible. Two-thirds thought the matter was "just politics," and 80 percent saw no reason to change their support to McGovern. After all, citizens thought, Nixon was going to win. Why would the president of the United States know anything about a botched break-in at Watergate?

McGovern pounded away, mentioning Watergate in every campaign speech, but he never could muster the support necessary to lead the New Democrats to the White House. Although the senator won his nomination with support of the left, he had to move back toward the political center to win the election, and his attempt was not credible. Moreover, and after numerous politicians had turned down the offer to be his running mate, McGovern chose moderate Senator Thomas Eagleton of Missouri. Eagleton had been hospitalized three times for depression, but failed to inform McGovern, and when the medical problem was revealed, the presidential nominee declared his support "1000 percent" for his running mate. Yet opinion polls revealed Eagleton as a liability, and McGovern changed his mind and chose a relative of the Kennedy family, former Peace Corps director Sargent Shriver. The reversal raised questions about McGovern's character and estranged supporters, who now saw the antiwar candidate as an opportunist, just another politician.

The "Eagleton affair destroyed any chance I had of being elected President in 1972," McGovern later wrote, but he never had a chance. McGovern was the most liberal candidate ever nominated by a major party. His views reflected the values and ideas of the sixties culture, and because they always were a minority of citizens, McGovern was doomed. In televised interviews his supporters shocked the silent majority by declaring war on tradition. Women demanded liberation, equality, and abortion. Gays advocated the end of all discrimination, even the right to marry. Although the candidate was vague on abortion, he stated that he favored "decriminalizing the use of marijuana," which rallied college students who hoped he said legalization but enraged most parents. If elected, he said, he would consider amnesty for draft resisters, which was popular with dissidents but angered millions of veterans and conservatives. He would reform welfare by giving every man, woman, and child $1,000 annually, a Demogrant, which appalled hardworking

The silent majority battled the sixties culture every week
in Norman Lear's popular TV show *All in the Family.*

family men, and he supported busing at a time when over 60 percent of white citizens opposed it. He attacked American foreign policy as imperialistic, supporting any "dictators, dope-runners and gangsters," and on the war he was scathing: "The Nixon bombing policy on Indochina is the most barbaric action that any country has committed since Hitler's effort to exterminate Jews in Germany."

Such declarations heartened many activists, but they also irritated millions who considered such words unpatriotic, who did not want their nation compared to Nazi Germany, and who did not want to take the blame for Vietnam. Aware of the mood of their constituents, many Democrats refused to endorse their party's ticket. As Governor Jimmy Carter explained, McGovern's views were "completely unacceptable to the majority of the voters."

The Republicans knew that and launched their attack. McGovern was the "candidate of the 3 A's: acid, abortion, and amnesty." His grassroots army was "a small group of radicals and extremists," who would "abandon prisoners of war and friends in Saigon," resulting in the United States "begging, crawling to the negotiation table." Nixon declared that he supported law and order and prayer in schools and opposed abortion and busing. He vigorously campaigned in the South and urged Congress to weaken or end the Fair Housing and Voting Rights acts. The Republican, who had mandated affirmative action goals and timetables with his Philadelphia Plan, now declared he supported the "merit system," and in an audacious move he called McGovern the "quota candidate."

Nixon proclaimed he was bringing about détente with the USSR and China and that he was the best bet for peace in Vietnam. Twelve days before the election, Henry Kissinger returned from Paris and surprised the public, declaring, "peace is at hand," a statement that made headlines around the world. Peace was not at hand, of course; the statement was a campaign stunt. Neither South nor North Vietnam agreed to U.S. terms and it would take three months of pressure on Saigon and the most intensive bombing of Hanoi of the entire war, during Christmas 1972, to force all parties to sign the Paris Peace Accords. Nevertheless, Kissinger's pronouncement was what Americans had wanted to hear for years.

Nixon won in a landslide: 49 states. Although he won only 10 percent of minority votes, he acquired two-thirds of the white male electorate, 70 percent of Southerners, and even a majority of the blue-collar and union vote, all demonstrating the success of his southern strategy. Females also voted overwhelmingly for him, for women's liberation was still a movement, not yet a political reality at the ballot box.

Yet, as in 1968, Nixon had no coattails. Republicans only picked up a dozen seats in the House, where they remained a distant minority, and the same was true in the Senate where they lost two seats. Two New Democrats were elected to the House, Andrew Young of Georgia and Barbara Jordan of Texas, the first southern African Americans in the House since Reconstruction. And other members of the sixties culture began political careers that would become successful later—John Lewis in Georgia, Gary Hart in Colorado, Paul Wellstone in Minnesota, Bob Kerrey in

Nebraska, John Kerry in Massachusetts, Barbara Mikulski in Maryland, Willie Brown and Tom Hayden in California.

As in his first term, Nixon would spend most of his time battling moderate and liberal Democrats. This time, however, liberals would cut off all funds for the war and would begin investigations of his administration. After his second inauguration in January 1973 the Senate Judicial Committee began hearings over the Watergate affair. Months later a White House aide divulged that the president taped his conversations, and the resulting battle over those tapes crippled the administration. Haldeman, Ehrlichman, and Mitchell resigned and were indicted, and for accepting kickbacks as Maryland's governor, Vice President Agnew left in disgrace. All the while the tapes revealed the dark side of Richard Nixon—hush money, dirty tricks, money laundering, obstruction of justice—and resulted in his resignation.

This was the Decade of Tumult and Change. Both LBJ in 1964 and Nixon in 1972 won overwhelming victories, only to relinquish their office disliked and distrusted, the latter disgraced.

Demise

The 1972 election also demonstrated the demise of the sixties. The hopes and dreams of 1960 had been replaced by the frustration and alienation of 1972. Almost 64 percent of the electorate voted in 1960, but 12 years later only 55 percent showed up at the polls, a disturbing trend that would continue for future elections. Youth turned away from political involvement, and low percentages of students voted. Vietnam, the Pentagon Papers, and eventually Watergate, had turned off the public, leaving behind a demoralized America.

Other events demonstrated the waning of the sixties during spring 1973. In February about 300 members of the American Indian Movement occupied the small village of Wounded Knee, South Dakota, the site where in 1890 the U.S. cavalry had massacred a few hundred Sioux in the last conquest of the Native American. The militants took 11 hostages and announced their demands: an investigation of the broken treaties made by the federal government; immediate improvement of conditions on reservations; and "sovereignty" over their own affairs, including the idea that Indian nations be considered independent. The siege dragged on for seven weeks, occasional shooting erupted, and the Nixon administration began negotiations that granted most demands and led to self-rule for Native Americans the next year, the Indian Self-Determination Act.

But unlike previous demonstrations, Wounded Knee received little support. Although college opinion polls then demonstrated that students felt Native Americans and homosexuals were the most discriminated groups in the nation, neither students nor other Native Americans rushed to South Dakota. Polls also showed that students were becoming more moderate and that discrimination was not as pressing to them as new concerns—the environment, consumer protection, and especially

American Indian Movement's armed occupation
of Wounded Knee, South Dakota.

women's equality. Moreover, students were turning away from the public issues of
the sixties and toward the private self-fulfillment issues that would come to mark the
seventies. "The students I've seen have been talking about more personal issues,"
said the president of Oberlin College. "There is a desire for greater quality of life."

During spring 1973 a final event occurred that symbolized the demise of the sixties era—the end of American involvement in Vietnam. Secretary of State William
Rogers signed the Paris Peace Accords in January. Negotiated by Kissinger, it provided for a cease-fire, U.S. troop withdrawal, return of U.S. prisoners of war, and
incredibly, a few billion dollars of American reconstruction aid to Hanoi. To get the
North to sign, the United States agreed that enemy troops did not have to leave the

South, and to get the Thieu government to agree, Nixon promised the American military would return in "full force" in case of enemy attacks. The Johnson administration could have had the *same* agreement with the North during negotiations in 1968, before Nixon and Kissinger prolonged the bloodshed searching for "peace with honor."

The treaty was a hoax, and soon all sides violated it. The North attacked, the South counterattacked, and the Nixon administration continued bombing. Nevertheless, the last American troops were coming home during spring 1973, and that included the prisoners of war, who were met by their wives and invited to an emotional homecoming at the White House.

The end of the sixties was logical. The cause for most of the protest—the war—was over. Racial and sexual discrimination had been legally outlawed and socially they were subsiding. And there were other reasons, which social scientist Peter Drucker predicted as early as July 1971. Although he admitted then that "a great many people . . . take it for granted that today's 'youth culture' is the wave of the future," he speculated that with the aging of the baby boomers "this country will return to a preoccupation with the traditional economic worries," especially jobs and savings.

Exactly. As the U.S. armed forces demobilized with the end of the war, unemployment soared, creating a shaky economy in 1973, when suddenly, the OPEC oil embargo forced citizens into long lines at gas stations. Petroleum prices quickly doubled, eventually quadrupled, sending inflation rates into the stratosphere, dismissing workers from assembly lines to unemployment queues, and resulting in the worst economic downturn since the Great Depression. Production was disrupted, then stagnant, and citizens learned a new economic term: *stagflation.* All this was happening while a record number of baby boomers were graduating from college and looking for jobs. The nation "will have to find jobs for 40 percent more people," predicted Drucker, "than in each of the past ten years." Not only white men with degrees were starting careers, so were more minorities and females than at any time in American history. The nation slipped into recession, and many activists, now exhausted after a decade of demonstrations, naturally turned away from public protest and toward personal interests, careers, and practicing the values of their sixties culture.

Finally, the sixties waned because activists had changed America. The era had reached its climax between 1970 and 1972, and compared to 1960, there was much less to protest against. Throughout the era activists had exposed hypocrisies, challenged traditions, and won significant victories. Jack Weinberg, who had championed the 1964 Berkeley Free Speech Movement, looked back on the era and simply summarized, "We had taken what we had as far as we could go."

The Decade of Tumult and Change was over, and America shifted into the uneasy seventies.

The Decade of Tumult and Change

"The '60s, a time of tremendous forces and changes," *Life* wrote in December 1969, "will be analyzed and argued about for years to come."

Indeed. The conservative view was announced as early as 1972 when the Republican platform labeled the decade "a nightmarish time in which the torch of free America was virtually snuffed out in a storm of violence and protest," a theme broadcast since by many talk-show hosts. Liberals have often disliked the excesses and violence but have concluded that many changes eventually were beneficial to the nation. "I think few generations cared more deeply about this country," wrote historian Leon Litwack in 1984. "It defined loyalty to one's country as disloyalty to its pretenses, a willingness to unmask its leaders, a calling to subject its institutions to critical examination. That, to me, is real patriotism." Minorities might agree with Roger Wilkins, who when asked what he thought of the era simply answered, "Wonderful. It was the time that freed my people." Former hippies might chuckle along with Carl Gottlieb: "Anyone who remembers the sixties wasn't there."

One thing is clear about the Decade of Tumult and Change: it produced a sea change—a significant transition in politics, society, foreign policy, and culture. Whether these changes are good or bad depends on the perspective of each individual, but like it or not, America is different, very different than it was in the fifties. That is the legacy of the sixties.

Politics

The sixties was a political reform era, one of the few in American history: the American Revolution granted liberties and placed democratic ideals into the world's first Constitution; the Jacksonian era expanded those liberties and granted the vote to

the common man; the Civil War ended slavery; the Progressive era increased governmental powers to regulate the economy and society, and began to protect
nature; and the New Deal introduced the safety net in the form of unemployment
compensation and social security.

LBJ's Great Society expanded the safety net by providing food stamps, Medicaid,
and Medicare. Since then, politicians and pundits have argued about the cost of these
programs and about state versus federal control. Conservatives have attacked them.
In 1997 Congressman Newt Gingrich labeled the Great Society "an expensive failed
tribute to the collective liberal imagination" and he claimed that antipoverty programs have done "more harm than good." Liberals, of course, have a positive view.
Johnson's domestic adviser Joseph Califano recalled mistakes, but also noted suc-
cesses: "We simply could not accept poverty, ignorance, and hunger as intractable,
permanent features of American society."

Evaluating whether LBJ's safety net was a success or failure would take a book
by itself; nevertheless, it is interesting to note that neither the conservative Reagan
administration in the eighties nor the Republican-controlled Congress in the
nineties abolished these Great Society programs. In fact, Senator Bob Dole voted
against Medicare in 1965 and three decades later as the Republican nominee for
president supported that and other Great Society programs—and so did George W.
Bush in the 2000 election. Why? Because the Republicans know the majority of
Americans have benefited from those policies and vote to continue them. Because
of food stamps, farmers can sell off their surplus and there are relatively few beggars
in America; because of Medicaid poor citizens are not denied health care; and
because of Medicare seniors do not have to fear that an illness will exhaust their lifetime of savings.

Most citizens also support many other Great Society programs. LBJ's environmental policies have resulted in cleaner air and water today than in 1965, even
though by 2002 the nation's population had increased by over 90 million. Citizens
have more public parks and lands, and the Great Lakes no longer are "dead" but
alive with fish. Education acts resulted in better funding for public schools, Head
Start, and the Public Broadcasting System. Various student loan and grant programs
have helped millions attend college, some 10 million today, which is almost two-
thirds of those enrolled. Federal laws resulted in cleaner and safer vehicles, and the
death rate in highway accidents has been cut in half although the number of automobiles has doubled in the last 30 years. The 1965 Immigration Act ended discrimination and opened the "golden door" to peoples of all nations, and perhaps most significant, LBJ's civil rights acts fundamentally changed race relations in America.

Much less successful, however, was the War on Poverty. Middle-class taxpayers
rarely have been enthusiastic about spending on the poor, usually equating poverty
with laziness, and the federal government in the sixties only allocated about $1 bil-
lion a year to fight poverty while spending almost 30 times that annually to fight in
Vietnam and about $25 billion to get to the moon. In fact, one study demonstrated

that if all the money allocated to fight poverty between 1965 and 1970 had been simply given to the poor, each individual would have received only between $50 and $70 a year. Thus, as Professor Irving Bernstein concluded, LBJ's attempts to end poverty was "not unconditional warfare; it was a skirmish." Perhaps historian Paul Conkin penned the fairest evaluation: LBJ's "welfare measures could alleviate some of the burden of the poor, but had little impact on broad changes in the economy and on the cultural roots of poverty."

The sixties altered the political parties, especially the Democrats. The New Democrats captured the party in 1972 and since then they have stood for civil rights, personal freedom, environmentalism, corporate responsibility, and a foreign policy emphasizing human rights. Activists pried open the party and wrestled control from white males who for years had been negotiating alone behind closed doors. At the 1960 convention that nominated John Kennedy almost all the delegates were white men, but the impact of the decade was apparent by the 1972 convention, and delegates in the 1976 event included African American Congresswoman Barbara Jordan of Houston and Mayor Tom Bradley of Los Angeles, Hispanic Governor Jerry Apodaca of New Mexico and Cesar Chavez, and of course scores of female delegates. The eventual nominee, Governor Jimmy Carter of Georgia, represented the end of Jim Crow—in the November election many white and black Southerners voted for the same candidate for the first time.

The sixties also changed the Republican Party. In the fifties the Republicans represented business and anticommunism. But LBJ's policies supporting school integration and equal employment opportunity, along with urban riots, contributed to white flight to the suburbs and charges of "reverse discrimination," which helped realign the two parties. Many white Southerners switched from the Democrats, who they had supported since Reconstruction, and began voting Republican; some white workers deserted the Democrats who had boosted and represented them since the New Deal. Moreover, the sixties culture and its new morality shocked the silent majority, and a response was a host of advocates promoting traditional values. Conservative Christians, along with activists opposed to the Equal Rights Amendment, abortion, and gun control, formed a conservative movement that reached its zenith in 1980 with the election of Ronald Reagan.

Yet the Reagan Revolution did not reverse the sixties. The president was very popular, but the majority of citizens, and the Congress, did not support his attempts to outlaw abortion and defeat the ERA, to cut environmental protection, to dismantle civil rights legislation, or to roll back the Great Society. In fact, sixties political values marched on during the eighties, and a central theme since has been inclusion. Both political parties have attempted to include all Americans in their primaries, conventions, elections, and cabinets. First Democratic presidents in the sixties, and later Republican ones, have named Hispanics, African Americans, and women to their cabinets and to the Supreme Court. The sixties ended the long era of white men controlling the body politic.

Minorities

America became multicultural—a legacy of the civil rights struggle—because for minorities, the sixties were a legal, political, and social revolution. In just a few years minorities overturned centuries of legal discrimination and obtained their rights guaranteed by the Constitution, an astounding achievement for any society. The Johnson administration, with support of the Supreme Court, integrated public facilities, ended all voting restrictions, and accepted the idea that men and women charged with a crime should be judged by a jury of their peers. The sixties killed Jim Crow, and since then citizens have witnessed the unprecedented election of people of all races and the rise of minority political power, from mayors and police chiefs of predominantly white cities, to governors, Congress, the cabinet, and the Supreme Court. Furthermore, black power advocates stimulated a flourishing of cultural pride that spread to Hispanics, Native Americans, and other ethnic groups, all of whom have embraced empowerment. The federal government answered ethnic demands by ruling against discriminatory practices by businesses and agencies and by enforcing bilingual ballots and education. Ultimately, the struggle challenged Anglo America, and the result was a new definition of *American*.

The struggle also diminished stereotyping and racism. That was apparent as early as 1975 when a cabinet member in the Ford administration, Earl Butz, made a racist joke and was forced to resign. Since then, a black leader who was hated by millions, mistrusted by presidents, harassed by the FBI, and assassinated—Martin Luther King Jr.—has become a national icon. Congress established a federal holiday observing his birthday, placing him on equal footing with Washington, Jefferson, and Lincoln. Numerous opinion polls since have demonstrated that racism, as measured by slurs and stereotypes, has declined markedly. For those who do not think that race relations have traveled light-years in America since 1960, compare white racial convictions before and after the sixties. Attitudes that had been held for centuries have changed considerably, even on very personal behavior such as interracial marriage. Or compare television programs, movies, or school textbooks depicting minorities in 1960 with today. America is more tolerant on racial issues than at any time in history.

Opinion polls in the nineties demonstrated that whites and blacks, three to one, felt race relations have improved and the nation has made significant progress. "Segregation is over," declared former Alabama governor George Wallace in 1978, "and it's better that it is over." A black adversary of his agreed. John Lewis, a marcher at Selma in 1965, who then was beaten bloody and since has become a U.S. congressman from Georgia, said about a return visit to that city a generation later:

> *The civil rights movement that I was a part of has, in a short time,
> changed this region. There are still problems, no question about it, but
> when you go around this area, you see people working together in a*

way that is simply amazing. . . . I'm telling you, they are entirely differ-
ent people now, and I think one thing the movement did for all of us in
the South, black and white alike, was to have a cleansing effect on our
psyche.

Minorities won their rights—but not equality. To address centuries of discrimination, President Johnson established social programs and boosted affirmative
action. King advocated an Economic Bill of Rights that would result in reasonable
education and employment: "It didn't cost the nation anything to guarantee the right
to vote, or to guarantee access to public accommodations, but we are dealing with
issues now that will cost the nation something." African American leaders called for
a Marshall Plan to aid and educate minorities, and Nixon established "goal and
timetables" for contractors to hire minorities. Such actions opened new jobs for
African and Native Americans, Hispanics, and Asians, but these programs were not
popular with many in the white majority, especially during recessions when the
nation's economy slumped and unemployment mounted. Many white politicians
heard these voters, labeled affirmative action regulations "reverse discrimination,"
and convinced the public that employment was based on federally mandated quotas.
Ever since, the so-called angry white males have attacked affirmative action, and
since the late 1980s the policy has been curtailed by state referendums and a more
conservative Supreme Court.

In the long run, minorities have benefited from affirmative action and equal
opportunity employment. Those policies, along with Title VII, contributed to a radical change in educational policies, resulting in stunning increases of the number of
minority college graduates. Businesses also changed. "At Chrysler Corporation," its
CEO declared in 1998, "we believe that workforce diversity is a competitive advantage." Most companies agree. Today, there are more minority managers, white-collar
workers and professionals than at any time in American history. As a result of policies that began in the sixties era, the nation created in a relatively short time, one
generation, a substantial black and brown middle class.

Yet in the first decade of the new millennium minorities still have not reached
equality in America. During the last 30 years white flight to the suburbs has acceler-
ated, resulting in larger urban ghettos and *resegregation* of schools and residential
areas. Recent studies have demonstrated that Hispanic suspects still receive more
brutal police treatment, and if guilty, stiffer jail sentences than whites, and that black
unemployment has remained double that of whites while minorities continue to lag
in education, jobs, income, and home ownership. "When you look at the data, yes,
we have made substantial headway," said the president of the National Urban
League in 2002, "but there are still—without a shadow of a doubt—substantial gaps
in every category, every vital sign."

In 1963 John Kennedy called on the nation to pass a civil rights law. He looked
into the television camera and asked his mostly white audience: "Who among us

would be content to have the color of his skin changed?" Although there is more racial sensitivity than ever before in the nation, Kennedy's question remains relevant: race still matters.

Women

Gender also matters, but less than ever before, for the legacy of women's liberation was that it rapidly and radically changed American society. Years ago the editor of *Ladies' Home Journal* published a statement that raised eyebrows. "The point is: this is 1970. All peoples and both sexes are free to reexamine their roles. They are free to grow where they have been stunted, to move forward where they have been held back, to find dignity and self-fulfillment on their own terms." Radical as it seemed then, the statement now is taken for granted. Since then, a "woman's place" is *her* decision.

Feminists confronted sexism, provoked men to reconsider their views, and along the way brought about men's liberation. Men have the freedom to choose if they want to be the provider, the decision maker, or if they would rather stay home with the children or remain single. Roles shifted, as demonstrated by polls in the eighties that a majority of citizens agreed that men and women should share housework and child rearing equally. Feminists also changed the family. In the fifties about 70 percent of families were traditional: a dad who was the breadwinner and a mom who was the wife, mother, and homemaker. By 1990 only 15 percent of families fit that description. More women than ever before are working, and although the economy was significant in pushing them out of the house and into the office, contemporary opinion polls demonstrate that a majority of females want marriage, children, *and career.* Critics complain that feminism strained the family, and it is true divorce rates have doubled since 1970; but another view is that people no longer feel obligated to spend their entire lives in loveless marriages. Whatever the case, pollster Louis Harris noted in 1987, "the country is witnessing a radical and even revolutionary change in the basic role of women within the family unit." Sex roles have not ended, of course, but because of the movement, America has become a more androgynous society with more flexible views on those roles than at any time.

Activists also were successful in winning legal and political power. Although feminists did not succeed in getting the Equal Rights Amendment ratified, they utilized civil rights acts and decimated discriminatory state and federal laws. During the seventies most states revised divorce laws, established the idea of common property and no-fault divorce, and accepted the notion that women were full and equal partners in marriage, not subordinate to the husband. Women also revolutionized American politics. Very few had been elected before 1970, but by 1990 women had become mayors, governors, congresswomen, senators, and Supreme Court justices. By the time a female becomes president, few will be concerned about the question, "Would you vote for a woman?"

Feminists liberated occupations and the professions. Most conspicuous was television. Before the sixties, men reported on women and actresses played housewives, but after the era, females have become the reporters while actresses are portraying professionals, from lawyers to doctors to presidential advisers. Most states and local governments legalized the concept of equal pay for comparable worth, and since then the amount females make compared to males, the earnings gap, has been narrowing. Meanwhile, feminists won legal battles against public institutions and corporations, attacking job and educational discrimination, and punching open the door of opportunity. Quotas keeping women out of colleges and professional schools have been abolished, resulting in a soaring number of female graduates. In 2002 women earned a record 57 percent of baccalaureate degrees, and between 1970 and 2000 the percentage of female attorneys, professors, physicians, and business managers increased from approximately 5 percent to over a third; many first-year professional courses now are over half female. Clearly, women—more than minorities—have been the main beneficiaries of affirmative action and equal opportunity; they are the ones competing against white males for appointments in college and professional schools, and for the jobs.

The argument here is not that the women's movement brought about complete equality, a condition reserved for utopia. In fact, as feminists note, there remains a "glass ceiling." Most top positions still are held by men, and liberation generally helped white middle-class women, having much less impact on the poor and contributing to the feminization of poverty. Nevertheless, activists significantly improved the status of women. They exposed private matters long suppressed— abortion, harassment, incest, lesbianism, rape, wife and child beating—forcing public discussion that resulted in a more open society. They challenged the traditional system of education and brought about more sensitivity in the classroom and in textbooks, and they inspired female writers who flooded the nation with new, exciting literature and scholarship. Moreover, in a relatively short time, feminists revolutionized the legal status of women while they changed relations between males and females that had existed for centuries, resulting in more freedom to define their own lives. Because of feminists, women also have more opportunities than at any time. "It changed my life," Betty Friedan simply wrote. The women's movement resulted in changes so profound—and so accepted—that to the ire of many older activists, young females today often take their equality for granted. Women should simply ask themselves, would I rather live in fifties America or today? Women's liberation was the most successful social movement of the sixties era—and of American history.

Students

On a smaller scale, the student movement also resulted in a form of liberation. The sixties generation raised fundamental questions about the American university. What rights do students have? What are appropriate courses for a college degree?

What role do students play in decision making at their university? Activism disrupted and then changed campus life, and at most colleges, gone are the days of in loco parentis, the barracks-regimented dormitory life, the mandate that the administration rules and the students are ruled. By confronting deans, activists forced administrators to listen, to become more flexible.

Furthermore, students in the various empowerment movements challenged an education based on Western civilization, provoking administrators to develop new classes to include African American, Chicano, Native American, Jewish, and women's studies. That prompted a debate. "About the sixties it is now fashionable to say that although there were indeed excesses, many good things resulted," wrote Professor Allan Bloom in 1987. "But, so far as universities are concerned, I know of nothing positive coming from that period; it was an unmitigated disaster for them." Conservatives declared that the nation since has been engulfed in "culture wars" and in an endless digression over what is and what is not politically correct. Others, however, note that with rare exceptions such as World War II, America usually is engaged in various culture wars—certainly in the sixties—and that current political correctness has resulted in more sensitivity about language. To historian Lawrence Levine the sixties resulted in the university "doing a more thorough and cosmopolitan job of educating a greater diversity of students in a broader and sounder array of courses . . . than ever before in its history." Whatever the case, students of the sixties confronted the educational establishment, and the result was more personal freedom on campus and a broader college curriculum.

Foreign Policy

The legacies of the antiwar movement also are mired in debate. As North Vietnamese tanks rolled into Saigon in 1975, winning the war and unifying their nation, Americans sank into resentment and cynicism. "I believed in Jesus Christ and John Wayne before I went to Vietnam," said one vet. "After Vietnam, both went down the tubes."

Most Americans just wanted to forget the long nightmare, but within a few years some conservatives were adopting a new approach. In 1982 President Reagan declared the war a "noble cause," and shortly thereafter Richard Nixon reinterpreted his own policy in his book *No More Vietnams.* "On January 27, 1973, when Secretary of State William Rogers signed the Paris peace agreements, we had won the war in Vietnam. We had attained the one political goal for which we had fought the war: The South Vietnamese people would have the right to determine their own political future." He and a new intellectual movement called neoconservatives claimed the United States lost the war because liberals would not let the military win the conflict and that they forced his administration to terminate aid to South Vietnam. Our troops were stabbed in the back by wimpy congressmen, an idea popularized after every defeat, and one boosted this time by actors in numerous *Rambo* and *Missing in Action* movies. Although these actors and the neoconservatives avoided service in

Vietnam, their ideas were warmly received by many who wanted to blame someone and by those who desired to accept another nationalistic myth instead of the truth: we lost. As we have seen, the military used an astonishing tonnage of firepower all over Southeast Asia, and the generals never developed a strategy for victory—if that objective ever was possible. Moreover, by 1970 two-thirds of citizens wanted to withdraw from South Vietnam, 80 percent by 1973, so legislators of both parties only represented the views of their electorate. Finally, after the Cambodian invasion there were no Rambos in the U.S. Army in Vietnam. "By '70," recalled Vietnam vet General Norman Schwarzkopf, "it was over. . . . Everyone wanted to get out."

Vietnam had two lessons concerning foreign policy: America was not invincible, which demolished the idea of the post–World War II era, and the presidents and their foreign policy experts were fallible. They could make mistakes, or as Robert McNamara confessed in 1995, "Vietnam was wrong, terribly wrong." To prevent such blunders Congress passed the War Powers Act of 1973. The act mandated that presidents inform Congress before sending troops into combat and then secure congressional approval for military operations lasting more than 60 days. The act reflected the public mood, for since Vietnam, citizens have supported the commander in chief in short campaigns, but they also have expressed skepticism about intervention abroad. President George Bush understood that mood in 1991, promising that the *allied* intervention to liberate Kuwait was "not another Vietnam," and then withdrawing U.S. troops as soon as feasible, ending Desert Storm. A decade later his son George W. Bush conducted a war against terrorism after the tragedy of September 11, attacking Afghanistan and then Iraq. Both presidents asked for and received congressional approval—a legacy of Vietnam.

The antiwar movement alone did not end U.S. participation in Vietnam, but it provoked citizens out of cold war allegiance, generated and focused public opposition, and influenced presidents Johnson and Nixon. After all, LBJ quit his job and Nixon withdrew from Vietnam, actions incompatible with their personalities and inconceivable without the antiwar movement. Since the demonstrations concerning Vietnam, thoughtful citizens and the media have questoned military action, asking the significant question: Is American involvement necessary, is it in the national interest, and will it enhance our security? In this sense, then, the antiwar movement was victorious, for as historian George Herring stated, "The conventional wisdom in the military is that the United States won every battle but lost the war. It could be said of the antiwar movement that it lost every battle but *eventually* won the war—the war for America's minds and especially for its soul."

The movement also won a new armed forces. A discriminatory selective service paired with an unpopular war forced Nixon to abolish the system and establish a lottery, eventually leading to a volunteer armed forces. Since, male college students no longer have to enroll in ROTC training and young men no longer have to serve two years in the military. Because of GI resistance within the services, the brass tossed out numerous regulations and traditions and erected a more flexible and especially professional U.S. military. The old army became the new army.

Culture

The sixties challenged many traditions, and as much as any group that is the legacy of the counterculture. Since the first hippies walked down the streets of Haight-Ashbury, critics have castigated them, blaming them for everything from the decline of the American family, to drug and venereal disease epidemics, even for AIDS. Sex, drugs, rock and roll. Freaks filled the void in another great American pastime: the search for a scapegoat.

No doubt hippie values and behavior contributed to social problems. Drugs, of course, always have been an American crisis—the reason for Prohibition—but hippies contributed by making casual use more acceptable. High school marijuana rates peaked in the late seventies, and since have been slowly and unevenly declining. Hippies also promoted casual sex, which along with pregnancy has soared to epidemic levels among teenagers.

Yet how much impact the counterculture of the sixties has had on students a generation later is moot. In 1969 *Newsweek* noted rapid cultural change and wrote that "television is the most subversive enemy of the old ways." A generation later in 1996, ABC interviewed high school students who claimed the reason for sex and drugs was contemporary—social pressures induced by the continual bombardment of sexy images and drugs in magazines, television shows, and popular films, along with "troubles at home." The next year ABC News called the media's message about drugs "confusing and contradictory," and pharmaceutical companies continue to bombard the media with ads for "medicines" or "mood enhancers," from Effexor to Prozac to Zoloft. Whatever the cause of social problems today, most likely social scientist Paul Lyons is correct when he noted, "Madison Avenue has done more to subvert traditional values and behaviors than any vanful of hippies and radicals could hope to accomplish."

The counterculture had a more lasting impact on the baby boomers and eventually on American society, since by 1969 it merged with various movements and created a sixties culture, which first subverted and then significantly altered cold war culture. Coming out of the Great Depression the older generation saved for the future, worked for the family, and followed the roles and the rules. But the sixties culture challenged that, encouraged experimentation, and what resulted was a different value system that has survived with the baby boomers. Surveys by the Daniel Yankelovich Group in the early seventies, confirmed in the late eighties by Peter Hart Research Associates, found that the combined events of civil rights, campus activism, the antiwar campaign, women's liberation, and the counterculture eventually altered the ethics of about 30 million people. The sixties culture is different from their parents. They are more skeptical about experts, leaders, politicians, and about institutions—the church, government, and military. They are more flexible, intro-spective, and tolerant, especially concerning race, living arrangements, and personal behavior. They are more open about their feelings and more liberated sexually. Women feel they have the same right to sexual satisfaction as men, as demonstrated by a revolution of opinion about premarital sex. The double standard is dead, and there is more freedom about sexual orientation than at any time. "At the level of social life and daily experience," wrote historian John D'Emilio, "it is not too much to say that, for millions of gay men and lesbians, the changes of the last three decades have been nothing short of revolutionary." Even during the conservative eighties, numbers soared of interracial marriages, gay couples, and single men and women living together. Cohabitation and other alternative living arrangements have become common, and so by 2002 almost 5 million couples live together out of wedlock; half of American women have lived with a partner by the time they turn 30. Being "nor-mal" is no longer a mandate for behavior: be yourself. Most people today are inter-ested in self-fulfillment, defining their own lives, and they often question authority: do your own thing.

Most of the counterculture values since have become accepted clichés, and they still influence the society. America is casual in dress and behavior, and states have repealed laws prohibiting various forms of sexual behavior between consenting adults. The daily diet includes a wide variety of health foods and corporations pro-claim on their packages "Organic" or "No artificial flavors or preservatives." Youth is not necessarily defined by age, as demonstrated by a legion of older joggers, hikers, swimmers, rock stars, and others participating in behavior unseen and inappropriate in the fifties. "How old would you be," asked Satchel Paige, "if you didn't know how old you was?"

Sixties activists also created a much more open society than fifties cold war America. Since 1970, citizens of all political persuasions dissent and demonstrations have become routine, again a vital part of democracy. Moreover, activists revived the old progressive idea: you can fight city hall. Taxpayers question authorities, and that has opened public offices to scrutiny, prompting numerous changes, especially with the police. No longer are protesters beaten. Police are more educated and depart-ments more integrated, reflecting their communities. Officers are trained in crowd control, and they work at improving their relations with all citizens.

Because of the activists—along with the major decisions of the Supreme Court during the sixties—Americans today have more personal freedom and privacy rights than at any time in the history of the Republic, so much freedom in fact that some have become bewildered and frustrated with all their options. "We have more choices now than ever," wrote columnist Robert J. Samuelson, "but they aren't necessarily easier."

The sixties, then, expanded choice. Like the Revolution, Jacksonian era, Pro-gressive period, and the New Deal, the sixties challenged traditions and eventually opened doors, this time to the majority of Americans, women and minorities. For most citizens the era expanded the American Dream. Since then these empowered citizens have had the choice to—or not to—compete for the opportunities that previously had been reserved for white males. That, naturally, upset many who had benefited from the traditions and the social roles, and the result ever since has been a "culture war" fought out in Congress, courts, city halls, boardrooms, even bedrooms.

Thus, years after the shouting stopped, the Decade of Tumult and Change is important to examine and to understand because it was another defining period in U.S. history. Activists confronted issues central to the Republic: equality or inequality, war or peace, national interest versus individual rights, personal behavior versus community standards. By raising these issues, the sixties legacy was to question the very nature and meaning of *America*.

Additional Reading

A library has been written about the sixties, so this section directs you to just a few books, many of them consulted while I wrote *The Sixties*. Also see my *The Movement and the Sixties* (1995), which has numerous quotes, citations, and a large bibliography, and Rebecca Jackson, *The 1960s: An Annotated Bibliography of Social and Political Movements in the United States* (1992). In addition, Web sites have been developing rapidly, changing quickly, and a good place to begin is Dennis A. Trinkle and Scott A. Merriman, *The U.S. History Highway: A Guide to Internet Resources* (2002), which covers thousands of sites and includes a CD-ROM.

Kennedy Years

A guide to the literature is James N. Giglio, *John F. Kennedy: A Bibliography* (1995), and see his *The Presidency of John F. Kennedy* (1991). Important books on the Kennedy administration include two works by insiders, Arthur M. Schlesinger Jr., *A Thousand Days: John F. Kennedy in the White House* (1965), and Theodore C. Sorensen, *Kennedy* (1965). A balanced view is Herbert S. Parmet, *JFK: The Presidency of John F. Kennedy* (1983), and for domestic policy see Irving Bernstein, *Promises Kept: John F. Kennedy's New Frontier* (1990). Also see Henry Fairlie, *The Kennedy Promise* (1973), and Thomas Brown, *JFK: History of an Image* (1988). A book that raises disturbing issues is Thomas C. Reeves, *A Question of Character: A Life of John F. Kennedy* (1991), and an exhaustive study is Gerald Posner, *Case Closed: Lee Harvey Oswald and the Assassination of JFK* (1993).

On foreign policy, see Peter Wyden, *Bay of Pigs* (1979), Peter Kornbluh (ed.), *Bay of Pigs Declassified* (1998), Graham Allison, *Essence of Decision: Explaining the Cuban Missile Crisis* (1971), Ernest R. May and Philip D. Zelikow (eds.), *The Kennedy Tapes: Inside the White House During the Cuban Missile Crisis* (1997), and Aleksandr Fursenko and Timothy Naftali, *"One Hell of a Gamble": Khrushchev, Castro, and Kennedy, 1958–1964* (1997). Also consult Gerald T. Rice, *The Bold Experiment: JFK's Peace Corps* (1985), Stephen G. Rabe, *The Most Dangerous Area in the World: John F. Kennedy Confronts Communist Revolution in Latin America* (1999), and William J. Rust, *Kennedy in Vietnam* (1985). An important autobiography is Robert McNamara's *In Retrospect: The Tragedy and Lessons of Vietnam* (1995).

LBJ

Consult Vaughn Davis Bornet, *The Presidency of Lyndon B. Johnson* (1983), Paul K. Conkin, *Big Daddy from the Pedernales: Lyndon Baines Johnson* (1986), and Robert Dallek, *Flawed Giant: Lyndon Johnson and His Times, 1961–1973* (1998). LBJ taped many of his White House conversations, and the transcripts appear in Michael R. Beschloss's *Taking Charge* on 1963–1964 (1997) and *Reaching for Glory* on 1964–1965 (2002). An interesting portrait of an aging president is Doris Kearns, *Lyndon Johnson and the American Dream* (1976), and for oral history consult Michael L. Gillette, *Launching the War on Poverty* (1996). An excellent introduction to LBJ and his policies is Irving Bernstein, *Guns or Butter: The Presidency of Lyndon Johnson* (1996), and see Irwin Unger, *The Best of Intentions: The Triumphs and Failures of the Great Society Under Kennedy, Johnson, and Nixon* (1996), while a more negative view is Allen J. Matusow, *The Unraveling of America: A History of Liberalism in the 1960s* (1984).

Warren Court

On the Supreme Court, see Bernard Schwartz, *Super Chief: Earl Warren and His Supreme Court—A Judicial Biography* (1983), *The Warren Court: A Retrospective* (1996), and G. Theodore Mitau, *Decade of Decision: The Supreme Court and the Constitutional Revolution, 1954–1964* (1967). Earl Warren's *Memoirs* (1977) are interesting, and see G. Edward White, *Earl Warren* (1982).

Civil Rights

General studies include Harvard Sitkoff, *The Struggle for Black Equality, 1954–1992* (1993), Robert Weisbrot, *Freedom Bound: A History of America's Civil Rights Movement* (1990), Aldon D. Morris, *The Origins of the Civil Rights Movement: Black Communities Organizing for Change* (1984), and Fred Powledge, *Free at Last? The Civil Rights Movement and the People Who Made It* (1991). The many fine autobiographies include James Farmer, *Lay Bare the Heart: An Autobiography of the Civil Rights Movement* (1986), Roger Wilkins, *A Man's Life: An Autobiography* (1982), and Ralph David Abernathy, *And the Walls Came Tumbling Down: An Autobiography* (1989). Excellent books on Martin Luther King, Jr., have been published, including Taylor Branch, *Parting the Waters: America in the King Years, 1954–1963* (1988), Stephen B. Oates, *Let the Trumpet Sound: The Life of Martin Luther King, Jr.* (1982), and David L. Lewis, *King: A Biography* (1978). Two shocking accounts of the misuse of the FBI are David J. Garrow, *The FBI and Martin Luther King, Jr.* (1981), and Kenneth O'Reilly, *"Racial Matters" The FBI's Secret File on Black America, 1960–1972* (1989). Civil rights organizations are examined in Clayborne Carson, *In Struggle: SNCC and the Black Awakening of the 1960s* (1981), August Meier and Elliot Rudwick, *CORE: A Study in the Civil Rights Movement, 1942–1968* (1973), and David J. Garrow's superb *Bearing the Cross: Martin Luther King, Jr., and the Southern Christian Leadership Conference* (1986). On certain locales, see William H. Chafe, *Civilities and Civil Rights: Greensboro, North Carolina, and the Black Struggle for Freedom* (1980), David J. Garrow, *Protest at Selma: Martin Luther King, Jr., and the Voting Rights Act of 1965* (1978), and Charles E. Fager, *Selma 1965* (1985). A fine oral history is Howell Raines, *My Soul Is Rested: Movement Days in the Deep South Remembered* (1977).

The long, hard struggle in the South is examined in John Dittmer, *Local People: The Struggle for Civil Rights in Mississippi* (1994), Doug McAdam, *Freedom Summer* (1988), and Mary Aiken Rothschild, *A Case of Black and White: Northern Volunteers and the Southern Freedom Summer, 1964–1965* (1982). And for Alabama, see J. L. Chestnut, Jr., and Julie Cass, *Black in Selma: The Uncommon Life of J. L. Chestnut, Jr.* (1990).

Three of the best books on women in the civil rights movement are Mary King, *Freedom Song: A Personal Story of the 1960s Civil Rights Movement* (1987), Sally Belfrage, *Freedom Summer* (1990 ed.), and Kay Mills, *This Little Light of Mine: The Life of Fannie Lou Hammer* (1993).

Stimulating books by black militants include Floyd B. McKissick, *Three-Fifths of a Man* (1969), James Forman, *The Making of Black Revolutionaries* (1972), Cleveland Sellers and Robert Terrell, *The River of No Return: The Autobiography of a Black Militant and the Life and Death of SNCC* (1973), and Bobby Seale, *Seize the Time: The Story of the Black Panther Party and Huey P.*

Newton (1970). For another opinion of the Black Panthers, see Elaine Brown, *A Taste of Power: A Black Woman's Story* (1992). A classic is Malcolm X (with Alex Haley), *The Autobiography of Malcolm X* (1965). A thoughtful study is William L. Van Deburg, *New Day in Babylon: The Black Power Movement and American Culture, 1965–1975* (1992).

Vietnam

Hundreds of books have been written on Vietnam, as demonstrated by the large bibliography by Lester H. Brune and Richard Dean Burns, *America and the Indochina Wars, 1945–1990* (1992). A fine place to begin is George C. Herring, *America's Longest War: The United States and Vietnam, 1950–1975* (2001 ed.); also excellent are Stanley Karnow, *Vietnam: A History* (1991 ed.), Marilyn Young, *The Vietnam Wars, 1945–1990* (1991), and Robert Schulzinger, *A Time For War: The United States and Vietnam, 1941–1975* (1997). Most authors view U.S. involvement in Vietnam as a disaster, and provocative studies include Frances FitzGerald, *Fire in the Lake* (1972), Loren Baritz, *Backfire* (1985), and Leslie K. Gelb and Richard K. Betts, *The Irony of Vietnam* (1990). For the fifties, see David L. Anderson, *Trapped by Success: The Eisenhower Administration and Vietnam, 1953–61* (1991), and for the next decade consult George Herring, *LBJ and Vietnam: A Different Kind of War* (1994), Lloyd C. Gardner, *Pay Any Price: Lyndon Johnson and the Wars for Vietnam* (1995), and Jeffrey Kimball, *Nixon's Vietnam War* (1998). On the military, see James William Gibson, *The Perfect War: Techno-War in Vietnam* (1987), Shelby L. Stanton, *The Rise and Fall of an American Army: U.S. Ground Forces in Vietnam, 1965–1973* (1985), Robert Buzzanco, *Masters of War* (1996), and for the army's views of itself, Douglas Kinnard, *The War Managers* (1985), and Andrew F. Krepinevich Jr., *The Army and Vietnam* (1986). Also of interest is William C. Gibbons, *The U.S. Government and the Vietnam War* (1986), Daniel C. Hallin, *The "Uncensored War"* (1986), John Prados, *The Hidden History of the Vietnam War* (1995), and Arnold R. Isaacs, *Without Honor: Defeat in Vietnam and Cambodia* (1983). For a more positive, "revisionist" view of American involvement see Guenter Lewy, *America in Vietnam* (1978), and Timothy Lomperis, *The War Nobody Lost—and Won* (1984). Revealing accounts of Nixon's policy are Frank Snepp, *Decent Interval* (1977), and the documents in Nguyen Tien Hung and Jerrold L. Schecter, *The Palace File* (1986).

The most complete book on the antiwar movement is Charles DeBenedetti with Charles Chatfield, *An American Ordeal: The American Antiwar Movement of the Vietnam War* (1990); also see Tom Wells, *The War Within: America's Battle over Vietnam* (1994), Amy Swerdlow, *Women Strike for Peace* (1993), Melvin Small, *Johnson, Nixon, and the Doves* (1988), and his short and readable *Antiwarriors* (2002). On dissenting politicians, consult David L. DiLeo, *George Ball, Vietnam, and the Rethinking of Containment* (1991), and Randall Woods, *Fulbright: A Biography* (1995). Concerning who fought, and who avoided Vietnam, see Lawrence Baskin and William Strauss, *The Draft, the War, and the Vietnam Generation* (1978).

Fine oral histories include Al Santoli, *Everything We Had* (1981), and *To Bear Any Burden* (1985). Wallace Terry, *Bloods* (1984), examines African American soldiers, Charley Trujillo investigates *Soldados: Chicanos in Vietnam* (1989), and for recollections of women veterans, see Kathryn Marshall, *In the Combat Zone* (1987). An important nurse's story is Lynda Van Devanter, *Home Before Morning* (1983), and for the Vietnamese view see two stunning books: Le Ly Hayslip, with Jay Wurts, *When Heaven and Earth Changed Places* (1989), and Truong Nhu Tang, with David Chanoff and Doan Van Toai, *A Viet Cong Memoir* (1985). An incredible veteran's saga is Ron Kovic, *Born on the Fourth of July* (1976), and an outstanding memoir is Philip Caputo, *A Rumor of War* (1977). A superb collection of letters is edited by Michael E. Stevens, *Voices from Vietnam* (1996).

It is doubtful that any war produced as much fine literature. Just for starters, try Tim O'Brien's *Going After Cacciato* (1979) and *The Things They Carried* (1990), Stephen Wright's *Meditations in Green* (1983), Gustav Hasford's *The Short-Timers* (1979), Larry Heinemann's *Close Quarters* (1977) and *Paco's Story* (1986), and from the former enemy, Bao Ninh, *The Sorrow of War* (1995).

Protest, Youth, and Counterculture

Consult Terry H. Anderson, *The Movement and the Sixties* (1995), which includes a large chapter on the counterculture based on their underground sources. Other authors who have examined those documents are Timothy Miller, *The Hippies and American Values* (1991), and Abe Peck, *Uncovering the Sixties: The Life and Times of the Underground Press* (1985). Charles Perry, *The Haight-Ashbury* (1984), understands hippies in 1967, as does Theodore Roszak, *The Making of a Counter Culture* (1969). *Communes U.S.A.: A Personal Tour* (1972) by Richard Fairfield is excellent, and see the documents in Mitchell Goodman (ed.), *The Movement Toward a New American: The Beginnings of a Long Revolution* (1970), and more recently, Alexander Bloom and Wini Breines (eds.), *"Takin' it to the Streets" A Sixties Reader* (2002 ed.).

Many activists have penned fine participant histories, including Todd Gitlin, *The Sixties: Years of Hope, Days of Rage* (1987), Tom Hayden, *Reunion: A Memoir* (1988), David Harris, *Dreams Die Hard* (1982), and for fun try Raymond Mungo, *Famous Long Ago: My Life and Hard Times with Liberation News Service* (1970). David Farber, *Chicago, '68* (1988), captures the spirit at the Democratic National Convention, and James Miller, *"Democracy Is in the Streets": From Port Huron to the Siege of Chicago* (1987), focuses on SDS leaders. An enjoyable edited book by former activists is Alexander Bloom, *Long Time Gone: Sixties America Then and Now* (2001).

Women's Liberation

Begin with Ruth Rosen's *The World Split Open: How the Modern Women's Movement Changed America* (2000), and then consult Barbara Sinclair Deckard, *The Women's Movement: Political, Socioeconomic, and Psychological Issues* (1983), Blanche Linden-Ward and Carol Hurd Green, *Changing the Future: American Women in the 1960s* (1993), and Winifred D. Wandersee, *On the Move: American Women in the 1970s* (1988). To get the flavor of women's liberation, read the documents in Robin Morgan (ed.), *Sisterhood Is Powerful* (1970). Also of interest are Jo Freeman, *The Politics of Women's Liberation: A Case Study of an Emerging Social Movement and Its Relation to the Policy Process* (1975); Sara Evans, *Personal Politics: The Roots of Women's Liberation in the Civil Rights Movements and the New Left* (1978); Cynthia Harrison, *On Account of Sex: The Politics of Women's Issues, 1945–1968* (1988); and Pamela Allen, *Free Space: A Perspective on the Small Group in Women's Liberation* (1970). On African Americans, begin with Paula Giddins, *When and Where I Enter: The Impact of Black Women on Race and Sex in America* (1984), and for a study of radicals see Alice Echols, *Daring to Be Bad: Radical Feminism in America, 1967–1975* (1989). A classic "memoir" is Sara Davidson, *Loose Change: Three Women of the Sixties* (1977).

Chicanos and Native Americans

Rodolfo Acuña, *Occupied America: A History of Chicanos* (1988 ed.), is a good place to begin, and also see Carlos Munoz, *Youth, Identity, Power: The Chicano Movement* (1989), Mario García, *Mexican-Americans: Leadership, Ideology, and Identity* (1989), and Francisco Rosales, *Chicano! The History of the Mexican American Civil Rights Movement* (1996). Armando B. Rendon captures the flavor in *Chicano Manifesto* (1971), and also of interest is Edward Rivera, *Family*

Installments: Memories of Growing Up Hispanic (1982), and Peter Matthiessen, *Sal Si Puedes: Cesar Chavez and the New American Revolution* (2000 ed.).

On Native Americans, consult George Pierre Castile, *To Show Heart: Native American Self-Determination and Federal Indian Policy, 1960–1975* (1998), and Troy R. Johnson, *The Occupation of Alcatraz Island: Indian Self-Determination and the Rise of Indian Activism* (1996). A book of interesting documents is Alvin M. Josephy, Jr., J., *Red Power: The American Indians' Fight for Freedom* (1971), and for sympathetic accounts of the movement, see Josephy's *Now That the Buffalo's Gone* (1982) and Vine Deloria, Jr., *Behind the Trail of Broken Treaties* (1974).

Environment

A short survey is Kirkpatrick Sale, *The Green Revolution: The American Environmental Movement 1962–1992* (1993). Much more substantial is Samuel P. Hays, *Beauty, Health, and Permanence: Environmental Politics in the United States, 1955–1985* (1987). Kenneth T. Jackson, *Crabgrass Frontier: The Suburbanization of the United States* (1985), is excellent, and two important academic accounts are Adam Rome, *The Bulldozer in the Countryside: Suburban Sprawl and the Rise of American Environmentalism* (2001), and Scott Hamilton Dewey, *Don't Breathe the Air: Air Pollution and U.S. Environmental Politics, 1945–1970* (2000).

Gays and Lesbians

Good surveys are Barry D. Adam, *The Rise of a Gay and Lesbian Movement* (1987), and John D'Emilio, *Sexual Politics, Sexual Communities: The Making of a Homosexual Minority in the United States, 1940–1970* (1998 ed.). A more journalistic account is Charles Kaiser, *The Gay Metropolis, 1940–1996* (1997). A significant legal history is William N. Eskridge, Jr., *Gaylaw: Challenging the Apartheid of the Closet* (1999); documentaries that relate the early flavor of the movement are Karla Jay and Allen Young, *Out of the Closets: Voices of Gay Liberation* (1972), and Jonathan Katz, *Gay American History* (1976). A more personal approach is Martin Duberman, *Stonewall* (1993), and numerous interviews appear in Eric Marcus, *Making Gay History* (2001 ed.).

Nixon

Melvin Small, *The Presidency of Richard Nixon* (1999), is a fine book, and also consult Herbert S. Parmet's *Richard Nixon and His America* (1990), Tom Wicker's *One Of Us: Richard Nixon and the American Dream* (1991), and A. James Reichley's *Conservatives in an Era of Change: The Nixon and Ford Administrations* (1981). Stephen Ambrose's three volumes of *Nixon* (1987–1991) is almost a daily record; an important revisionist work that emphasizes Nixon's domestic policies is Joan Hoff, *Nixon Reconsidered* (1994). Other books of interest are Robert Litwack, *Détente and the Nixon Doctrine* (1984), and especially Jonathan Schell, *The Time of Illusion: An Historical and Reflective Account of the Nixon Era* (1975).

After Watergate numerous insider accounts were published, including Raymond Price, *With Nixon* (1977); John Dean, *Blind Ambition* (1976); John Ehrlichman, *Witness to Power* (1982); and H. R. Haldeman, *The Haldeman Diaries: Inside the Nixon White House* (1994). Stanley I. Kutler, *The Wars of Watergate: The Last Crisis of Richard Nixon* (1990), is the most complete book, and see his *Abuse of Power* (1997), which transcribes numerous White House tapes and demonstrates "the President knew virtually everything about Watergate . . . from the beginning." Bob Woodward and Carl Bernstein, *All the President's Men* (1974), remains a compelling story.

Filmography

A quick and uneven survey of popular films of the sixties is Ethan Mordden, *Medium Cool: The Movies of the 1960s* (1990).

Compared to today's standards, films then were rather mild, and this is obvious when readers view what were considered classic shockers of the fifties such as *The Wild One* (1954), *Rebel Without a Cause* (1955), or *The Blackboard Jungle* (1955). More interesting were later movies that rebelled against the cold war culture and McCarthyism, and that included such superb films as *Twelve Angry Men* (1957) and *The Manchurian Candidate* (1962). Three excellent movies that confront atomic holocaust are *On the Beach* (1959), *Fail-Safe* (1964), and the classic *Dr. Strangelove* (1964). Merging nuclear war with the increasing power of the military is *Seven Days in May* (1964), and a delicious spoof on the cold war is *The Russians Are Coming, The Russians Are Coming* (1966). Two notable more recent attacks on society in the fifties are *Pleasantville* (1998) and especially *The Truman Show* (1998).

A few excellent films were produced on race relations. To start, see *To Kill a Mockingbird* (1962) and *In the Heat of the Night* (1967). A period piece is *Guess Who's Coming to Dinner* (1967) and, more recently, *Mississippi Burning* (1988), which is effective but got the story wrong because the FBI in 1964 was racist, part of the problem.

Hollywood produced numerous films on the sixties culture, and the first one to appear might have been the best, *The Graduate* (1967), which revealed the gap between the Depression/World War II generation and emerging sixties culture. During the late sixties Hollywood made five uneven but interesting films: wanderlust biker hippies were the topic in *Easy Rider*, the counter-culture merged with draft resisters in *Alice's Restaurant*, burned-out campus radicals appeared in *Getting Straight*, free love California style was *Bob & Carol & Ted & Alice*, and some interesting scenes of the 1968 Chicago Democratic Convention were in *Medium Cool*. The industry did produce some classics that portray the revolt against the Establishment: *A Thousand Clowns* (1965) mocks the business world and their 8 to 5 day, and *King of Hearts* (1967) is a bizarre attack on war, in this case World World II. *One Flew over the Cuckoo's Nest* (1975) hammers institutions, and a rare classic that captures the views of the sixties culture is the black comedy *Harold and Maude* (1971). All of those were very popular on campuses then, and all asked, What is sane? Finally, three interesting rock concerts are *Monterey Pop* (1968), *Woodstock* (1970), and the end of the era, *The Last Waltz* (1975).

Later, during the Reagan years, filmmakers tried to look back at the era and produced two movies about activists who met for a weekend in the eighties. The Hollywood version is mediocre, *The Big Chill* (1983), but the low-budget John Sayles film is poignant, *Return of the Secaucus Seven* (1981). Also of interest is a sixties radical in *Running on Empty* (1988).

Vietnam has generated scores of films, and according to Tony Williams and Jean-Jacques Malo, *Vietnam War Films* (1994), about 600 that in some way concern conflict. The worst one is John Wayne's *Green Berets* (1968), a cowboy plot placed in Vietnam that provoked laughter among combat troops, and almost as bad is Sly Stallone as a one-man army in *Rambo* (1985). Stallone's earlier *First Blood*, about a returning vet hitchhiking through a small town, is provocative but flawed. Hollywood began making important Vietnam movies during the late seventies, including Burt Lancaster as a crusty combat vet in *Go Tell the Spartans*, the tale of three friends in *The Deer*

Hunter, and the metaphors and surrealism of what remains the finest Vietnam War film, *Apocalypse Now.* During the eighties vet Oliver Stone made other important films, especially *Platoon* and *Born on the Fourth of July,* which remains the best film capturing the clash between World War II and Vietnam vets. Other veterans portrayed a doomed reconnaissance mission in the interesting *84 Charlie Mopic* (1989), and also superb are *The Killing Fields* (1984) of Cambodia and *Dear America: Letters Home from Vietnam* (1988).

Concerning women's liberation and male/female relationships, a classic is *Diary of a Mad Housewife* (1970), complete with a demanding husband and a suffering wife, and also excellent is *Alice Doesn't Live Here Anymore* (1975). A black humor male response is *A Boy and His Dog,* and young males' views about sex in the early seventies are revealed in *Carnal Knowledge* (1972).

On Watergate, see *All the President's Men* (1976).

Photo Credits

Index